T0267174

GYPSIES
AND
JESUS

GYPSIES
AND
JESUS

A TRAVELLER THEOLOGY
STEVEN HORNE

DARTON·LONGMAN+TODD

First published in 2022 by
Darton, Longman and Todd Ltd
1 Spencer Court
140 – 142 Wandsworth High Street
London SW18 4JJ

ISBN: 978-1-913657-94-9

A catalogue record for this book is available from the British Library.

Printed and bound in Great Britain by Bell & Bain, Glasgow

CONTENTS

ACKNOWLEDGEMENTS

Nowadays, my mum Sue – the eternal volunteer and cleaner of churches – is likely to give you a meal or a bag of food. But when I was little, she gave me a nickname, 'Little Professor'. It took 30 something years to get close to living up to that name, but I finally got there, mum. Thank you. I hope you're proud.

Getting 'there' was a trial, and along the way from desert to doctorate, I met many magical strangers who helped mould me from a shapeless ball of clay into someone who felt like they could 'sit at the table'. Some of those magical folks are: Revd Dr Ivan Khovacs; Professor Robert Beckford; Dr Maria Diemling; Revd David Stroud; and Professor Thomas Acton.

And last but by no means least, I want to thank Emma and my children. You are my sunrise and sunset, and the wind in my sails. If I had a pound for every time you've shown me patience and given encouragement to me during this process, I could probably buy us a house we can all fit in and pay off the credit card. You're incredible, and quite simply, I could not have done this without you. Thank you.

ABSTRACT

They are a people who have been separated from God; they are a people whose sin has left them unclean; they are a people in need of unconditional love. This is how many Gypsies, Roma and Travellers (GRT) view those outside of their community ... Yet for more than 500 years, GRT people have been persecuted, misrepresented, enslaved and even murdered in whatever land they reside by the very people they now preach to. A life embalmed in the belief of radical grace and immovable faith has, for Gypsies and Travellers, given a refreshed emphasis to Christ's instruction of 'turning the other cheek'. This book lights the touch paper on the grace-filled, intimate and unheard core of GRT religiosity that is Traveller Theology.

Traveller Theology identifies and threads cultural strands (beliefs and customs, narratives and histories, and rituals and traditions) from Gypsy and Traveller culture into a coherent message that speaks of collective piety and cultural purity. Testimonies from members of the GRT community develop this message further, revealing the absolute centrality of religious conviction at the heart of Gypsy and Traveller communities. All of these factors are supported by a biblical exegesis to produce an exciting, revelatory and at times sobering book that, for perhaps the first time, hands over the reins of Gypsy-Christian identity to Gypsies themselves.

TABLE OF FIGURES AND IMAGES

INTRODUCTION

'I once asked an Irish Traveller to tell me about his culture.
His response was unexpected and wise in a way that I was
beginning to recognise as "Traveller". "OK but can you tell
me about yours first?" Immediately I realised what a difficult
and seemingly impossible thing I had just asked. With a
smile he continued …'[1]

JOHN 18:34

I stood at the front of the lecture theatre and looked out at 200 curious, bewildered and excited faces. As I opened the floor to questions on Gypsy and Traveller culture, a tsunami of questions started with a trickle before multiple hands and voices flooded the room. A hand raised and a young man stood up, flicking his long fringe back from his face. 'So, a large number of Gypsies and Travellers have a Christian faith, but how can that be when they always leave rubbish wherever they stop, and fight with the locals?' …

The hundreds of young trainee teachers sat before me had, for the most part, the best intentions and they wanted to do what they could to change the world of the pupils they would go on to educate and develop over the coming years. Their somewhat naïve positivity was refreshing, but revealing. However, in spite of their optimism, they had only ever experienced a limited social narrative about Gypsies and Travellers. For them, the one common denominator of their

[1]   G4S / HMPS, 2016, p. 6.

13

information and social development in this area so far was the media and press. This informal and often skewed 'education' had permeated their attention and shaped their social discourse. I continued talking to the young man with the floppy fringe.

He meant well and he gave the impression he would lead a class effectively. His downfall though, like so many of us when exploring this area, was that his question came not from his own experiences but from hearsay, from tabloids, and from TV financed by sensationalism. As I stood before the crowd, his sincere question of wrongful conviction took me to my saviour's side. In my mind's eye I watched as the words emerged from Pilate's mouth, 'Are you the King of the Jews?' I paused and waited for a moment. My hands were not in shackles and my back bore no stripes, but I knew this was a moment whereby 'guilty', regardless of what I said, would be the decided outcome. So, following Christ's example, I replied as Jesus did before Pilate, and returned the question. 'Do you say this of your own accord, or did you hear others say it to you?' There was no reply.

The social narrative and the tangible fate of Gypsies, Roma and Travellers (GRT) has forever remained at the whim of those outside of Gypsy communities. Since the emergence of said communities, gorgers (non-GRT people) have controlled the lands in which Gypsies resided, they have penned the stories and started the rumours, and they have placed the nooses around Gypsies' necks. Pressures such as these have unsurprisingly caused a collective cultural introspection, more commonly observed as a deliberate separation by GRT communities from their gorger counterparts. However, maintaining a deliberate and managed separation for the best part of a 1000 years is not achievable without a definitive cultural identity and, perhaps most importantly, a form of collective anchoring.

TAKING BACK THE PEN

Through the storms of political oppression, religious damnation, and social assassination, the anchorage among nearly all GRT communities around the world which has remained throughout (and is seldom addressed), is a unique religious and spiritual cosmology. Like precious diamonds that have emerged through incredible and extended pressure, so too has Gypsy Christianity formed. Whilst external forces have determined the periphery of GRT culture, religious identity and practice has reactively formed and located itself deep inside the heart of GRT communities. The seed of Christ has been planted, has taken hold, and the result is a people whose collective identity is rooted in a distinct and often secretive code of purity, nomadism, nature and purpose.

Religious engagement has allowed Gypsies and Travellers to bridge the gap between themselves and gorgers through a common language of Christianity (and in some remote areas, Islam). Furthermore, the combination of resisting gorger control and welcoming divine interjection has resulted in a strengthening of Gypsy identity that is secure in its Christological foundations. Religious engagement by GRT groups in this manner spans many centuries. Of note is the Evangelical movement in Europe from the late 1950s onwards, which has spawned a global GRT Christian revival and a growing body of international GRT religious literature.

However, the vast amount of *readily available* religious GRT texts, for the most part, occupy sociological books and journals. Whilst theological themes are present in some of the explicitly Christian material, many are primarily concerned with ecclesiological matters and questions concerning both the need and the sincerity of Christian conversion by GRT people. Interesting to note at this juncture is that a large percentage of the aforementioned dialogues have been undertaken by gorgers.[2]

Of course, this is not a criticism; any awareness is better than no awareness. And besides which, Gypsy and Traveller culture is often

---

[2] A 'gorger' is a non-Romani person (Hancock, 2013, p. xx – xxi).

oral in its nature.[3] The consequence of this being that many religious and theological contributions by GRT people are seldom recorded, explained or shared in readily available, mass-produced formats or via a broader academic sphere.

This book will place a spotlight on the heartbeat of Gypsy community, retaking the pen that has for so long caused so much damage to so many people. In this rewriting of one part of the GRT script, the pen will formulate a Traveller theology; a Traveller theology among *many* others, but for all to see (Matthew 5:14–15).[4] Exploring Gypsy religion and belief structures in this manner will help resistance to dominant narratives concerning GRT communities. In this way, Traveller theology is not just an exercise of reading that is concerned about understanding and learning, but is about resisting oppression, democratising theology and encouraging inclusivity. Inclusivity issues include both the theological process and academically-originated theology, a global domain in which Gypsies and Travellers are underrepresented.

A lot of existing material is predominantly focused upon social issues or perceived issues of social injustice. This creates a frustrating situation for Gypsies whereby the already negatively-perceived Gypsy is now only known by their issues, complaints and suffering. The negativity is magnified whilst the stories of family, music, simple

---

[3]   GRT communities are widely considered to be an 'oral' community. Cultural values, history and traditions are often passed on orally, rather than through text or other means. Sometimes this is undertaken to ensure the security and privacy of some communities. In his analysis of a particular part of London, historian Jerry White notes the 'Gypsy connection' amongst some of the people resident there, describing their oral tradition as being 'overwhelming' despite having no clear documentary evidence' (White, 2003). Clark & Greenfields (2006, pp. 110-111) highlight some of the oral tradition that White speaks of as relating to specific stopping places used frequently by different Travellers.

[4]   'You are the light of the world. A city set on a hill cannot be hidden. Nor do people light a lamp and put it under a basket, but on a stand, and it gives light to all in the house'. All biblical references in this book are taken from the NRSV Bible (National Council of Churches, 1998).

living and community are forgotten. Furthermore, there is often a big difference between the authentic GRT experience and that of the romanticised accounts from both Traveller and gorger sources. This often results in an augmented reality of sorts that either trivialises and/or disparages Gypsy and Traveller culture. As such, this book will take into account those things that have built common ideas about Gypsy and Traveller culture, including social, political, religious, historic, and personal accounts. I'll also use personal anecdotes and experiences from my familial, personal and professional links with the Traveller and Gypsy community spanning over 35 years.

ONE LAST THING BEFORE WE START ... WHY 'TRAVELLER'?

Before we leave this introduction and head into the main content, it's worth looking at the title of this book again. I've been told in recent years (by gorgers, no less) that it's now offensive to use the term 'Gypsy'. It's not. Feel free to ask either the millions of people around the world who identify as Gypsies, or World heavyweight boxing champion, Tyson 'The Gypsy King' Fury. So do we use 'Traveller' instead? This causes further issues. For example, another question I regularly get asked is 'Aren't all Travellers Irish?' No, they're not. As you can see, there is a degree of confusion as to what terms to use. However, there are also social dangers in incorrect ascription. So, it's important for us to make some clear definitions before we go any further.

The decision to choose 'Traveller' (rather than 'Gypsy' or 'Roma') in the title of this book is as historian Becky Taylor suggests, 'not simply a matter of semantics, since individuals and whole communities are still routinely deported, moved on or discriminated against on the grounds that they are, or are not, Gypsies / Roma / Travellers'[5]. Whilst 'Traveller' is still a descriptive term historically ascribed by gorgers, it

---

[5]   Taylor, 2014, p. 11.

carries little or no offence. However, the term 'Gypsy' is considered by some to be derogatory, partially owing to its roots in discriminatory and racialised labelling following a supposed immigration at one stage from Egypt.[6] Even so, in some studies Travellers preferred to describe themselves as Gypsies. The reasoning behind this includes, but is not limited to: a belief that they would always be recognised as Gypsies regardless of title given or their status in society; deciding to 'settle'; and recognising the pejorative implications and connotations that are affiliated with the title 'Gypsy'.[7]

In the UK the term 'Traveller' is often used interchangeably with the term 'Gypsy', 'Romany', 'Romany Gypsy', 'Roma', or even 'Rom' – by both Travellers and gorgers alike.[8] Where appropriate this book will reflect that interchangeability. However, it must be noted that a percentage of Travellers and Gypsies wish to be identified and addressed by a specific term. For the most part, the term 'Roma' (or 'Rom' – meaning 'man') will not be used; this is due to the term being predominantly associated with Gypsies living throughout Europe – particularly Eastern Europe.[9] Although many aspects of the ancestry and historical narratives of Gypsies and Travellers are shared with their European cousins, the current political and social environments can be markedly different in Europe to those in the UK. If references towards Roma and Europe are required, then it will be included where necessary, appropriate, and contextually relevant.

In light of this, I will be mostly using the parameters of the definition given by Liégeois and Gheorghe (1995) which delivers

---

[6] 'Gypsy' has certain racial connotations, as it derives from 'Egyptian' and was based upon the Gypsies' dark skin and colourful clothing (Okely, 1998, p. 1).

[7] Bhopal & Myers, 2008, p. 8.

[8] For example, Romany-Gypsy, Irish Traveller, Scottish Traveller, Rom, Roma, etc.

[9] Among the estimated global 11 million people identifying under the Romany banner there are numerous other collectives and 'Gypsy' identities, including but not limited to: Romanichal (England); Sinti (Central Europe); Manouche (France); Gitano (Spain); Bayesh (Croatia); Kalé (Wales and Finland); Romanlar (Turkey); and Domari (Palestine and Egypt).

separate definitions for Gypsies and Travellers. 'Gypsy' is associated with ethnic groupings whose ancestries originate in the Indian diaspora somewhere between the eighth and tenth centuries; whereas 'Traveller' commonly refers to collectives who assert a predominant and indigenous European source whose culture has been characterised by nomadism, fluidity in occupations and self-employment.[10] It must be noted that the definitions of 'Gypsy' and 'Traveller' vary between different sources, meaning that there may be some dispute as to whether Liégéois and Gheorghe's definitions are strictly applicable to English Romanies and Travellers.

Before we move on to the start of our journey together, it's worth making a key point regarding ethnicity and race. In Britain, Traveller and Gypsy groups are protected by race-relations legislation and are recognised individually and collectively as ethnic minorities.[11] Defining 'ethnicity' in GRT studies is challenging because of the multiplicity of separate ethnic GRT groups (for example, Irish Travellers, Roma, and English Romanichal). To reflect this, I will employ a broad application of the term 'ethnicity' and an understanding that ethnicity is defined as being a collective identity which includes religious, national, and cultural forms.[12] In doing so, there is a conscious recognition that defining Gypsy and Traveller ethnicity involves several recognisable factors that are both variable in nature and in constant flux with other GRT groups and the outside world. These factors include among others: nomadism, language, the relationship between GRT and gorger society, and self-identification.[13] So, with that said, let's make haste, pack up the camp and load the trailer, we've got a long journey ahead …

[10]   Liégeois & Gheorghe, 1995, p. 6.
[11]   Clark & Greenfields, 2006, p. 19.
[12]   Clark & Greenfields, 2006, p. 297.
[13]   Bhopal & Myers, 2008, pp. 13 – 18.

CHAPTER ONE
GYPSY CHRISTIAN HISTORY AND BIRTH OF THE GYPSY CHURCH

'On the evening of that day, the first day of the week,
the doors being locked where the disciples were for fear of the
Jews, Jesus came and stood among them and said to them,
"Peace be with you."'(John 20:19)

IN THE BEGINNING

God created; God spoke; God was the Word. For many people, the foundation of their journey of faith begins with a past tense. Often, to understand ourselves and the position we find ourselves in we look to the past. We contextualise our present by sharing stories and presenting facts, and in doing so we recall the footsteps that led us to where we now reside – figuratively, literally, spiritually. Our stories make us, identify us, and set us apart. They are in constant flux and transition – a state of permanent impermanence. Even the account of God is subject to such rules of impermanence; from hovering over the face of the young Earth's waters to laying in a manger in Bethlehem. One God and always the same God, but many stories and stages.

Gypsy culture is rich in-part because of its amplification of the past. Many well-known Gypsies are known *because* of their recollection of past events and their ability to tell stories of loved and respected ancestors. 'This is our way. We start with the past.' Sitting by a fire and sipping on a cup of tea, the softly spoken words of an old British Romani imparting his wisdom to a young(ish) theology researcher were loud and clear. And so it is with this account. We begin with the past. In doing so, we see our collective journey with greater clarity and marvel at how the Creator has led us, saved us, and continues to guide us.

> For me, 'In the Beginning' starts in a small makeshift paddock, somewhere in a secluded Kent woodland. 'Now, keep looking forward, hold on tight to the rope, and don't let go.' Unbeknown to me (a nervous and small five-year-old boy standing next to an equally nervous young Cob named Rambo), I was moments away from my having my first riding lesson (if you can call it that). There was no saddle or stirrups; just a blue nylon rope for a rein and a makeshift hackamore.[14] In one swift movement, my brother picked me up under my arms and sat me on the horse. 'Remember what I said.' With that, he took another long drag on his cigarette, stood slightly back, and slapped the horse on the backside. The aptly named Rambo shot off like a rocket. Hurtling towards the end of the paddock, I instinctively pulled on the reins. Nothing happened. My brother, who was already laughing, yelled out, 'Pull harder!' I pulled as hard as my arms would allow.
>
> An interesting thing happens when you yank on a horse's reins, particularly if the horse disapproves. They will often force their head down whilst slowing or stopping. Rambo opted for head down and stopping on the spot, which induced a swift demonstration of Newton's third law. My then tiny frame proceeded to launch through the air to the height and speed the likes of NASA and Elon Musk would approve of. I cleared

---

[14]   A hackamore is a type of horse headgear that uses a heavy noseband of some sort, rather than a bridle which uses a bit.

the paddock fence and prepared for impact. Thankfully I landed in some bushes. Concerns for my wellbeing were oddly demonstrated by my brother and cousins through raucous laughter and howling. My brother walked over, picked me up, dusted me off, and said, 'Let's go again.'

So, what's the point in my story coming first? It's simple really. Beyond the emotive hooks of a story (happy, sad, exciting, scary, etc.), in all of our stories there are demonstrations of principles and values, examples of character, and indications of what may come. These stories are in all of us. We are all divinely-inspired notes played out in God-breathed symphonies more commonly understood as our past, present and future. Regardless of colour, race or nationality, we share one source.

That is why we begin this Gypsy story looking at how that source became the heartbeat of a nation with no land and no armies. Real recognises real. Likewise, struggle recognises struggle. Look for the struggle in this account and you will find your empathy; find your empathy and you will see the struggle of others. When you do that, we will be ready for the next chapter. With that said, let us start …

BEFORE THE GYPSY CHURCH

A few years ago I found myself handing out food and supplies to the refugee residents of the French Calais 'jungle'. Like many others, I had seen the images on the news of terrified people fleeing war-torn Syria and other parts. Along with a friend, I set about raising money and gathering supplies with the intention of making the cross-Channel journey to where many refugees had gathered. The familiarity of their plight and indeed their path had not escaped my attention. Around 700 years previously, my ancestors had made a near identical journey, fleeing war and persecution and running firmly into the arms of uncertainty.

The Roma – or *Gypsy* - diaspora began with movements south

into Persia and north-westerly into Eastern Europe around the year 1300AD,[15] after a fleeing of sectarian violence in India. By the year 1400, Roma were present in many fringe nations to the west of mainland Europe. Of note is a significant number of Roma present at a place called Modon (located in southern Greece). Modon was a key stopping-place, for the pilgrimage to Holy Land was part of the Byzantine Empire.

The Roma's time in Modon would prove to be significant to their identity (both self-conceptualisation and in how others perceived them) and to how they were accepted and travelled across Europe. Being a major passageway for Christian pilgrims, the harbour city of Modon attracted numerous people from a plethora of nationalities. At some stage, cultural stands crossed and the Roma began to absorb Christianity and utilise it as a blanket form of identity and as a mode of operation. This enabled the Roma, to some degree, to 'hide in plain sight'. Meanwhile, the swallowing of the 'red pill'[16] of Christianity enabled a spirit of revelation (Ephesians 1:17) to work its way through the Roma's camp – both tangibly and metaphorically.

Persecution against the Roma grew, primarily taking two forms. First, localised hostility from residents of Modon and certain groups in the area (mostly, European/Germanic armed forces who had an established presence in the area). It was during this period that the dark-skinned Roma, along with their flamboyant brightly coloured clothing, was likened to that of the traders who regularly travelled across from Egypt. From then on, many referred to the Roma settlement as 'little Egypt',[17] and the Roma people as 'Egyptians'. Translated into the Greek mother

---

[15] Hancock, I. (2001), p. 516.

[16] The 'red and blue pill' concept is a pop culture reference drawn from the movie *The Matrix* (1999), whereby the lead character Neo is offered a red and a blue pill; the red pill enables one to experience the full revelation of the 'truth' with the condition that one can never unlearn what one has learnt. Whereas taking the blue pill is an agreement to forever live in ignorance of the greater truth and choosing to accept the current state as all there is to know.

[17] Fraser, A. (1995), pp. 51 – 55.

tongue, Egyptian would read as '*gyptiós*'; *gyptiós* would then later encounter Anglo-Saxon and become 'gypsy' – the plural of course being 'gypsies'. The Roma had first become refugees; then they became victims of racism – racism that would continue to the present day.

After continued persecution and the advance of Byzantine Empire,[18] the Gypsies prepared to enter central and eastern Europe; a journey that would culminate in their arrival in England and Scotland. The long and perilous journey would cement Christianity as the primary religion of Gypsies and Travellers.

Representatives from the various Gypsy clans were allegedly granted an audience with Pope Martin V in 1422CE, where they obtained papal letters. Said letters granted them safe passage wherever they went, but ordered them to seven years of nomadic penance for their supposed adoption of pagan (Islamic[19]) practices; 'for seven years they should go to and fro about the world without ever sleeping in a bed'.[20] In Gypsy culture, one's word is as valid as any contract. However, there is power within the tongue that goes beyond what is heard; in Gypsy communities, verbal utterances hold spiritual power and can be used to bless and curse. This belief operates both ways. In the instance of Pope Martin V, the decision to 'curse' Gypsies into a perpetual state of nomadism would be one that would last ad infinitum.

As the Gypsies made their way across the continent they entered Bavaria in 1424CE where their entrance was documented in a diary by a Priest named Andreas of Ratisbon:

[18]   Ibid, p. 55. By 1500 CE Turkish forces had taken control of the area and captured Modon.
[19]   Whilst in France, Andrew 'Duke of Little Egypt' presented letters that carried the signature of the pope. The letter gave details of the conquering and subsequent conversion of the Travellers by Christians; it was followed shortly by an attack from the 'Saracens'. Following no attempt to defend the land or resist conversion, the Travellers converted to Islam and then reverted back to Christianity once they had left the land (Taylor, 2014, pp. 43 – 44).
[20]   Shirley, J. (1968), pp. 217 – 218.

'They were near to Ratisbon, and were succeeding each other, sometimes to the number of 30, men, women and children, sometimes less. They pitched their tents in the fields, because they were not allowed to stay in towns; for they cunningly took what did not belong to them. These people were from Hungary, and they said that they had been exiled as a sign or remembrance of the flight of Our Lord into Egypt when he was fleeing from Herod, who sought to slay him.'[21]

Many of the reports emerging at the same time as Andreas of Ratisbon's account spoke of crimes committed by Gypsies – particularly of theft. Indeed, as Andreas reports 'they cunningly took what did not belong to them.'[22] Consequently, the protection that the papal letters had afforded began to wane during the fifteenth century as varying nations became hostile towards the Travellers. By 1497CE the Imperial Diet of the Holy Roman Empire intervened, accusing the Gypsies of espionage and ordering them to be expelled from all German territories. With the expulsion came the general permission to enforce violent actions upon them if they returned; Gypsies were entering a process of becoming outlawed from multiple states.[23]

The year 1505CE saw the first reports of 'Egyptians' arriving and settling in Scotland, followed by reports in England. By the late 1520sCE the influx of Gypsies was increasing rapidly and by the end of the decade public opinion (from the settled population) had become hostile.[24] King Henry VIII was in the process of reconstructing England's Church as he saw fit, and removing any traces of

[21] Fraser (1995, p. 75) records this particular excerpt from Andreas of Ratisbon's diary in a translation from the original Latin of Oefelius, A. F. (1763) 'Andreas, Presbyter Ratisbonensis, Diarium sexenale' in Rerum Boicarum Scriptores. Vol. 1 (1763), p. 21. Augsburg.
[22] Ibid, p. 75.
[23] Ibid, pp. 88 – 89.
[24] Keet-Black, J. (2013), p. 13.

'superstition' and 'abuses' from the pulpit to the parishioners.[25] Henry would take exception to the influx of nomadic people arriving on British shores who were reported operating as 'palm readers, fortune tellers and sorcerers', activities that the church strongly opposed.[26] Henry's solution emerged in the construct of the Egyptian Act 1530, which would officially deem it illegal to be a Gypsy in both identity and practice. The Egyptian Act specifically targeted those who practised the 'crafty sciences' and those who were 'feigning knowledge in palmistry'.[27] Furthermore, it presented 'solutions' to deal with the Gypsies and gave limited options to those affected by the bill; they were to either voluntarily leave the country within 16 days or face deportation.[28] Failure to abide by the ruling would result in the Gypsies' goods being confiscated and distributed to the local authorities and the imprisonment of the Gypsy.[29] The rapid demonization of the Gypsy community increased as the reformation was gathering pace. Henry's well-documented and problematic relationship with the Roman Catholic Church and the subsequent split from the Holy Roman Empire consequentially resulted in

[25]   Haigh, C. (2006), p. 1456.
[26]   Richardson, J. & Ryder, A. (2012), p. 6. In addition, the description of Travellers as palm-readers and fortune-tellers is a common theme through many literary pieces that touch upon early Traveller history. The link to so-called 'exotic cultures' (such as Egypt) and their associated practices (fortune telling, dancing) were popular at fayres, and enabled the Travellers to earn money. Therefore the association with such acts was actually profitable and thus maintained as an identity by many Travellers – many of which most likely did not genuinely practise such activities. The association with 'exotic occupations' (such as fortune telling) is specifically mentioned in the 'Statute of Henry VIII, 1530' – 'The Egyptians Act' (Okely, 1998, p. 3).
[27]   Keet-Black (2013). See p. 13.
[28]   The 16-day deportation ruling was applicable to newly-arrived immigrants and those Travellers who could not prove their birth had occurred in the British Isles. For those Travellers who were of British birth, they were given 40 days in which to leave the country. The eventual punishments for disobedience to the Act were the same for both native-born and immigrant (Fraser, 1995, p.131).
[29]   Ibid. See pp. 130 – 131.

the papal letters of protection utilised by the Gypsies becoming worthless.

By 1554 the penalty for being a Gypsy who refused to leave the country had escalated to capital punishment.[30] The move to execute 'Egyptians' had been an additional edit to an Act bought in during 1547 that enforced brandings and enslavement of 'master-less men' to prevent the 'Sojourners' from settling in one place for too long. Philip and Mary, who now held the throne, defended their continued drive against the Gypsy population by using their 'Christian' voice and associated power to demonise the Gypsies, employing Christianity as a measure against Gypsy practice; '[they (the Gypsies) use] their old accustomed devilish and naughty Practices and Devices, with such abominable living as is not in any Christian Realm to be permitted...'[31]

By the seventeenth century, slavery (as an industry) developed as a pressing issue for Gypsies.[32] The Church was now complicit in the state-enforced usage and implementation of slavery against Gypsies. Nearly 150 years prior to this, Pope Nicholas V had issued a decree named Dum Diversas; an act which actively encouraged and enabled slavery, and was essentially geographically limitless in terms of its application. Dum Diversas gave the following permissions:

'We grant you by these present documents, with our Apostolic Authority, full and free permission to invade, seek out, capture, and subjugate the Saracens, pagans and any other unbelievers and enemies of Christ wherever they may be, as well as their kingdoms, duchies, counties, principalities, and other property and to reduce their persons into perpetual slavery.'[33]

---

[30] Okely, J. (1998), p. 3.
[31] Fraser (1995), p. 130; Keet-Black (2013), p. 13.
[32] Bhopal and Myers (2008), p. 30.
[33] Cameron, J. (2014), p. 6.

The initial stage of slavery in the sixteenth century adopted the form of forced labour for Gypsies, with the inclusion of an attachment to a 'master'; by the turn of the seventeenth century it had developed into the traditionally understood 'chattel' slavery. A change in legislation in the early 1700s stopped the deportation of native-born Gypsies, preventing another full-scale diaspora. The legislative alteration was inadequately enforced, and there remained for some time a percentage of Gypsies sold into slavery and shipped back across Europe as well as to the Caribbean and the Americas, where they would be sent to plantations in exactly the same manner as their legally and socially recognised African counterparts.[34]

The religious, political and social spheres of the Reformation period within the UK enabled an environment of hostility and segregation towards the Gypsies, who were compelled to conform to the expected state 'identity', denying of oneself (as a Gypsy), and refusing association with anybody identifying as Gypsy.

Both the Catholic and Protestant Churches were (perhaps unknowingly) causing a redaction of Gypsy culture. Martin Luther's introduction of the 'Protestant work ethic'[35] helped to change traditional approaches to the poor, as secularisation and the questionable spiritual value of almsgiving came into effect.[36] Previous legislation such as the Egyptian Act 1530 placed Gypsies in the same category as beggars and vagabonds because of their methods of obtaining finances. As a result, Gypsies were seen as 'poor' and were thus treated in the same way as other people in the same social category. The developing humanist Renaissance championed the tenets of success and activity; poverty and laziness were subsequently seen as having an inseparable association with each other and provided grounds – both spiritually

---

[34] Hancock, I. (2000), p. 9.
[35] Max Weber in 1904 coined the term in his book *The Protestant Ethic and the Spirit of Capitalism*.
[36] Taylor, B. (2014), pp. 52 – 53.

(through a particular theological 'work ethic' hermeneutic[37]) and socially, for rejection and condemnation. The negative connotations to the development in 'labour' interpretation resulted in a trifecta (Government, the Church, and the general populace) of hostility towards the Gypsies and other 'poor' elements. The option to leave the British Isles was a fallacy, as much of Europe was enforcing equally severe restrictions and punishments on the 'idle wanderers'.[38]

As the Reformation continued, Europe witnessed the rise and divisions of nation states and a reactionary 'religious freedom' from Rome, resulting in a subsequent 'strengthening [of] the authority of national monarchies vis-á-vis Rome'.[39] The evolving situation created a fundamental issue: the nations needed to define loyalty and belonging – to the state and to the church (more specifically, which denomination one identified with, i.e. Catholic or Protestant). The concept of national identity caused further issues for the Gypsies, who were now subject to enhanced political suspicion as a result of their nomadic practice and lack of definable national identity. Gypsies became a scapegoat for the political elite who used their war of denominational affiliations to oust those who could not be defined so readily. Becky Taylor highlights a particular incident where the Tudor state passed blame on the Gypsies for plots towards Elizabeth I and the harbouring of spies; the accusation of Gypsies being spies soon developed and spread through Europe. A law was passed in Germany that categorised Gypsies as spies, severely limiting their potential movements throughout the continent; that law read as follows:

[37] The Apostle Paul alludes several times (directly and indirectly) to working hard. Paul predominantly refers to physical labour rather than spiritual, but proposes that the physical rewards the Christian in ethical and spiritual capacities. See the following: Ephesians 6:7; Philippians 2:14; Colossians 3:22 – 25; 2 Thessalonians 3:6 – 13; 1 Timothy 5:8; Titus 2:9 – 10; and 2 Timothy 2:15 & 24 (NRSV).

[38] Jerónimo Castillo de Bobadilla emphasised in 'Política para Corregidores' the importance of defining the reference *vagamundo* (vagabond) as something that should include the Travellers (or Gypsies as Bobadilla expresses), as they were 'a suspect people who wandered idly and had no masters' (Pym, 2004, pp. 21 – 35).

[39] Taylor, B. (2014), p. 56.

'when credible proof exists that they are scouts, traitors, spies and explore Christian countries for the benefit of the Turks and of other enemies of Christendom [it is] strictly forbidden to allow them to travel in or through their states to traffick, to give them safe conducts, escorts or passports'.[40]

The emergence of a politicised Christianity offered little in the way of tolerance for Gypsy culture and identity. In spite of this, Gypsies continued to practise Christianity and to develop a particular religious fervour through worship and ritual. Gypsies continued to travel throughout the British Isles practising Christianity relatively freely, with records evidencing the baptisms of Traveller children as widely-spread as Suffolk and Devon.[41]

Barring the actions of a few parishes and chapels, there was an overall consensus of hostility towards Gypsies. This failed to deter many Gypsies who continued to practise a conglomeration of spiritual(ist) practices and Christian traditions. During the nineteenth century, the London City Mission proved to be a highly vocal element within the Church of England that actively expressed their concern over the continued social difficulties faced by the Gypsy community. They instead provided and encouraged the uptake and participation in education, met basic welfare needs and delivered a message of Christian hope and salvation. A number of Gypsies who partook in tarot card reading and other psychic phenomena for income purposes[42] were said

---

[40] Ibid, p. 56.

[41] Keet-Black (2013) highlights numerous Acts bought in to limit Travellers' movements. She shows that in spite of the various Acts, Travellers showed tenacity in their adaptions to attacks upon their way of existence (p.13).

[42] Practising spiritual 'gifts' amongst the community occurred less frequently in comparison to practising upon the public through fayres, travelling shows and other enterprises. This is potentially because of the superstitious nature and subsequent caution associated with such phenomena within Travelling culture. Such cautions may be due to demonization by the church or because of negative personal experiences associated with so-called 'dark arts' (Keet-Black, 2013, pp. 31 – 33) (Dawson, 2000, p. 26).

to have rejected such practices and adopted the counter-teachings of the church,[43] with many reported to have gone on to become missionaries and evangelists.[44] The Gypsy community began to produce several key evangelical figures; they were to ignore the Catholic rejection of the 'Little Egyptians' and begin preaching the gospel themselves.

A CHURCH IS BORN
Salvation and Cultural Redemption

During the twentieth century an Evangelical movement amongst Gypsies began in France, initiating a Christian-Gypsy revival that would eventually become global in its reach. Prior to this there had been a history of Gypsy/Traveller engagement with Christianity going back centuries. However, factors such as the Evangelical development point towards a collective cultural shift among Gypsies from mostly animistic and primal expressions of religion and faith, to an adherence and cultural adoption of organised religion. With this cultural religious realignment comes many new relational and operational factors between Gypsies and the world around them, the communities among them, and the God above them.

The relationship between God and Gypsy – or a *Gypsy/Traveller theology*, is expressed through various avenues. For one of the earliest proponents of the Evangelical movement – Rodney 'Gipsy' Smith - this expression came by way of a lifetime in ministry and an autobiography[45] in the early years of the twentieth century, some time before the predominantly French revival began. For Gypsies and gorgers the message and examples given by Smith, potentially offer different meanings. For Gypsies (particularly of the time), a clear message is delivered of the need for repentance and salvation.

---

[43]   The Church had already made its position clear through the considerable volume of legislation it had either propagated or supported over the previous five centuries.

[44]   Keet-Black (2013), p. 40.

[45]   Lazell, 1970.

For gorgers, there is a rejection of the social narrative that says *all* GRT people are sinful and corrupt, and instead it is an opportunity to see an example of Gypsies serving as an example for a 'lost' majority. However, there is an overarching (and potentially unintentional) point; and that is, beyond the extraordinary and miraculous tales, and beyond Smith's oratorical and evangelical skills, is an almost ordinary engagement with Christianity.

Gypsy Christianity, whilst not always conventional, is present, is familiar, and is largely devoid of non-orthodox belief and practice. Much to the curious outsider's dismay, it is not always the exotic spectacle that some may perceive it as being. Mapping GRT religion from that standpoint demonstrates key features that may otherwise be missed. These features are theological in nature, hence detail a 'Traveller Theology'. However, in the early days of Gypsy-led ministry by the likes of Smith, certain key cultural themes consistently emerged that are still relevant/familiar today. The fact that many of these themes (listed below) could be considered as stereotypes should not be reason to dismiss them. Stereotypes are merely harmless identifying traits *until* they are used to separate and segregate. The list, which isn't comprehensive, is as follows:[46]

- A preoccupation with cleanliness, purity, and polluting things/ practice.
- A love and affiliation with nature.
- The existence of an innate religious sense.
- Family as a central part of community and identity.
- Horses as a symbol of the wandering life.
- State-led education considered 'dire'.[47]

What is often ignored when presented with these components, and what Smith would have wanted emphasised, is the centrality and

[46] Lazell, 1970, p. 19.
[47] Lazell, 1970, p. 39.

significance of religious conviction in Gypsy circles. And whilst Smith's personal theology could be criticised for being somewhat elementary,[48] his message is clear: What is desirable and good is a wholesome Christian life; there is almost a nobility to converting others or being converted; and that a rejection of sin is a step closer to God. For Smith, these elements trumped the essential 'Gypsy' elements mentioned above. There is no indication during the birthing pains of the Gypsy church that Christianity replaces these cultural elements, but it does highlight the Christological-centred theologising among GRT Christians. The urgency and reverence for salvation, repentance and cultural evolution from Gypsy communities that Smith relentlessly pursued would later be replicated in Europe, and then across other parts of the world.

France, in the mid-twentieth century, was rapidly becoming the hub of a European Gypsy Evangelical and Pentecostal revival. Although the tangible voices of key proponents such as Smith were long gone, their influence remained. The newly emergent Gypsy revival hurtled through its infancy and quickly established itself as a force for conversions – both in and outside of the community. Matéo Maximoff, a Romani Kalderash and key figure in the Gypsy revival, proposed that Gypsies are moving towards a position whereby they are trying to wake up 'the slumbering conscience of the [gorger] Christians'.[49] Gypsy Christianity was no longer limited to the evangelisms of one man – namely, Gipsy Smith, but was forming a collective new identity – a Gypsy Church.

Ecclesiology, Particular Beliefs and the Early Gypsy Church

The revival was spreading across Europe. In the UK, the absorption and application of the Gospel by English Romanies (Gypsies) and

[48] 'He preached for conversions; he believed that was his ministry. He believed he could do little in the way of building up the church through the teaching of doctrine – and that was not his job!' (Lazell, 1970, p. 96).

[49] Maximoff, 1965, p. 152.

Travellers (Irish, Scottish) had not gone unnoticed. Questions of ecclesiological concern began to emerge – in part to understand the phenomena and the Gypsy position, but also to regain (gorger) control. No doubt the control would have been labelled as the good shepherd of the European flock leaving the 99 to save the one. However, Western Christianity was already facing an identity crisis across the pond and panic was undoubtedly setting in. James Cone and his suggestions of a Black Christ was too much for many to swallow. No one in the 1960s and 1970s had gone so far as to suggest that Jesus could also be Gypsy, but I imagine the thought was not too far from their lips.

Elwood Trigg,[50] an academic and Episcopalian Vicar, proposed that in the instance of British Gypsies there has been a series of failures in the process of evangelising and providing lasting social reform. These failures were due to a number of factors, including but not limited to: ineffectual evangelism; questionable integrity of certain Missionaries (both Gypsies and gorgers); poor understanding of unique cultural characteristics; lack of commitment from larger church bodies; and problems with elements of Gypsy culture itself. Trigg's conclusion was, with some irony, that the gorger-led Evangelical movement which once sought to destroy essential elements of Gypsy culture, could now be the very thing to save it. Gypsies had taken Christianity, and like everything else they touched, had gotten more out of it than seemed possible. Even so, Trigg's position and concerns emerged from a gorger culture and a gorger church; the dilemma of whether Gypsies and Gypsy culture *actually* required/require conversion or salvation, is another question ...

The growing Gypsy Church was still relatively formless, albeit a few larger organisations that served to plant missionary Churches. Growth was strong, but as with any fast-developing entity, foundations can be fragile. In *Gypsy Demons and Divinities: The Magical and Supernatural Practices of the Gypsies*,[51] Trigg used his ally status to

[50] Trigg, 1968.
[51] Trigg, 1973.

attempt a process of reclaiming, redressing and reimagining the religious landscape of Gypsies. Trigg established that Gypsies were for a long time considered so primal and devoid of morality and wherewithal that it was inconceivable they could hold any spiritual and/or religious beliefs; the Christianity they professed to hold in their early European history (approximately 1400 CE onwards) was merely a cover. The result was a combination of demonization, accusations of occultism and paganism, and extensive missionary work by gorgers to 'convert' Gypsies. The 'old' question of whether Gypsies had any beliefs – religious, magical or otherwise was being refuted by academics, allies, and by Gypsy communities themselves.

Historically understood Gypsy beliefs (ghost life, omens, taboos, myths and superstitions) were more suggestive of 'a magical emphasis than of a religious one'.[52] However, the reality on the ground was now contestable, given the rapidly changing locale of Gypsy beliefs over the nineteenth and twentieth centuries from tribal-esque to definitively religious and denominational. As for the current period (twenty-first century), given the immense development and change in Gypsy beliefs over the past 50 years or so, such beliefs are now more suggestive of a theological emphasis over and above a 'detached' religious – or indeed a magical prominence. Ecclesiologically speaking, for Gypsies, Roma and Travellers, this draws the first of many lines in the sand. The collective evidence is irrefutable: there can be no doubt that comprehensive and unique religious practices have existed amongst Gypsy and Traveller collectives for centuries. Furthermore, (Christian) religious practice among Gypsy communities is not only still undertaken, but Gypsies have seized the leadership in the evangelical campaign among Gypsy and Traveller communities.

GRT religiosity has on the whole transitioned from one form to another; from syncretic superstition and magical practice to collective religiosity, most commonly framed by traditional Christian practices

52   Trigg, 1973, p. 27.

and doctrines. The days of Gypsies or Travellers in the UK partaking in the worship of vampire gods, or holding fears of grave robbers, have long gone.

Gypsy engagement with gorger-led ministry is, in the first instance, an exchange of sorts. This of course is not unfamiliar. Evangelical Pentecostalism in any construct offers a transactional account of salvation: Forgiveness in exchange for repentance, and eternal life as a reward for replacing oneself with Christ as Lord over one's life. However, the assumption that 'Church' in its current guise is something that is both attractive to Gypsies and is a 'best fit' in which Gypsy and Traveller Christian expression can operate, should be met with caution. Persistent cultural nomadism coupled with other historic traits, such as high illiteracy rates and self-governance, suggest that 'true' unbridled Gypsy Christianity could be something vastly different to the unbending, near on 2000 year old model of institutionalised worship currently offered.

Indeed, herein resides the first pillar of a Traveller theological foundation: as God moves and adapts to the nature of His creation (hovering over the waters; hanging from a cross), so creation must move and adapt to the will of its God and Creator. All creation – including the church, is permanently impermanent; we are all spiritual and metaphysical nomads.

Growth of Gypsy Christianity and the Gypsy Church

As the Gypsy Church began to grow, several factors became clear: that there exists a distinct and growing Gypsy church body, and that it is autonomous in its nature, unifying in its construct and an important element of Gypsy culture.[53] In France, Pastor Clement Le Cossac,[54] an instrumental figure in the Gypsy Evangelical Church, served as a pioneer, conversing with senior Gypsy figures across Europe and initiating large outreach

[53]   Acton, 1979, pp. 11 – 17.
[54]   Acton, 1979, p. 17.

events which would serve as a model for many other Christian 'fair' events, often characterised by a large dominant marquee in a field and surrounded by tents and caravans. Church in this form both went to the people and it drew the people in, often from far and wide. As Abraham went where his flocks could be fed, and the Ark floated to where it encountered firm foundations, so Gypsies would (and still do) travel to where there was life. Church still had walls and a roof, but it also had wheels underneath and a horse at the front.

During the early 1980s, 'Light and Life Gypsy Church'[55] was founded by British Romany Gypsy, Davey Jones. Along with other figures of note (Pastor Jackie Boyd, Revd Bernard Mends, et al.), an apostolic phenomena of Gypsy revival began to take place in the UK, demonstrating the power of Christianity to transform an entire culture through everyday actions of faith. However, it was not all fair weather and smooth sailing. Jones' theology and thus his ecclesiological stance seemed to be for the most part based on his own personal experiences and preferences. Jones' unwillingness to 'allow women to enter ministry'[56] and other conservative factors were of course reflective of a larger, pre-existent dogma and conveniently synergistic with 'traditional' Gypsy cultural conservatism. This perhaps offers some explanation as to why Jones would believe that a gorger-originated exegesis should direct a newly birthed Gypsy church.

All of these factors have at various stages been documented, discussed and analysed. However, as Professor Thomas Acton, identifies,[57] there appears to exist in European institutions a kind of 'forgettory'; a structured and intentional 'amnesia' that allows Roma and Gypsy historical and religious narratives to be reversed, altered, or forgotten, with little or no consequence for gorger people. As such,

---

[55] *Light and Life* is a large UK-based Gypsy-led Pentecostal Evangelical movement and Church body.

[56] Locke, 1997, p. 91.

[57] Acton, 2017.

there is an academic argument to make for continuing the reflective, investigative and contributory process that has been undertaken by key academics such as Acton. Further to this, such collective amnesia among larger institutions and the Church highlights the importance for 'story telling' and historical recollection among traditionally nomadic collectives such as Gypsies, Roma and Travellers. However, as a warning: many current studies are often localised and consequentially assumptive, resulting in the creation of mass generalisations. Failing to place such studies and testimonies historically, socially and in the hands of GRT people themselves allows for the normalisation of racism towards GRT people to continue.

As the Gypsy church expanded among Western nations, several distinctive traits amongst Romani congregations emerged; traits which are still consistent with current GRT congregations. As such, this historical story now catches up with the present day. These characteristic identifiers include aspects such as:

- In North America, Roma were (and are) more likely to join gorger-led congregations, whereas this is not the case in Europe.
- Roma have become self-led, training their own Pastors, etc.
- The (Holy) Spirit as a source of religious truth, favoured over biblical or written truth.

Gypsy Pentecostalism was not content to simply be a static attraction or alternative religious option. Instead it became a vehicle of ethnic mobilisation. After all, Pentecostalism is not only a significant element in Gypsy Christian expression, but it is also arguably the fastest growing orientation of Romani Christianity in general. Gypsy Christianity has grown from its roots of spiritual and cultural anchor to that of an inherent method of engagement with mass society.

A Traveller Theology emerges

To underestimate the centrality, impact and importance of Gypsy Christianity, in any form, is a foolish error. For those in the back who might not be hearing me clearly enough, or might be missing the significance of this understanding, let me make it clear: Christianity can serve as a bridge between GRT and gorger society. Different Romani religious groups are reaching out to each other across Europe, indicating in many ways a connectedness of Gypsy ethnicities via the body of Christ.

The interconnectedness of Gypsy communities across the globe is of course cultural and ethnically centred. However, that cultural and ethnic identity is collectively grounded in and facilitated by a shared unobstructed relationship with its Creator. It would seem that the many Gypsies and Roma, excluded from participation in the luxuries of renaissance and modernism, have bypassed the shackles of intellectualism and as a result, held on to a primal connectedness with the Father. A connectedness that many in the modern world have lost touch with.

So, could it be that the oppressed GRT people, much like we see in James Cone's theory,[58] know the 'God of the oppressed' in a different (not better or worse) manner than those who are considered privileged? And could it be that the survival (and now, flourishing) of GRT people in their own right, is evidence of God fundamentally aligning Himself and identifying with the oppressed, as demonstrated through the biblical, prophetic tradition? For Cone, his ideas of material elevation and social liberation becoming indicators of salvation, would probably see him deny GRT people of that alignment. The key issue here is perception and positioning. Regardless of ethnicity, social position or anything else, we have all sinned and fall short of the glory of God. This has left us all oppressed when we consider the magnitude of an eternity without Christ.

[58]   Cone, J. (1986).

However, as God through the person of Jesus Christ identifies with the oppressed, we (GRT) too identify with Christ. We are not told to leave the Cross behind but to pick it up each and every day. We are not instructed to sit still in comfort but press on and run as to win the prize. Therefore, remaining in suffering and clinging to the foot of the Cross are our only moments of stillness – everything else is transitory. As such, our liberation moment is not evidenced by the ending of our suffering but by our defiance in the face of adversity. Despite our thirst we turn our heads at the sponge of sour wine (Matthew 27:48), and as we hang either side of our Creator, we look to Him and cry 'remember us Lord as you come into your Kingdom' (Luke 23:42).

So, we find the script to this historical journey we have just encountered to have been flipped. It's the moment in the movie when we realise all is not what we once thought it was. It transpires that the claims of oppression made on historical and socio-political grounds were not the accounts of the Gypsies but of those who observed them.

For many of these 'allies', their drive to see oppression of GRT communities disappear is admirable and often welcome. However, without a Traveller theological interpretation, the eschatological understanding of those outside of the community circumvents such oppressive 'events' as finite; oppression is seen as something fixable and with an end date. In some respects, that may be the case.

However, we must tread carefully and not assumptively when engaging with material and historic realities. It's too easy to assume that the removal of oppression equals liberation, and that liberation is the end goal of all who are oppressed. When we do, we risk separating our temporal human experience from the eternal nature of Christ. For Gypsies and Travellers, understanding Christ's crucifixion and sacrifice as both an unfolding and eternal event (rather than ahistorical), continual participation in them is possible. And with that participation comes everything – from joy to sadness, from love to indifference, from cleanliness to sin. Life, in this respect, is not theorised and intellectually pondered. Life is engaged fully. Christ is engaged fully.

SUMMARY

Every story has a beginning. Too often our anxious minds dwell in the 'what next' or the 'I wish I had'. It's a very human way of looking at things. However, our Creator has already shown us the blueprint of how to remember, understand and interpret the past. Personally I cannot recall reading Genesis and thinking, 'Why did God float above the waters?'. I was more interested in the magnificence of simplicity in what was being described, and in what was coming next. I knew that the violence and splendour of light hitting the face of the Earth for the first time would turn out all right because the book carries on past Genesis, and well, we're all here, reading this. Yet too often we fall into the temptation of lamenting and calling upon God and/or our memories and asking, 'Why did you do that? Why didn't you choose x/y/z?'.

Revelation doesn't just occur in the text – it also occurs because of the text. The text exists. Our 'text' exists also. However, our 'text' exists in the annals of our minds and memories, and for GRT communities, our 'text' exists in the words of our story tellers and in the songs of our people. It is heard around fires; it is seen through photos on walls and ink in skin; it is felt through physical endurance; and it is experienced in the hands of our Creator.

So, much like time spent talking to a counsellor or confessing in our prayers, Revelation – or 'revealing' – becomes a process of healing. Our past, when re-contextualised in the mould of God's greater plan, loses its sting of condemnation and hurt. On one hand the revealing you have just read represents nearly a thousand years of pain, oppression and rejection. On the other hand, it represents the transformative grace and love of a God who lifts up the broken and remains faithful to those who call on His name.

Our Story

This account begun with a people isolated from their lands by war, who travelled the silk path to Europe in search of safety and a new home. The multitude encountered a God of grace and they took Him into their hearts. The multitude grew and then separated, making new destinies for themselves in European nations and beyond, taking the Gospel of Jesus Christ with them wherever they went. The multitude formed many new tribes; tribes that one day would be collectively known as Roma, Gypsies and Travellers. Centuries would pass, and the tribes would be separated by land, by governments, and by tribal conflict.

However, one day the isolated people who had travelled so far for so long, would turn inwards and call with greater conviction upon that which had loved and guided them from the beginning. The Gospel would begin a slow process of reuniting them. They would take that Gospel message, and return it to the very people who had rejected them, knowing that those who caused pain needed love and salvation the most. With little surprise, many outside of their communities rejected them. But now the people grew with faith and confidence, their identity secure in their Creator and in the 1000 year heritage He had given them.

Still, a war of words waged on. 'How can these people act differently?' asked some of the outsiders. 'Most of them look the same as us'. And then, as a period of political and social unrest swept the Western world, a realisation set in among the outsiders; 'We're all equal to one another' they said. With that, the multitude raised their voices, pointed to themselves, and looked the outsiders in the eye, shouting, 'Then treat us as equals. Listen to our story. See how we are all brothers and sisters.' The outsiders looked puzzled. 'How can we all be brothers and sisters with you? You are Gypsies.'

'Sit down by this fire. Here, have a brew and some food. I'll tell you all about it ...'

CHAPTER TWO

I AM NOT CAIN: THE PERCEIVED SIN OF GYPSIES

*'And I will make justice the line, and righteousness the plumb
line; and hail will sweep away the refuge of lies,
and waters will overwhelm the shelter' (Isaiah 28:17).*

*'"When one Romani is guilty, all Romanies are guilty".
It shouldn't have to be that way.'*[59]

INTRODUCTION TO TRAVELLER SIN AND OTHERNESS

Among other things, this chapter will introduce sin as a key theme in GRT spiritual and cultural understanding. Examining modern populist Gypsy imagery – both imagined and factual (but very often discriminatory and stereotyped) directly confronts what is sometimes a 'taboo' area in academic GRT sources/studies but almost always the leading component in media and tabloid products. In this respect, understanding – rather than apologetics - is the intention; a more complete, rather than selective, theological monograph, is the intended outcome.

Gypsies, Roma, and Travellers are often categorised as 'other' – both officially in national censuses, and unofficially in the capacity of our minds

---

[59]   Hancock, 2013, p. 104.

and imaginations. They are not alone, often they are joined by people with disabilities, with different coloured skins, with people of different social class, and with people whose sexuality isn't heteronormative. The phenomenon of categorising others is mostly never malicious, but it can be destructive. The sword of inclusion is a powerful one and whose fine metal is a virtuous material. Yet such a sword is double edged – it identifies yet it also separates. However, it is not only used by those who wish to highlight those who may be persecuted, but it is also, particularly in the modern era, used by some to 'other' themselves, and in doing so, protect themselves from further harm.

There is much to be said for our natural in-built primal instinct of preservation for our family and kin, for protecting the borders of our 'village'. However, in the contemporary modern environment that many of us find ourselves a part of, we are blessed with the capacity to reflect and appreciate God's creation beyond that of our own interests. In short, our 'fears' of being overrun by invaders or obtaining enough food for our families is not something that the majority of people in the developed West have to be worried about. When we remove those fears, we can see that we all share the same planet but we do not all share the same experience.

Unfortunately this phenomenon is not limited to social and physical factors. As the director of our words and deeds, our minds have also put in place a practice of spiritual othering. Using various methods of justification (biblical exegesis; doctrinal interpretation, etc.), we have at times closed the door to who can access the Father, by monopolising salvation and forgiveness, and deciding what the standards of being 'Christian' are, based on the changing topic of the day. Again, often our intentions are well meaning – we want everyone to experience Christ's love. However, our interpretation and explanation is almost always the result of our experience and does not accommodate the incredible variation of life experienced and understood by others. That does not mean we are wrong when we seek to defend and implement orthodox dogma, but simply that others also hold their own 'truths'.

When the subject is considered to be 'other', seeing that subject for what they *actually* are rather than they are *perceived* to be (by us or others), is often challenging. The initial hurdle to systemic change in both others and in ourselves is recognising that the 'other' does not share the same positive experience that we do. Their truth is different to our own. This chapter is not and cannot be the 'systemic change' bought about by recognising the 'other' or Gypsy for what and who they are without our restrictive vision. However, this chapter in particular is an opportunity to practise the first step of this process: recognising that GRT people have been and are being 'othered', and being willing to look at the perceived sin of Gypsies with a view to expanding our theological periphery vision. At the very least, this allows us to see where God, who sets the plumb line of righteousness (Isaiah 28:17), decides the line in the sand is to be placed.

When we enter the territories of others – physically and metaphorically, directly and indirectly, we encounter unfamiliar and sometimes unwanted surroundings. Our call to such places is sometimes because of a divine prompting; a nudge by the Spirit of God to minister to a specific group, or evangelise in a particular area. As such, it's helpful to know both the lay of the land and the context in which it stands. There is of course the danger of hearing troublesome reports and being dismayed by them (Numbers, 13:27-28), or even worse, hearing a call but running in the opposite direction! Fearful spies or encounters with the belly of a whale aside, mission often calls for exploration, and walking with our Saviour requires courage. These areas of exploration will from here on in be referred to as the 'Edgelands'.

Entering the Edgelands

The 'edgelands' concept is not new. In recent years it has become the basis for a research theory, developed and proposed by Frances Rapport (2005) et al. In the edgelands the boundaries of conventional and new methods are synergistically woven in metaphorical 'new territories', allowing for both new and greater levels of personal, communal, and cultural expression.[60] Both Tessa Muncey and Rapport et al. cite British activist Marion Shoard, who utilises metaphorical imagery taken from the UK to mentally position and assist the reader in both visualising the *edgelands and to also understand its political, academic, and social value:*

> We are aware of the great conurbations. But not of the Edgelands ... Between urban and rural stands a kind of landscape quite different from either ... Often characterised by rubbish tips, superstores and *Gypsy* encampments ... for most of us most of the time this mysterious no man's land passes unnoticed in our imaginations, it barely exists ... But if we fail to attend to the activity of the interface we forfeit the chance not only to shape ... change but also to influence the effects of it on other parts of the environment.[61]

Other theologians of note also press into this edgelands space, recognising that if we are to a) enact spiritual change in ourselves, and (b) we are to understand how Creator God works in others, we must continue to move from our own experiences and take residence, if only for a little while, in the territories of those who are not us. We must break bread with the rich tax collectors, we must sit down by the pool with the diseased, we must pray for those who persecute us and we must suffer with those condemned by others to die. This is not liberation theology. This is the Gospel.

Professor Robert Beckford's criticality in Black theology is in many contexts an example of occupation in the edgelands. Beckford chooses to move beyond the taxonomy of 'typical' Black theology, allowing for a present engagement with the Black church and community, creating a politicised and constructive theology.[62]

---

[60]   Muncey, 2010, p. 28. Also see Rapport, Wainwright, & Elwyn, 2005, pp. 37 – 43
[61]   Shoard, 2002, pp. 117 – 125. Also see Rapport et al, 2005, p. 37; Muncey, 2010, p. 29.
[62]   Kee, 2008, 152 – 155.

However, it could be argued that the liberation (theology) radicalism that both formed the core narrative of Black resistance is also one that is established and familiar. Thus, despite presenting itself as a theologised resistance and mode of liberative social empowerment, it *is* known and therefore resides *outside* of the edgelands.

Theologians have examined the world and interpreted it accordingly. However, as the late Black theologian Alistair Kee suggests, interpretation is fine, 'but the point is to change it'.[63]

As Christians, we must commit ourselves to pressing into the edgelands and the unknown, remembering that in encountering uncomfortable truths (in others and ourselves) we are rewarded with refining understanding. In short, let's understand God in others, not by our external interpretation but by getting among those 'othered' and allowing their witness to be our truth. On multiple occasions, Beckford has provided great examples of how operating within the edgelands creates tangible impacts. His persistent criticality in Black theology and culture positions his own theological praxis as prophetic; his continual engagement with musicians and artists creates an environment of reclamation for aspects of 'God-given human life'[64] such as sexuality.[65] So, when the question is Black, the answer cannot be White. And when the question is Gypsy, the answer cannot be gorger.

We can successfully navigate the endangerment of limitation in response and understanding by eschewing the theoretical in favour of reflection from experience. As members of the body of Christ, we have a duty to employ deep criticality in order to dissolve illusions through analysis. When we stand in the Hall of Hewn Stones and we watch the rushed midnight trial of our fellow humans, we have a choice: We can either stand on the periphery, quietly condemning the outlandish media demonization of society's refugees; or we can enter

63 Kee, 2008, p. 155.
64 Beckford, 1998, p. 77
65 Beckford, 1998, pp. 75 & 77.

the Edgelands and instead seek to understand, without flinching or reaction, what is meant when the already-condemned, in reaction to their accusers, responds with 'You have said so' (Matthew 26:64).

Whatever side of the fence we stand on, as believers in Christ, we must remember that it is the Father who operates as our judge, and not Caiaphas. And so our theological court is one that is, to coin a contemporary phrase, a 'safe place'. This safe place provides adequate room for subjective criticality and expression in otherwise problematic areas of social and religious discourse, such as sin and sexuality.

By contextually and theologically understanding relevant behaviours, traditions and practices, a process of exploring the edgelands of Traveller activity can begin. It is important to note that the process of positioning the culture and community in a greater state of exposure is not synonymous with a dismantling of borders and divisions between Gypsies and gorgers. Such boundaries are necessary; their tangibility – evidenced by the necessity of the creation of this book, does not serve as a tool of division but as a method of cultural and religious preservation for Gypsies and Travellers.

Reinforcing this narrative, Liberation theologian, Miroslav Volf, questions the benefits of radical inclusion which 'seeks to level all the boundaries that divide'.[66] The GRT method of 'border protection' stands in stark contrast to secularised approaches, such as Michel Foucault's attempt to unravel 'binary divisions' and 'broaden the space of the "inside" by storming the walls that protect it'.[67] Volf's imagery of the protective walls is succinctly expanded upon when he next suggests that '[w]ithout boundaries we will be able to know only what we are fighting against but not what we are fighting for'.[68] If objective examinations and explanations are to remain objective (even in the face of the author's complex subjectivity), cultural examinations must resist cultural appropriation.

[66]   Volf, 1996, p. 62.
[67]   Volf, 1996, p. 63.
[68]   Volf, 1996, p. 63.

TRAVELLER PERCEPTIONS OF SIN
Matthew 7:3

Since their emergence into Europe, Gypsies have been associated with criminality; associations that are both popularist and overwhelmingly unjust. Associating deviancy with 'others', particularly nomadic others, relates back to our collective psyche of protectiveness over our territory – our territory of land, our territory of values, our territory of kin, and our territory of religious conviction. Perhaps for many of us, the privation of rootedness in a given settled locality (that is seen both figuratively and literally in GRT communities) causes us to reflect on our determination to be fixed in our lives – be it our jobs, our homes, our marriages. However, many would argue that their perceptions of GRT people as deviant emerges from experience.

It is then worth mentioning at this juncture that, for example, in the UK there are (officially) around 300,000 Gypsies and Travellers, however, on the ground this number is closer to around half a million. Could it be that all 500,000 Gypsies and Travellers in the UK are guilty of the crimes to which they are accused? Of course not. But that is the 'elephant in the room' logic we are faced with. Theologically speaking, when we partake in such a narrative – whether in mind or deed, we ignore the very premise of our collective need for salvation. We choose to recognise the sin in others but ignore our own. It's not say that there isn't a speck in our neighbour's eye, but that in our own eye is a log (Matthew 7:3).

Condemnation, in this instance taking the form of an historical accusation of blanket criminality, would be assumed to be the preserve of the powerful and pure; a (insert race here) privilege. It may come as some surprise then to learn that the majority of Gypsies and Travellers believe in their own superiority despite their subordination, marginalisation, and the internalisation of anti-Traveller racist comments and stereotypes.[69] This is sometimes observed in the implementation of descriptors such as 'country folk' and 'gorger'. Such terms are mild demonstrations of the Gypsy and Traveller's sense of authority vis-à-vis the majority of non-nomadic people. However, the use of pejorative words is not what is of concern here. Instead it is the asymmetry of social control and the subsequent distinction between accusing one or the other of sin, and the subsequent committal of said sin. In recognising this balance, Robbie McVeigh would suggest that 'we must contrast the capacity of the overwhelmingly dominant settled population to racialise, marginalise and discriminate against the nomad with the incapacity of the nomad to operationalise any anti-sedentary prejudice he or she may hold'.[70] This, then, is the tension between response and responsibility; between accusation and necessary action; between sedentary life and nomadism. At this point, it is important to define how sin is being understood and implemented.

Ownership of Sin

Interpreting and defining a Christian understanding of sin can be challenging and contentious. In its simple form, sin can be understood as 'the purposeful disobedience of a creature to the known will of God'.[71] The nature of this definition may include the idea that sin is not only action, but also inaction (sins of omission), and most profoundly, a state of being (i.e., of being born into a condition defined by 'the fall', alluded in the notion of 'original' sin[72]). From there, sin can be broadly divided into two categories.[73] The first category is concerned with the *source* and *nature* of sin. The second category is concerned with how

---

[69]   McVeigh, 1997, p. 12.
[70]   McVeigh, 1997, p. 12.
[71]   The purposeful disobedience of a creature to the known will of God' (Livingstone, 2006, p. 545); essentially an intentional transgression of some sort.
[72]   Genesis 3.
[73]   McGrath, 2011.

the differing doctrines of sin *function* in certain religious communities and theological systems where the language of sin is incorporated.[74]

Early discussions from Augustine helped to establish the primary positions on sin, in regard to a person's relationship with God and the intrinsically linked tropes of grace and salvation.[75] These tropes require a greater attention to be placed upon where sin originates (for example, generational) and where sin resides (either the individual is responsible for their sin or something external to them caused them to sin). However, this must be undertaken with the knowledge that sin as inborn corruption, whether in Augustine or Calvin's understanding, is the very target in Christ's saving grace; and that only Christ, through a process of grace (resulting in salvation) can accomplish this task.

Theologian Darlene Weaver explores the tension of the ownership of sin (and thus responsibility of said sin) and whether it is either placed *in* the person or *external* to the person. Weaver concludes that certain individual 'sins' should not be ignored and re-categorised.[76] This creates a situation whereby sin, regardless of its origin or current locale, requires a degree of personable ownership. However, personal ownership of sin in some Gypsy and Roma communities can be culturally unfamiliar. For example, passing blame for discrepancies to the object, the catalyst, or another individual is a normative process among Kalderash Roma. Lee (2001) provides examples of this phenomena:

> A Gypsy man falling into a river and drowning – it will be said that 'the water killed him'; if by accident he is electrocuted – it will be said that 'the electricity killed him'; if he commits an act that wouldn't take place if he were sober – it will be said that 'the whisky (or other drink) takes control of him.[77]

[74] Weaver, 2001.
[75] Weaver, 2001, pp. 473 – 474.
[76] Weaver, 2001, p. 498.
[77] Lee, 2001, p. 205.

This method of explanation is considered to be reasonable, since 'the [Gypsies] believe that visible or invisible forces can act on their own to influence actions of people'.[78] In English Romanichal circles, the dynamic of blame attribution is often less consensual than that of our European cousins – the Kalderash, who employ a 'tribunal Kris' method of justice[79]. 'Justice' in the English Gypsy sense is more contested, personal, and vengeance-based. In a practical sense, this might play out in the form of an organised fight or the theft/destruction of another's property. Whilst this distanced relationship with sin is understood within GRT communities, the challenge comes when criminality or sin occurs between GRT and non-GRT communities.

Fig. 1   *Appleby: Sin and Crime*

I took this photo at the world famous Appleby Horse Fair. Note the Evangelical marquee to the left of the picture, warning against sinning, whilst directly to the right is the Police mobile CCTV

---

[78]   Lee, 2001, p. 205.

[79]   A Kris is a form of court, where matters of conflict are resolved 'in house'.

'Crime Prevention Unit'. It was quite fortunate for the composition of my picture that the GRT people on the Trap are moving from the conviction of the law to the grace of God.

Common areas of contention or 'sin' in Gypsy and Traveller communities, as noted above, will sometimes have a particular rationale and explanation. Some of these areas have a habit of dominating public preconception. It's worth then having a look at a sample of the common stereotypes that fuel public imagination. These have been grouped and addressed below and are broadly entitled as: 'Conflict'; and 'Thieving and Deception'. It should be noted that another key theme which was considered was 'Illegal Settlements'. The theme of settlements/camps is pivotal for a number of factors, and as such, it is discussed in greater detail later in the book. In the following sub-sections, each area will be briefly addressed with one or more examples given.

RESPONSES TO CONTEMPORARY STEREOTYPES
Conflict: People

Sitting in an old, abandoned Church hall, the irony of the situation was not lost on me. In the past, the walls surrounding me must have witnessed gatherings for virtually every human event of significance – wakes, wedding receptions, birthday parties, and much, much more. However, today was markedly different. Today was no celebration. It was to be a moment of retribution, of justice, and of hoped-for peace. To my left stood a man in his late 30s who I'd met only weeks before. His brother stood silently, holding his brother's wrists whilst wrapping black tape around his knuckles. Meanwhile, another relative of the man in question stood close by, shouting words that would put fire in the belly of the man who, in all honesty, didn't look like he wanted to be there.

The weed-covered courtyard to the hall, which once welcomed new brides and grooms, and saw the lives of the deceased celebrated, would in a few short moments facilitate a bareknuckle fight between two men who had fallen out some time ago. So much had happened between the original altercation and now, that the original 'sin' was pretty much forgotten. What was certain is that as long as the 'rules' of the fight were observed fully, then the sins of each man and his family would be absolved. The rules were simple: No outside interference. Traditional boxing only – no elbows, biting, or kicking permitted. Break apart/stop fighting when instructed by the designated referee (often a respected neutral figure). When a fighter falls to the ground, step back. Fight until someone wins, someone gives up, or the fight becomes a stalemate. At the end of the fight, respect the referee's decision and shake hands with the opponent.

I was fully aware that what I was witnessing was not commonplace in GRT communities in the contemporary period, despite what TV programmes, newspaper headlines, and online material would have people believe. And it was by no means sensational or public. There were nine people in attendance – including the fighters and the referee, and the location was disclosed a day beforehand. It's important to state a couple but rather obvious key points at this stage, concerning the aforementioned list. Furthermore, it's not right to assume that all GRT people condone such behaviours. In fact, in the current age, many are likely horrified by such behaviours and would sooner deny their existence. However, the reality is, every culture has violent actions that seem at odds with what the majority believe in or accept, yet they exist and are often believed to symbolise or mobilise benefits to the larger collective. Sometimes these violent actions look like fights, other times they look like government policies, and sometimes they look like Priests and Levites crossing the street to avoid the beaten outsider.

Often, narratives of honour, values and tradition provide the rationale behind conflict within the GRT community. And in dealing with those conflicts, gorger systems of justice – for some Gypsies and Travellers, sometimes miss the mark. Not because they are ineffective, but because gorger systems and processes are *based* on values, whereas Gypsy methods of justice are the *embodiment* of those values. For some, five minutes of hand-to-hand conflict is a purer, simpler, honourable and more transparent form of resolution than court hearings, processes of suing, family counselling, and custodial sentences. This doesn't mean conflict is right or acceptable; however, it does make it understandable.

Biblical instruction is insistent on avoiding quarrels in processes of resolution, opting instead for methods favouring both holistic and legal practices, such as talking and entering processes involving courts or panels (Deuteronomy 1:16 and 17:9; Exodus 18: 21 – 22). Opting for resolution to emerge via oral discussion is given precedence, with the decision to enter into confrontation seen in some instances as the result of sin, rather than the action of fighting itself being the actual sin; 'Only by pride cometh contention: but with the well advised *is* wisdom' (Proverbs 13:10).

Exegetically, it is tempting to mine and present any aspect of virtue (rather than pride) in the physical acts; something which speaks of self-sacrifice and provides evidence of an altruistic motive. However, in this sense pride can covertly infiltrate into acts of Christian behaviour and even into God-focused motives.[80] C. S. Lewis describes this pride as 'spiritual cancer: it eats up the very possibility of love, or contentment, or even common sense'.[81] As mentioned earlier, a 'tribunal Kris' is particularly commonplace in Europe, where discussion between elders, leaders and those in conflict is favoured over physical resolution. Negotiations in one form or another is, culturally speaking, the preferred method. So why then does the narrative of 'violence and Gypsies' persist to permeate our understanding of GRT people and 'others'? One quick test to give us an indication is to think of the story of Cain and Abel.

Here's a quick experiment for you to do: In one short sentence and out loud now, describe the story of Cain and Abel. Done it? Good.

[80]   Lewis, 2012, p. 12.
[81]   Lewis, 2012, p. 125.

Did you mention Cain, killing his brother Abel? The likelihood is you did. Why not instead mention the grace of God in protecting the sinner, Cain, after he had been sentenced to wander the Earth? Why not explain the story as an example of giving God your best? Why not describe the incredible situation of the first 'real' humans encountering life in the newly fallen world[82]? The reality is, we often choose (consciously or unconsciously) to recall and magnify the sins of others, in the vain hope of alleviating the pressure of guilt accrued from our own transgressions. In looking down on others (in this instance, Gypsies and Travellers), we (gorgers) operate in our position of privilege and effectively say, 'Look, Lord, they have only brought to you vegetables, whereas I have bought you the finest new-born of my flock. Look, Lord, they have murdered, yet I am clean from sin'. However, when we examine the positions of Cain and Abel, we are faced with a plot twist that turns the tables upside down.

Cain is the firstborn and the older brother, and therefore he is born with privilege and status. He holds the authority and he leads the bloodline after his parents. Yet it is Abel, the symbolic 'shepherd' and protector of flocks, who is favoured by God. But how so? Metaphorically speaking, in this story is it not so that the Gypsies and Travellers are Cain – the despised murderer? And are not the gorgers, Abel – the one whom please the Lord with his offering? The issue is that Cain's response is so often our collective response. We see the activities of others that conflict with our own understandings of God and justice and right and wrong, and we grow despondent when the justice of God isn't served upon them. Our countenance drops and our rage rises. In our own self-defined righteousness, we apply our own justice. In the instance of Gypsies and Travellers questionable behaviours, the common response is to 'murder' GRT society and condemn its values.

[82]   Adam and Eve were created by God – not born, and were living in 'Paradise' – not the fallen world that we know today.

When these patterns of destruction are allowed to continue, they become the norm. We lessen the status of our fellow God-created human beings to 'less than', and we are presented with a new category – that of the 'other'. The other is placed beyond the walls of the larger populous and into the Edgelands. Yet those who have condemned others remain oblivious to their *own* perilous position, unaware that it is actually *them* who now carry the mark of Cain, wandering in a desperate wilderness where the challenging realities of a fallen world are seen as personal and unfair. In quiet desperation, we ask both God and ourselves, what is wrong with my offering, Lord? If asked in sincerity, the response is gentle but affirmative: First, do not judge your brother. That is for God to do. Secondly, in your moment of offering, check your heart and not your neighbour. Did Abraham not offer the life of his own son? Did Paul not propose an offering of Praise? Did Christ not offer Himself? The nature of our offering can generate many questions, but they are not ours to answer. Our concern is our own heart and not the heart and values of others.

At times, our sacrifice may take the form of physically defending our family's honour, other times it may appear as working many hours to provide, or indeed cutting back on work to be present for our children. So in conflict, we do not find justification, nor do we find status, but we do find rationale. We sin, but we are not sin. May God's grace be sufficient for us.

Thieving and Deception

The narrative that proposes Gypsies, Roma and Travellers are thieves and commit deception is arguably the most dominant and historical accusation held against GRT people. It is historical, comprehensive, and troublesome and has defined public perception for centuries. In the UK, the mode of theft 'traditionally' associated with GRT people has been broad and varied, and includes everything from metal theft to the stealing of children. One tabloid journalist (J. Norton) gave 'warning' to the readers about the probability of kidnapping in relation to their children:

> For centuries, the wandering Gypsy folk have frightened parents all over the world … adult Gypsies should not, on any account, be allowed to associate with white children in such a restricted area as a schoolroom or a playground. The confined spaces lend themselves too well to eventualities that might well cause fear [of their being kidnapped] in the heart of any parent.[83]

The arbitrary use of influence and power in condemning Gypsies in a blanket fashion is not new or unfamiliar. Such measures have, according to historical records, been practised for centuries. Furthermore, these historical practices do not appear to stand alone; instead they have been intertwined with religious authority and rationale, and thus carry with them potential ecclesiological implications. Hancock acknowledges that the 'necessary' crime [of theft] is a legacy from a time when it was one mechanism for subsistence and survival'.[84] However, to consider theft as a cultural identifier or definitive characteristic of Gypsies and Travellers is a failure to contextualise the social and historic factors against the possible moral standing of the accused. Crime (in this case, theft) is a social issue, and cannot be attributed to an ethnicity. Crime is always going to be the likely outcome for any collective that faces social exclusion and is denied the standard benefits of a society.

Justifiable theft is, theologically speaking, challenging. What is theft for one person is survival for another. There is some evidence among the many Romani maxims and proverbs that have passed through generations of Traveller families and societies, which speak of a collective sense of injustice. Because of the lack of apparent meaning, the Romani name for these sayings is '*garade lava*', translated

[83]   Hancock, 2013, p. 94.
[84]   Hancock, 2013, p. 97.

as 'hidden words'.[85] An example of one of these 'hidden words' is "'The non-Romani steals a horse, the Romani steals a horseshoe" (like the differences in society, Romani theft is correspondingly minor when compared with non-Romani theft)'.[86] Such a phrase does not remove responsibility for said actions but provides perspective on the potential rationale behind acts of theft that may occur. A variant of the above phrase is the following: 'The Romani steals a chicken, the non-Romani steals the farm'.[87] Again, issues of necessity versus greed and the inter-relationship between Travellers, the larger society and survival play out through this direct, simple, yet loaded phrase.

However, explanatory factors such as these could be seen by outsiders as a matter of self-justification and as an attempt by Gypsies to remove theft from its relationship with sin. Nonetheless, in the face of Christ's redemption, there is a distinction between sinner and sin. This struggle is seen with St Paul, as he battles with the sin that resides in him (Romans 7:14 – 25). Paul's sin, much like the accusations he received of being a murderer (Acts 28:4), is based on actions from his flesh and not on his identity in Christ; he may or may not have committed murder, but either way his spirit will not be condemned as a murderer by God. Historically, Gypsies and Travellers have been collectively condemned; their 'spirit' (community) receiving the same accusation and treatment as their 'flesh' (individuals). In this way, 'a Gypsy and a theft' has evolved to become 'Gypsies are thieves'.

ASSOCIATING SIN WITH TRAVELLERS' 'OTHERNESS'

A distinctive and destructive public discourse has resulted in Gypsies and Travellers being synonymous with theft. Whilst there remains a proportionally higher representation of GRT people in the current judicial system, the historical record (social, political, religious and theological) that has created such a scenario may be flawed, biased

[85] Hancock, 2013, p. 145.
[86] Hancock, 2013, p. 148.
[87] Hancock, 2013, p. 148.

and discriminatory. The biblical plumb line determines that 'all have sinned and fallen short' (Romans 3:23). In spite of this, historical and cultural stereotyping and expectations (or lack thereof) by the settled population towards Gypsies and Travellers suggests that GRT people may be seen as 'falling shorter' than other ethnicities and races.

In this respect, Gypsy sin is unsurprising to the gorger; it is merely a consequence of Gypsy inadequacies. It would appear that the ethos behind this contentious social narrative is applicable to any group of people, with the greatest consequences often falling upon those existing in some form of social and/or historical separation. Philosopher and Black Liberation theologian, Cornel West, identifies the relationship between sin or 'flaws' and differences of race and ethnicity through a comparison involving North America and Black people:

> To engage in a serious discussion of race in America, we must begin not with the problems of black people but with the flaws of American society – flaws rooted in historic inequalities and longstanding cultural stereotypes … As long as black people are viewed as 'them', the burden falls on blacks to do all the 'cultural' and 'moral' work necessary for healthy race relations. The implication is that only certain Americans can define what it means to be American – and the rest must simply 'fit in'.[88]

Negative portrayals of ethnic and racial 'others' in America has created patterns of low confidence and self-destructive behaviours amongst black youths and communities.[89] A similar effect operates among those identifying as Travellers and Gypsies in the UK, resulting in an impoverishment of self-belief, self-realisation and spirituality – collectively and individually. It would seem that interracial interdependency is inescapable. However, when the powerful (i.e. the

---

[88]   West, 2001, p. 6 – 7.
[89]   Martin, 2008. Also; Howitt, 1986, pp. 60 – 61; Donaldson, 2015.

larger population) enforces racial and social hierarchies in a nation where such interdependency exists, we are doomed to paranoia. This in turn has positioned suspicion as a default response from Gypsies to both gorger society as a whole and to a non-nomadic Church.

Such a response has produced a necessity for movements such as the *Light and Life*[90] Church and the European Evangelical revival. Richard Twiss, a Native American theologian and author, provides an interesting parallel to this situation, presented through his Native American indigenous perspective:

> However, suspicion and fear run both ways. Indigenous people have a lot to fear about the 'white man's religion'! Conquest, racism, hatred, prejudice, exclusion, forced assimilation and ongoing institutional injustices are just a few of the fears that come to mind.[91]

Martin Luther King Jr's statement concerning 'one garment of destiny',[92] highlights an aspect of the fear held by Gypsies and Travellers when expectations of assimilation and amalgamation arise, and reveals the complexity in the ethnic and racial equation. If Travellers are expected to be locked into King's single garment with the 'white' majority, then the chances of their social and religious freedom are reduced to nil. Anti-assimilation for the Traveller, therefore, is not a rejection of gorger culture but an intentional act of preservation for one's own culture and faith. Furthermore, a vacuum is created by the discourse of positivity towards 'gorgerness' and conversely the negatively debased historical and contemporary ideas of blackness and Gypsiness.[93] In this vacuum Travellers and Gypsies are subject to

---

[90]   Ridley, 2014.
[91]   Twiss, 2015, p. 20.
[92]   West, 2001, pp. 146 – 147.
[93]   'Gypsiness' is loosely defined as Gypsies expressing 'the Gypsy worldview, enact[ing] appropriate Gypsy behaviour, and maintain[ing] the Gypsy/Non-Gypsy boundary'; Silverman, 1988, p. 274·

marginalisation and exclusion by whites *and* blacks. This situation is identified by Malcolm X as a form of 'social death', where the 'hybrid' or 'mulatto' become symbols of 'weakness and confusion'.[94] One form of evidence which demonstrates this dynamic in operation is the Church's drive towards converting the 'savage' Gypsies during the eighteenth and nineteenth centuries.

The action of associating the Travellers' ethnicity with a sinful existence, often without merit or warrant, has shaped and directed how Travellers have been proselytised by a gorger Church. The result is centuries of evangelistic teachings and drives, focused on saving and redeeming the uneducated 'heathen Gypsies'.[95] However, whilst such evangelical drives have evidently had some successes, the collective modus operandi of Gypsy and Traveller communities suggests the existence of a persistent construct of *pre-existing* and continuous Traveller theological identity. This identity, often overlooked for its apparent 'sinfulness', operates both as a response to anti-Traveller and anti-Gypsy political, social and religious agendas, and as a form of deliberate separation.

A tenacious spiritual resistance and resilience has taken place whereby the Traveller, confident in his or her security in Christ (or as a Traveller), has retreated to the Cross (or camp). It is by the Cross and in the process of crucifixion where suffering is shared with Christ and Creator; liberation has not happened for the Traveller by pursuing a 'Promised land' of integration but by clinging to – even embracing – the Cross. The Crucifixion therefore is more than an active moment of reflection. It is the entirely intentional and purposeful decision to remain firmly in the Cross event, forsaking an assured existence of social acceptance and societal norms for the chance to live a life at the margins. In these Edgelands is Christ. It is at this point, with the Cross, that the contradictory nature of the Christ's absence is matched

---

94   Silverman, 1988, pp. 147 – 148.
95   Keet-Black, 2013, pp. 38 – 45.

in full measure with His unrestricted, unlimited and unrequited love; the Traveller's grief is also *His* grief. Furthermore, the Traveller's 'sin' has created a scenario whereby one is both close to Christ in one's suffering, but also in spiritual peril because of the sin itself[96] (Romans 6:23). However, the Gypsies' gospel is a gospel of continual grace that unlike their European masters, meets Gypsies where they are – in the margins and on the edges – literally, figuratively, and spiritually.

Issues of identity and 'otherness' (particularly in regard to ethnicity) are central in much of the rationale behind understanding Gypsy and Traveller behaviour as different, wrong, sinful and flawed. There are strongly developed social action policies designed to engage and support Gypsies and Travellers. However, these processes are often driven by an agenda of assimilation and dependence; the Traveller usually being required to submit in some way to another's 'ideal'.[97] Gypsies and Travellers then feel coerced into modes of engagement and worship which have unacceptable religious and social costs attached to the supposed benefits – costs that are simply too high. In getting the accuser to remove the title of 'thief', Gypsies must allow gorgers to steal their culture. In the presence and persistence of such a dynamic, GRT people appear to be perpetually judged as flawed and bound by accusations of sinfulness.

SUMMARY

For centuries, GRT people have been collectively condemned as thieves and accused of savagery. However, in the process of accusing the other of being Cain (the murderer whose offering is less than), bridges have been burnt. The curse, has for some, become a self-fulfilling prophecy. Many Gypsies and Travellers have been excluded from mainstream society, resulting in a forced defiance of certain rules just to survive. The accusers, now justified in their accusations,

[96] With reference to being in state of 'spiritual peril' due to sin. Also; Burns & Newman, 2012.
[97] DfES, 2003, p. 7.

subsequently look astonished when the excluded parties do not (and cannot) participate in singing from the same hymn sheet. This phenomenon, which sits in stark contrast to Jesus' blanket of inclusive love, is an all too familiar dynamic for many minority groups. One response in our contemporary times has been an increased awareness of inclusivity and diversity. However, this most Christian concern of shared love for all is not without its own issues.

In our necessary but insatiable pursuit of inclusion, we have created an unexpected by-product, and that is 'othering'. By purposively identifying those who are different in some way to the expected norm, a system of social and religious hierarchies have formed. We have inadvertently created a society of rulers and ruled. Some victims find themselves as such because of their lack of influence, whilst others choose to reside in victimhood. Either way, the place of residence for the 'others' is located squarely in the Edgelands – the place beyond the walls of common culture.

It has become all too easy to demonise those who follow other paths and dwell in different places – physically, spiritually, mentally. If only we would remember that when we pick up our Cross each day, we are embracing both God's promise of love and the fallen, suffering state of our fellow man. Sometimes that suffering takes the form of a sin, of an addiction, of a destructive habit. Our task is: To heal, not hurt. To listen, not speak. To embrace, not reject. To direct, not dictate. Our task is to love. Our task is to love. Our task, is to love.

'Sin' is a moral, theological motif. Illegality is a legal, judicial and sometimes civil category. Too often as Christians we have combined sin and illegality, and then taken it upon ourselves to serve as both the Sanhedrin and Pontius Pilate. We forget that we hold in our possession the living Word of God. A sword and a tool that can draw lines in the sand that no accuser can pass, lest they have no sin in themselves. For those that fight for honour, for those that accuse and condemn others, for those that steal to live, and for those that make the commandments their corner stone, remember that we have all fallen short. When we accuse the other of being Cain, we do so at the risk of revealing to others our own sacrifice. Let's choose to work on our own offerings, safe in the knowledge that when we humble ourselves (and not others), God can work through us. Sin needs to be driven out, not illuminated.

Among our differing tribes, races and peoples, there will always be positions of difference – in opinion, action and thought. As alluded to earlier, at times separation is helpful, particularly when a vulnerable group needs to protect its borders from external pressures and influences. Sometimes however, those same borders are more than just a line of defence or isolation; they are a method of equilibrium. Within Gypsy and Traveller communities, an unwritten equilibrium exists, which governs every aspect of life. An inherent code that has persisted through every generation. Faith serves as its anchor, Christ operates as its rudder, Holy Spirit fills its sails, whilst family and community form its deck. In Romani circles it is more commonly known as '*mokhhadi*' (meaning, *purity and pollution*). In the next chapter, we will see how even the most deepest, personal and unique parts of our very being can be examples of God breathing through His creation. At times our differences may separate us from each other, but through our language of Christ we are reunited. Now we will begin the process of examining that language as it plays out in Gypsy and Traveller culture.

CHAPTER THREE
PURITY AND POLLUTION: I HAVE CALLED YOU BY NAME

'What agreement can exist between the temple of God and idols? For we are the temple of the living God. As God has said: "I will dwell with them and walk among them, and I will be their God, and they will be My people. Therefore come out from among them and be separate, says the Lord. Touch no unclean thing, and I will receive you."' (2 Corinthians 6:17)

AN INTRODUCTION TO MOKHHADI

'For the last time, Steven, stop answering me back!' I knew I was in trouble because my mother had used my full name. However, the autistic nature of my 10 year-old brain felt extremely frustrated; how could I get my point across and explain my rationale if I could not answer her back? Clearly, upon reflection in my room later that day, I was missing the point. Unfortunately, I was convinced that my mother was also missing the point, so I let her know. It did not end well for me! I was not intentionally being disobedient, nor was my mother being unfairly harsh. We merely had different understandings and interpretations of the same situation. These differences, without their contextual explanations (my mother's usage of a classic idiom, and my unrealised and undiagnosed possible high-functioning autism), led us both to dig in and hold our own.

We've seen how differing interpretations of wants, needs and beliefs led to the creation of Gypsy churches. Indeed, the phenomenon of difference sparking new growth has been going on for much of the church's history. It's interesting how biblical hermeneutics that are usually focused on the same ecumenical standpoints, are often the catalyst for both church splits and multiplication of both congregations and denominations the world over. Our divisions, are, of course, spiritually and theologically significant to the foundations of our collective and individual faith journey. On a micro level, they determine the direction of our walk, and our relationships with God. On a macro level, such divisions determine our walk with other people, and with the structures, laws, and social standards of our living places. Sometimes we give those structures, laws and standards names, such as capitalism, the criminal justice system, and feminism, for example.

Then of course, we as specific groups (for example, Church bodies, sports teams, families, Universities) follow yet further 'codes' of practice based on our beliefs. At times these fall in line with those larger collective structures, laws and social standards, and at other times they do not. When it comes to our theologising – both individually and collectively, often our spiritual being and physical nature become unified. If we *search* for this unified nature through prayer and the scriptures, we will find God. If we *express* this unified nature, we will find those who share similar identities to us, and we will draw near those whose hearts are open. Often this looks like an established Church congregation/denomination, other times it looks like a family, and yet other times it can manifest through forms such as a collective racial or ethnic stance. This is the formula of how our deepest physical and mental identities are able to manifest theologically. This phenomenon, in its most simple form, is actually the crux of theology: God *speaks to* humans; humans speak *of* God; humans speak *back to* God; record and repeat.

PURITY AND POLLUTION

As outsiders to particular groups and/or identities, such as the ones mentioned above (Church denominations, etc.), every once in a while we are presented with a new presentation of a unified nature that touches on our own experience with the Creator. For example, in the 1950s/60s this happened in the form of Black theology. The experience and understanding of one collective resulted in another collective looking at itself and asking challenging and life-altering questions. So, how and where did this powerful impact come from? Well, if the equation has God in it, God is usually the answer! Does this mean, in this example, that Black theology had *everything* right? No, of course not. It does however highlight that when theological identities manifest, they usually share the same principles of miracles in the Bible: biblical miracles tangibly bless the recipient, but importantly they always impact the faith of the observer. So, if you're white/non-Black and you've ever read any Black theology and you're holding some form of guilt because you're struggling to engage fully, just remember that no matter how hard you try or how sincere your intentions, you can never fully 'experience' Black theology. However, as a non-Black person, that's not the point. The point is to be challenged and changed.

GRT culture in all its forms has, to some degree, a unifying nature that has existed since the beginning of the Gypsy ethnicity. It is in many ways an unwritten code that governs: behaviour, values, principles, health, sex and sexuality, gender roles, relationships with outsiders, and interaction with the outside world. It has evolved over the centuries as GRT communities have themselves evolved, and its relationship with Christianity is both synonymous and synergistic. Whilst many of its particular practices are unique to GRT culture, its principles and ethos are something which can benefit many more outside of the community. This unwritten code is often simply understood, acknowledged and/or felt, rather than named. However, for the benefit of this text and those unfamiliar with it, I shall use its original Romani name – *mokhhadi* …

Defining Mokhhadi (Pollution)

To Gypsies, Gypsy culture is sacred. As such, maintaining particular historical ways of living – even if they seem dated, pointless or at times bizarre, is an essential and often unquestionable choice. Some of these life choices, such as the decision made by some to remain nomadic (or semi nomadic), is often met with political resistance, public condemnation, and usually a degree of bewilderment by some outside of the community. However, the adherence to these practices are not just important because they have been practices for centuries and are deeply ingrained within GRT society, but they are unquestionable because of their symbolic and spiritual meaning. In many instances, that deeper meaning was born from physical necessity. So, in the instance of nomadism, moving on at regular periods meant that early Roma groups could escape spreading wars, leave hostile places, find new work, and maintain a degree of anonymity. However, as those needs diminished, the growing role of religion in the hearts and psyche of many GRT people, took over and placed a greater degree of spiritual importance on such practices. Like everything else under the sun though, many of these ideas were not new.

The idea of 'pollution and purity' (or, 'mokhhadi') stems from the Indian ancestry of Gypsies and was originally drawn from Hindu traditions.[98] Unlike its Hindu origins though, its manner of application in Gypsy and Traveller households has been likened to that found in Orthodox Jewish homes.[99] When positioned among Central Asian and East Mediterranean regions where other world views and systems of pollution, purity, and 'contagion' exist and operate,[100] mokhhadi starts to look a little more familiar. The Romani term 'mokhhadi' (or 'chikli'[101]) essentially means 'ritual purity'[102] and remains an element of

[98]   Dawson, 2000, pp. 3 & 9; Hancock, 2013, p. 75.
[99]   Clark and Greenfields, 2006, p. 41.
[100] Douglas, 1966.
[101] Chikli' is a synonym of 'mokhhadi'. Saying mokhhadi out loud can be considered impure.
[102] Dawson, 2000, p. 9.

Gypsy identity to this day. However, adherence to particular practices (such as males and females washing in separate basins) is undertaken by fewer and fewer Travellers as new generations emerge.[103]

Reflecting historically, it's clear that at some point there was a transition from a Proto-Gypsy ritual purity that was formed from its Indian and Hindu roots, into a common practice whose convictions were located in a Christian-Judeo framework. It's uncertain at this stage as to whether these 'convictions' pre-existed in a similar form prior to securing Christianity as its host. However, what is certain is the clear influence and appearance of certain 'traditional' church practices and teachings. With the rise of Christian support for Travellers and Gypsies in the nineteenth century (accommodation, food and educational provision), I would propose that the final remnants of any explicitly Indian elements would have been lost during the Victorian period, potentially earlier, with Christianity (including Church instruction) taking its complete grasp by the end of the nineteenth century.[104] The rise of influential Victorian preachers in Britain and their messages of instruction were the first attempts by an outside body towards a formal and positive outreach for Gypsies. Certain messages would have been complementary to the practices endorsed and implemented and indeed considered necessary by the Gypsy communities. These messages related to aspects such as hygiene, ritual purity, cleanliness and separateness – both physically and mentally. Charles Spurgeon, speaking on 14 December 1890, delivered a sermon entitled *Camp Law and Camp Life*. In his opening statements (with the Deuteronomic accounts as his backdrop), Spurgeon had the following to say with regards to personal and spiritual cleanliness:

---

[103] Clark and Greenfields, 2006, p. 41.

[104] It should be noted that I am referring primarily to the UK. In very remote pockets of Europe, there has been and still is some Roma communities who have adopted Islam as their main faith.

What I admire in it is that God the Glorious, the All-Holy, should stoop to legislate about such things. Such attention was very necessary for health and even for life, and the Lord, in condescending to it, conveys a severe rebuke to Christian people who have been careless in matters respecting health and cleanliness. Saintly souls should not be lodged in filthy bodies. God takes note of matters which persons who are falsely spiritual speak of as beneath their observation. If the Lord cares for such things, we must not neglect them...Dear Friends, the great thing that I would bring out at this time is the *spiritual* lesson of the text—*how the Lord would have His people clean in all things*. The God of Holiness commands and loves purity— purity of all kinds...Filth may be expected in persons of unclean hearts, but those who have been purified in spirit should do their utmost to be pure in flesh, clothes and dwelling.[105]

The use of the term 'Camp' in Spurgeon's message refers to aspects such as any home dwelling, person or Christian spiritual walk. However, in spite of the universal application of this sermon (i.e. it is not explicitly aimed towards Gypsies), applying strands of this teaching to the traditions of cultural purity in GRT culture facilitates a clear (albeit muted) conversation between seemingly mundane behaviour and intrinsic reasoning. As theologians and explorers of faith, we often want to find deep and complex mysteries behind these collective patterns of behaviour and faith practice. But the reality is that the hermeneutical properties of that 'intrinsic reasoning' are made possible by the imperceptibly congenital nature of the activity. In short, simple living makes for a rich Christian theology.

The use of Spurgeon's sermon, however, is of course in *comparison* to the greater, settled populace. Consideration (for the purposes of contextualisation) should therefore be given to not

---

[105]   Spurgeon, 1890, p. 1.

just the differences between Traveller and gorger communities, but also the *similarities*; in this instance – cleanliness and hygiene. The similarities in the Traveller's situation is not an attempted assimilation but an expression of uniqueness in the common human experience. Through an emphasis of cleanliness, separation, and tangible purity, Gypsies and Travellers have not created a new Christianity, but have simply made a purposeful reappropriation of Christian concepts in everyday non-religious Gypsy practices.

Interestingly, despite *mokhhadi* being a linking belief system among Gypsies, Roma and Travellers all over the UK and throughout the world, it is seldom discussed and rarely even referred to as '*mokhhadi*'. Indeed, on one particular research trip, I spoke to a number of young Travellers who just looked bemused when I spoke about purity and pollution. To put this into context though (and for any sexual health practitioners reading this), a young mother on the same site (a mother of one of the young people in question) who when asked how she would broach the issue of talking about reproduction with her daughter, replied with a story about storks delivering babies and being able to buy new-borns. If I hadn't heard the same thing elsewhere on multiple occasions, I would have thought it was a joke. 'My ma told me that story and it didn't do me no harm, now did it. You'd know though, we don't talk about things like that till we needs to. It ain't proper.'

Mokhhadi represents the elements of pollution and purity, of acceptable and sub-standard, of GRT and gorger. Whilst these dichotomies are disruptive in some areas, they are useful in establishing and maintaining borders between GRT and gorgers and in determining what is and isn't acceptable for GRT people. In a world that is growing ever more connected – both physically and virtually, there is perhaps some argument to upholding some of the dichotomies that we as individuals and collectives practice. Our *differences* don't divide us; however, *what we do* with those differences defines us. We are called to be in the world but not be part of the world (John 15:19); our acting (or not acting) upon our differences is what separates us from the world. We are called to follow God, but it's our actions that set the benchmark of whether we are sheep or goats (Matthew 25:31-46). Our understanding of God and subsequently our relationship with Him determines our *faith*. Our value systems (and as such, our actions) are born from that faith in God. So whilst our actions cannot secure our salvation or earn God's mercy and forgiveness, they can and do demonstrate how we understand our relationship with the Father. In many ways then, *mokhhadi* is a non-verbal expression of a love language that seeks to keep the 'Temple' free from defilement and the individual closer to their source.

How Mokhhadi Functions

On one hand, *mokhhadi* is a methodical practice that is intended to maintain health (physical, mental, spiritual) and order (social, familial, religious). On the other hand, it is a spiritual practice that incorporates superstitious beliefs and practices, liturgical actions (Christian, and others), and particular exegeses. There is an understanding that time spent in gorger environments has a draining effect upon spiritual energy. Conversely, one's 'spiritual batteries' are recharged and 're-purified' by spending time in an all-Traveller/Gypsy environment.[106] It is in this environment and context of 'spiritual and physical wellbeing that the Indian origin of ... [Gypsy] people is most clearly seen'.[107] The physical aspect requires the observance of rules that take many forms and that deal with elements of daily life. Typically these include but are not limited to: water and waste separation; the cleaning of clothes and bed linen/towels; preparation of food and drinks; washing and hygiene/appearance; menstruating and childbirth; interaction with animals; cleanliness of the home environment; and separation of males and females at particular times (such as at weddings and social environments).[108]

---

[106] Hancock, 2013, p. 75.
[107] Hancock, 2013, p. 75.
[108] Clark & Greenfields, 2006, pp. 23 and 41 – 42; Keet-Black, 2013, p. 20.

PURITY AND POLLUTION

Everyday cleanliness is of paramount importance when the living quarters for an entire family is sometimes permanently located in a trailer. As such, ideas on pollution can initially adopt a practical appearance. For example, concerns over hygiene mean that the toilet that is found in most caravans is almost always never used by Travellers, who often will remove them or simply use the space for additional storage. And whilst nowadays this specific example is only applicable to a small number of Gypsies (with the majority occupying fixed housing), the principles remain. Indeed, the old adage that says cleanliness is next to godliness has perhaps never rang truer than it does in GRT circles. Physical cleanliness and separation represents many external factors but is also, as we will see shortly, indicative of the spiritual self. Of course, by shining this light upon a largely unknown factor, another less positive and assumed factor is also brought to light. Historical derogatory stereotyping that suggests Travellers and Gypsies are dirty is simply untrue and unable to stand up to even the mildest scrutiny. This isn't an empty statement. Upon conducting research on numerous camps, researchers found in almost every instance the trailers and their immediate surroundings were 'spotless'.[109] Furthermore, Research by the Cardiff Law School suggested that less than 3 per cent of Travellers are responsible for excessive waste and rubbish being left on the outskirts of camps and on illegal settlements.[110]

On the surface, it's easy to only see the *practical* application of *mokhhadi*. Our vision is such that we are conditioned to see difference in others and in the world around us. Doing so allows us to appreciate fineries in comparison to our own familiarity, it allows us to rapidly identify danger, and it facilitates value judgements, which in turn cements our own way of living as just and correct. Digging just a fraction deeper allows us to see *ideological* values. Sometimes this is laid bare. For example, a Church may have a 'mission statement', or

[109]   Dawson, 2000, p. 12.
[110]   Dawson, 2000, p. 12.

77

a club may have a dress code. These ideological values can give an indication as to where our hearts are, and what our behaviour is likely to be in a number of situations. In Gypsy and Traveller communities this might look like the separation between Traveller and gorger; or the deliberate separation between males and females at parties, weddings and in certain other gatherings. These unwritten rules exist in part to avoid the breaking of taboos, such as sexual intercourse before marriage, which is seen as both polluting and as something akin to a gorger lifestyle choice. It is important to note that these approaches to daily living are not in retaliation to gorger people, but are in place to help maintain respectability and avoid 'polluting' circumstances.

Postmodernism and the age of enlightenment has brought with it far more freedoms for many than was otherwise enjoyed beforehand. And whilst many of our progressive attitudes towards sex and sexuality are both necessary and good, in many communities a high number of 'taboos' remain. If however we are still sitting here reading this and thinking 'but in this day and age X and X should be able to do this, and Y and Y shouldn't have to do 1, 2 and 3', then we must look at ourselves as a church, as a religious body – indeed, as a series of religions and States, and understand that we created and imposed such doctrines and dogma in the first place. In the name of God we bound the freedoms of countless generations so that we could control values, practices and lives, and in doing so we positioned ourselves as God and our institutions as the golden cow. Our lesson from history is that we should first choose to unconditionally love and listen before we give ourselves the mantle to instruct others in how they must now live.

For many GRT communities, the majority of 'taboo' avoidance practices and specific gender roles are not damaging and if anything help to maintain Gypsy culture. Many Gypsies would be shocked to see the lack of such standards among gorgers, adding further reasoning to maintain separateness. This 'lack of standards' among gorgers has sometimes been understood to include things such as the breaking of marriage commitments, a lack of care for the elderly, and moral corruptness. As such, *mokhhadi* is more than a form of reasoning with just physical consequences; it is something that invokes moral corruptibility from questionable actions. Pollution beliefs thus appear to present themselves on three different planes: the physical; the ideological; and the spiritual – or body, soul, and spirit. It is at this stage that *mokhhadi* is perhaps better understood as being a pyramidal structure, based upon an understanding of relationship between the human and the divine. In something akin to Abraham Maslow's 'Hierarchy of Needs',[111] there are certain stages in which the implementation of *mokhhadi* evolves – from a purely *physical* construct to a purely *spiritual* construct. In this instance, the evolution 'upwards' produces a 'Neoplatonic' layering, whereby any progression towards the top of this '*mokhhadi* pyramid' results in a greater degree of spiritual self-actualisation. Or put simply, as we draw nearer to Christ, we become more like him; our salvation becomes more assured. It's not our works that allow us to progress closer to Christ, but His grace and our desire to be like Him. However, pollution can occur at any level on the journey towards Christlikeness, and will undermine the other layers wherever it occurs – all are susceptible. As such, it is important for the Gypsy or Traveller to maintain purity at all levels. There is a greater chance of achieving this when the Traveller maintains a separation between gorger and Traveller, or, when we occupy the Earth but are not part of it.

The Pollution Narrative in Christian Terms

It is at this stage that it is more beneficial, relevant and arguably more understandable to modify and translate the terms 'pollution' and 'purity' into the contemporary Christian context in which they are used. Doing so does not negate or ignore the culturally historic roots of the terms ('*mokhhadi*', or 'ritual purity' still remain); it simply makes the terms accessible and more reflective of how they are understood

---

[111] Maslow, 1943.

in the present era. As such, the term 'pollution' can also be referred to as 'sin'. Meanwhile, the term 'purity' may at times also be referred to in a more relevant and context-specific state rather than a generalised application; so, 'purity' still exists, but is also understood as 'forgiven', 'clean', 'pure', 'grace', and 'love'.

The biblical precedent for the application of these concepts in a 'real world' scenario can be found in the book of Leviticus, where instructions on communal and personal holiness (in the Mosaic 'Camp' model) are developed. Rules for living are presented that deal explicitly with purity, going beyond the universalistic applicability of the Ten Commandments whilst remaining in the specificity of the intended audience – the tribe of Levi (the Priestly order). Theologian David Pawson provides a great exegesis, suggesting that many people interpret the moralistic standing of the Levitical rules for living 'in terms of good and bad'. However, as Pawson suggests, they should instead be understood in terms of the distinctions they make between what is *unclean and clean*, and between what is *common and holy*.[112] It is not that to do one or the other will make one 'good' or categorise the other as 'bad', but that all actions are either holy or common – clean or unclean. For the most part, the Gypsy narrative subscribes to this perspective. This has ramifications for the outcome of seemingly innocent or well-intended actions. Take, for example, the schoolteacher who delivers a lesson on sex education to a class consisting of both Travellers and gorgers. Although the motive for delivering the lesson resides in a desire to educate and inform, for the majority of the Traveller children present it will be shameful and inappropriate to engage in discussions concerning sexuality and sexual health.[113] So, whilst the act itself may be 'innocent', the partaking of the class is considered an unclean act, which creates a 'common' – rather

---

[112]   Pawson, 2007, pp. 142 – 143.

[113]   Bhopal and Myers, 2008, pp. 107 – 108.

than 'holy' action, as no holy act can be unclean.[114]   In this way, one of the arguments for separateness by the Traveller from gorger society is presented more clearly, through a process of ideological and spiritual reasoning, providing further insight into both the perceived relationship between Traveller and gorger, and between Traveller and God.

From a purely textual description, the application of *mokhhadi*-based practices and beliefs can appear to be draconian and socially restrictive. However, the honouring of such traditions is drawn from an embracing of one's cultural heritage, where a unified security and freedom can be found.[115] As such, the honouring of purity traditions becomes a source of freedom, where 'superstitious' acts and Hinduistic practices amalgamate to form a collection of conservative ideas, presented in an open and vibrant context. Consequently, for an external audience such acts and beliefs can potentially challenge and/or threaten certain societal ideas and the hegemony of 'traditional' British Christianity.

THE MULATTO AND THE DIDIKAIS: PURITY AND POLLUTION IN RACE

Judging others is, for the most part considered wrong by most, except for, well, when it isn't. Many people have moved on from judging others over their sexuality, but some of those same people will condemn others for eating meat or failing to recycle properly. The Bible can at times be a little grey when it comes to judgement. One moment we are being told to refrain from judgement (Matthew 7:1), whilst at other times we are actively encouraged to employ a host of judgements against our fellow believers. That last point is poignant for the next part of our journey through the purity and pollution

---

[114]   Pawson, 2007, p. 144.

[115]   Such a phenomenon is not unique to Traveller groups. Many collectives of people are united and strengthened in their unique shared beliefs and world views. See previous comments by F. Barth (1969, pp. 14 – 15).

narrative, as we begin to pack up and move our exploration beyond the camp (see Chapter Four – 'Sojourner'). As we hold our fellow believers to account, so do we maintain borders and control within our other structures. During some of my PhD field research, I was subject to judgements that some would find offensive, whilst others would see them as necessary. Although there are many issues with the idea of an actual 'pure' Gypsy race, the concept still persists among many communities. And with that idea comes judgements and internal boundaries, with purity and pollution serving as both the judicial system and the border control.

GET THE MAN A TEA

One part of my field research saw me head to the county of Suffolk; an area to the East of England, known for its rural pastures and famed for its archaeological finds. I was on my way to meet Billy and Charlotte;[116] a married couple with four children, living on an officially registered Traveller's site. They identified as Catholic and could be considered 'traditional' in their approach and understanding of Traveller life. Billy was a builder and a landscape gardener; however, he also had various other sources of income including logging and selling second-hand vehicles. Charlotte primarily worked as a housewife but also supplemented the family's income by doing haircuts for some of her friends and family and by customising baby accessories with lace and sequins (such as bibs, clothing and prams).

Approaching the site, one's initial indication of entering a different environment was the stark difference between the new housing development I drove through and the unkempt local-authority owned country lane, leading to where Billy and Charlotte lived. The road ran for a mile or so before reaching the site. Nearer the approach, rubbish including general waste, rubble and appliances filled the sides of the small lane, forming yet higher mounds around both sides of the

[116]   All names used, unless otherwise stated, are pseudonyms.

entrance to the site. Two large brick-built pillars marked the entrance, whereupon the waste was no longer present. Instead, the space was filled with an immaculately kept private road situated in an ordered and structured development. Initially I couldn't see any adults, just a few children playing on bikes in the distance. The overall cleanliness of the site would continue into the individual trailers and caravans filling each plot. This was not unusual in terms of typical Traveller sites that I had been to, but was in stark contradiction with the stereotypes that portrayed Travellers and Gypsies as 'dirty people'.[117] From my experience, cleanliness on this scale often indicated a greater application of *mokhhadi*. As such, I knew that on one hand my Christianity would serve as my bridge, but on the other hand, I was about to be grilled over my identity.

Regarding the site, as much as this was a settlement, it was, theologically speaking, better understood as a 'camp'. The Traveller – or sojourner, who had escaped multiple forms of Pharaohs and Egyptian lands, was now settled, for the time being. The camp had been established, and with that came divinely-inspired rules and conditions[118] (Deuteronomy 23:12–14). Later conversations with the Travellers living on the site revealed that there were technically no specific rules for camp 'hygiene', but that there were 'rules' in operation. These rules, as with many Gypsy and Traveller conventions were passed on through imitation, recorded through conversation and memory, and kept alive through tradition. Appeasing God in these various practices meant keeping the right spirit (i.e. the Holy Spirit) on side, so to speak, which also meant avoiding attracting unwanted spirits; spiritual purity and pollution was part of the same

---

[117]   Hancock, 2013, p. 100.

[118]   This passage is an example of God's instruction to keep the camp clean; in this instance, to ensure human waste is kept outside of the encampment. The reasoning is located in verse 14; 'For the Lord your God walks in the midst of your camp, to deliver you and give your enemies over to you; therefore your camp shall be holy, that He may see no unclean thing among you, and turn away from you'.

family as spiritual safety. Being on site provided the visual link to this phenomenon, in this instance in the form of a 'missing' trailer. There was no trailer number 13, in between trailers 12 and 14. How common this is on other sites is a little unclear, but it was something others had mentioned. Other aspects of *mokhhadi* had served as a barrier or gate to particular taboos; the belief in the unlucky or cursed nature of the number 13 was no different. Avoiding it meant that bad luck, and perhaps the devils that facilitated that bad luck, could be avoided and/or kept at bay.

Billy and Charlotte's plot in which the primary trailer and the secondary caravan (which housed their 17 year-old-son) were located was immaculate. Several times a day, Charlotte or her eldest daughter (aged 11 years) would sweep the yard, often, it would seem, when it was still clean. In spite of a continuous cleaning regime, Charlotte was always well turned out; her hair, make-up and clothing spotless. She would change her clothing once or twice a day, and always before Billy arrived home on the days that I was there. It is not to say that the changing of clothes throughout the day is a common trend, but it was indicative of the trend towards personal and external hygiene.

As I arrived on the first day I was welcomed by Charlotte. She invited me into her trailer, we spoke for a short while, and then I was offered a cup of tea. Some time later, other family members arrived and I was once again offered a tea. I hadn't clocked it the first time, but this time, I saw the sleight of hand and the blocking of my line of sight. I suspect most people wouldn't have noticed or perhaps even cared; I had seen and I did care. As the mugs were taken from one of the cupboards above the cooker area, Charlotte took another mug from a cupboard below the sink. It was all done very smoothly and quickly and would not have even been apparent as having any significance, had it not been for the fact that there were still several mugs in the 'main' cupboard. The same practice occurred in relation to crockery during the serving of meals; again, my plate or bowl was taken from the lower cupboard whereas the rest of the family's crockery was taken from the other cupboard. The plates, bowls and mugs were virtually identical barring one or two details. There was a distinction and separation in how I was being treated compared to those who were either family or 'full-blooded' Traveller/Gypsy – not a didikais such as me.[119]

I raised the issue with Billy and Charlotte. I was informed that as a guest they were using 'the best china' for me. This clearly was not the case, but they seemed a bit embarrassed that I'd called them out on it, so I let it drop. Many folks I know wouldn't have let it slide, but a gracious reply often results in a generous response. I was extremely grateful that I had been offered food and drink whilst visiting, however, there was a marked difference between the matching fine plates and cups being used by the family and of that being used by myself. In addition to the crockery situation, there were other instances, such as where I could and could not sit whilst in the trailer. Again, whilst there was no mention of any explicit rules or instructions, I was always encouraged to sit in the same place, or leave my shoes in the same spot. Such practices have not been uncommon in the past, but I was surprised to see aspects of *mokhhadi* implemented so consistently in one place.

Although not explicit, elements of the separation of the 'pure blooded' Gypsy and of the gorger and 'didikais' were being implemented in the camp towards me. Maintaining standards of purity and cleanliness in both the physical realm (personal and property) and the mental realm (spirituality and logic) is not something people can just switch off, even if they are doing their best to hide it from their experienced visitor. In many ways, *mokhhadi* is a syncretistic amalgamation of tradition and religious conviction. Those traditions and convictions have existed in one form or another for over 700 years. As such, despite the best intentions of my hosts, the synthesis of the

---

[119] 'Didikais' is a half-blood Traveller or Gypsy. For example, someone who has a Traveller father and a 'gorger' mother, is a didikais. Didikais is a Romany word and not broadly used nowadays, although its meaning is still relevant in Traveller society (Taylor, 2014, p. 17).

family's inherent Christianity and their traditional practice was subtle but apparent. It often manifested through many avenues, including conversations and, as seen above, through normal daily activities.

The Mulatto and the Didikais: Whose Ethnicity is it anyway?

There was no doubt about it; in spite of one of Charlotte's family members introducing me to the site as 'a man of God ... doing the Lord's work,'[120] and Billy informing folks that, 'his dad's a Gypsy', I found myself drawing back to how I had been subject to what was essentially an 'outsider's' treatment. The perception of GRT ethnicity *in* the community is an interesting subject. It's true that ethnicity does serve as an identifier and/or operates as a method of collective inclusivity, but, as seen on the camp, it can at times be used as a tool to establish to what degree one is a 'pure blooded' Gypsy or Traveller. This isn't a GRT exclusive phenomena. Within Black culture exists the concept of the 'mulatto'. The mulatto is the in-between, the answer and the problem, the 'bastard black son of the white slave owner'.[121]

In my own personal circumstance, I was neither fully accepted by my hosts nor was I entirely rejected; I was like them but not of them. I was, as David Mayall described, 'of diluted blood'. And from the differing treatment I was receiving it appeared that, as Mayall would suggest, I was also partially responsible for much of the injustice 'directed towards the clean-living Romany' who were 'superior in manners, morals and occupations' in comparison to 'their degenerate and impoverished mumply-brothers'.[122] This opinion had originally been formed and developed during the nineteenth century. Undertaking a particular and intentional process, self-appointed gorger 'Gypsiologists' introduced the idea of race, ethnicity, and nature into their works.[123] Through their work a 'racial hierarchy' was

[120]   A comment from one of Charlotte's family members.
[121]   Bantum, 2010, pp. 14 – 19.
[122]   Mayall, 1988, p. 78.
[123]   Taylor, 2008, pp. 8 – 10.

developed. This could initially be viewed as a positive move towards firm, racial identification for Gypsies and Travellers. However, as historian Becky Taylor reveals, it was 'Detractors of [the] Gypsies' lifestyle as much as supporters [who] deployed ideas of "race" and "nature" in their writings'.[124] Racialising Traveller and Gypsy people in this way allowed for the introduction of the concept that 'racial purity' and 'true' Gypsy blood was declining. This declining process took place through various methods, including intermarriage with 'degenerate members' – or gorgers.[125] The result was the Gypsy equivalent of the mulatto – the 'didikais', or 'half-breed'. [126]

Remembering the origins of our past – including the myths and legends that formed that past - doesn't always heal, but it certainly helps. In the immediate sense, I was feeling a sense of discomfort, betrayal even, that my hosts didn't fully recognise my ancestral past as being as valid as their own. But I had to remind myself of the truth I'd come to realise, that the human phenomena of insistence on exclusivity is born from a desire for inclusivity. Their rejection of my 'Gypsy' status was not a rejection of me but a cry for recognition of their humanity. Their vulnerabilities and painful past didn't require pandering to but instead needed space to be heard with Christ-like compassion. With some irony, the reminder of my own 'mulatto' situation was actually being played out in Billy and Charlotte's situation. As Travellers and Gypsies standing among the larger, settled population, *they* were the mulatto – or didikais. In the UK, Travellers and Gypsies can be considered as 'the white other'; often physically similar to the larger host – however, always culturally different and/or segregated.

In the setting of (particularly Eastern) Europe, things are a little different; as well as the aforementioned barriers, there are definitive physical identifiers that separate Gypsy from gorger. Derek Walcott (1974) identifies a similar situation among individuals from the

---

[124] Taylor, 2008, p. 8.
[125] Taylor, 2008, pp. 8 – 9.
[126] Taylor, 2008, p. 8.

Caribbean islands, where ancestry and history – and thus identity, has created 'increasingly exotic hybrids', that in Walcott's words, look like 'broken bridges between two ancestries, Europe and the Third World of Africa and Asia'.[127] The transition and movement of Gypsies from India to Europe and beyond, and subsequent integrations and inter-ethnic and racial relationships has indeed created a situation whereby Gypsies and Travellers are as Walcott suggests, 'broken bridges', or as Chris Bongie (1998) would describe – 'islands'.[128] Bongie presents the mulatto as an island – and conversely, the island as mulatto. GRT people and their culture can, in this sense, be understood as an island, in the sense that it must be viewed as a place of 'defined boundaries and dangerous isolation'. Islands are figures that must be viewed in a double light'.[129] From one perspective, Gypsies and Travellers occupy a complete, unitary and unified identity. However, from another perspective, Gypsies and Travellers are a fragmented, exiled and related part of a greater whole – be it the country in which they reside or the religion to which they belong. The 'island' metaphor as identity 'begs to be figured as either positive or negative exile'.[130]

On its own standing, *Gypsy as mulatto* will always be unique and will dichotomously exist through the physical, the mental and the spiritual, in a state of 'belonging with' and 'separated from' the larger space in which it resides. As such, despite its uniqueness, 'Traveller' or 'Gypsy' in itself can only ever be 'less than' – not in a detrimental way, but in a state of always just falling short, of just 'missing the mark'. However, not all is lost! Without the Creator, the created doesn't exist; without Christ, we are all incomplete. Gypsy, gorger, Black, White, straight, gay, rich, poor – without Christ we are just the antithesis of our full potential; to be complete, to reach our synthesis, we need

[127]   Walcott, 1974, p. 20.
[128]   Enz, 2006, p. 383.
[129]   Enz, 2006, p. 384.
[130]   Enz, 2006, p. 384.

Christ – the thesis of our being. For whilst 'Traveller' or 'Gypsy' in the modern context can be considered to be a mulattic creation, consisting of a synthesis of ideas, 'a mixture of parts that mitigate two contrary poles'; it is 'Jesus' body ... that renders the idea of dichotomous poles incoherent'.[131] Christ becomes the vehicle through which the mulattic position is both legitimised and made complete, whilst any negative forms of separation are made null and void. Christ does not cause any detraction from the Traveller-mulatto equation, but rather He *adds* to it.

In this way, Christ, *is* mulatto;[132] Christ is Traveller, Christ is Gypsy. Christ being mulatto does not and could not add to the scope of who Christ is, but it does represent a crucial juncture for our identity. Recognising Christ as mulatto helps us to bridge the gap between islands and the mainland, between isolation and shared living; between unbelief and unrestricted love. Christ is with us in our separation but He is also our destination of hope and unification. Christ is with us in our unbelief, as He was with Thomas (John 20:27), yet He is also the author and finisher of our faith (Hebrews 12:2). He is with us in our suffering, as we are with Him, clinging to the foot of the Cross. And He is with us in our redemption, and we are with Him in His resurrection. We need the Cross event to make sense of the contradiction we all occupy – for the filth of sin to occupy our flesh and the purity of love to dwell in our hearts. The godforsakenness of the cross does not sit alone but is woven from the same (and contradictory) outpouring of love. On the Cross Jesus' identification is with the suffering, with the abandoned, with the outcasts and with all who suffer. The contradiction is the facilitation of the unification of suffering (the Cross event) and love (Christ's sacrifice).

131   Bantum, 2010, p. 112.
132   Bantum, 2010, p. 112.

SUMMARY

Billy and Charlotte were participants in a cultural practice that kept them with Christ. Their 'journey' *to* Christ could never be fully completed in this life, but their journey *with* Christ could certainly be undertaken through the daily picking up of their purity 'Cross'. Would their acts of *mokhhadi* save them? Of course not. But there was no denying that these subtle and widespread acts of voluntary spiritual flagellation were serving to keep them clinging to the Cross. Christ risen is our hope, but Christ sharing in our suffering is our reality. We didn't meet Christ through the kind actions of others – they were absent. We met Christ through His passion, through His crucifixion, and through His death. However, in that place of suffering we encounter a love like no other and we cement our identity – as individuals, as communities, as ethnicities and as a people. As believers we are united by and through our suffering, we are emboldened, and we are reminded of both the grace to exist in our authentic forms now and the grace to enter paradise in our next form.

In the meantime, our journey remains here, in the present. How and what we do in that time not only determines our future but also that of the generations to follow. We are presented with many choices each day, including whom we welcome and how we welcome those who are not from our 'camp'. Our lives, intertwined with the suffering and hope of Christ, are in constant flux. Both our physical and spiritual forms are moving and are at work, and for generation upon generation of Gypsies and Travellers, this could not be truer. With that said, our 'work van' is now on the move and our tools of history, sin and purity are loaded up. Whether Gypsies at work or Christians in the world, we are sojourners, temporarily residing in a world that is not our own. As we head into the next chapter, we will see what that world looks like, and how, if we are to be happier and healthier, we must be comfortable with the permanent impermanence of everything we know and love.

CHAPTER FOUR

NOMADISM AND THE SOJOURNER: PART ONE – THE PERMANENT IMPERMANENCE OF CHRISTIAN LIFE

'Hear my prayer, O LORD, and give ear to my cry; hold not your peace at my tears! For I am a sojourner with you, a guest, like all my fathers.' (Psalm 39:12)

'Let us then know, that the sons of Cain, though deprived of the spirit of regeneration were yet endued with gifts of no despicable kind.'[133]

DECODING TRAVELLER NOMADISM
The Problem with Memes and Soundbites

As I flicked through the prints in the gift shop, hoping to find something to fill that odd-shaped frame I had under the stairs, I was greeted with nothing but pure cheese. And not the kind of cheese you'd put on a board or stick in a picnic, but the eye-rolling empty-well variety that had about as much impact and depth as a 99p Valentine's card. *'Life is a*

---

[133]   Calvin, 1848, p. 218.

Journey.' 'It's not the amount of days in your life but the amount of life in your days.' For sure, life is a journey of sorts, and quality over quantity in life is an equation I live by. But if I were willing to put one of those quotes up in my picture frame, I may as well draw an emoji or write the word 'Love' in bright colours and let the visitor to my house enjoy their own interpretation of my 'quick fix' pearl of wisdom. Messages that imply movement are, for GRT people and people of faith in general, representative of (meta)physical, spiritual, religious and biblical truths. Recognising that factor when I perused the prints, it saddened me a little, as I was reminded in some way that our text talk, fast food, short-hand was now permeating nearly every fabric of our society, including some of our churches and parts of our theology.

It's fair to say that it's been a while since humanity was first blessed with Augustine's compendious three-word definition of theology, 'faith seeking understanding'. However, Augustine's words are of course not left sitting solo and left to the imagination of the reader. They are merely the gateway into an exposition of the proof of God's existence. It's hard sometimes to know when to pluck edifying philosophical lessons from the barrage of warm and fuzzy soundbites we encounter in our modern lives. After all, you can't seem to throw a metaphorical stick these days without hitting a motivational quote somewhere online or on social media. Augustine didn't leave that question open to the general public; he wrote books to explain and discuss and to learn and to grow. So why did the two aforementioned cards bother me so much? Are we not allowed to have well-meaning quotes anymore? Of course we are. And are we to be offended by every little thing that despite holding a different meaning somehow was purposefully designed to agitate our race or collective? Of course not! What bothered me in this instance was the lack of emphasis and urgency in the message. Perhaps 'Life is a Journey' could have had an asterisk beside it which directed the reader to the bottom of the page, whereupon it would have been followed up with:

Life is indeed a journey, but at times it can be terrible whilst at other moments it can be blissful. Either way, none of it is guaranteed – least not tomorrow - and so you need to make each moment count and everything should be done with purpose. Stop letting life pass you by as if you have your eyes shut and that you will see your next birthday. Bloody wake up! Go and tell your loved ones you love them. Do that thing you've always wanted to do. And stop being attached to everything – it will only cause you suffering.

Of course, that kind of message is not going to sell many cards. Besides which, it could be argued that each one of those sentences could form their own individual pretty motivational cards or memes. Unless, of course, you actually live within the parameters of those words of advice ... Within the Bible we are reminded that our lives are but a vapour, here for a short moment and gone the next (James 4:14). Furthermore, we are reminded that whilst we are here, we are to avoid attachment to things and people (Matthew 6:19-20; Luke 14:25-27; Luke 18:24-30). Urgency, attachment, purpose and direction: these are the factors of our journey and should be the subheadings of our lives. Within the GRT community, that journey has historically been a tangible and perpetual one. However, like the journey from the depth of Augustine's 'faith seeking understanding' to the one-liner, figure-it-out-yourself motivational memes of today, the impermanent nature of GRT communities has also changed, albeit for the better. Those changes are journeys and movements in themselves and represent in some ways a lived-out resistance to attachment.

Furthermore, within those accounts are stories of acceptance and rejection by others outside of the group. GRT, non-GRT, believers, unbelievers – we are all at times strangers in the land and at other times we are the hosts. Sometimes however, we find ourselves permanently at the edge, unable to access or engage with what we're told is the 'norm'. At those times the instruction to be in the world but not part of it (Romans 12:2) seems to be more of an ill-fated fulfilled prophecy, rather than a step towards holiness. We have all been there at some point, mentally, spiritually or otherwise, travelling through the wilderness of missing out on the assurance of stability, sitting in the cold emptiness of depression born from isolation. But what for those odd few of us who seem to thrive when the chips are down? What for those who intentionally occupy suffering in the *name* of something bigger than themselves, who seem to actually pursue difficulty? Either way, if the suffering/excluded party isn't us, they always receive a name or a label. To name something outside of our own sphere, provides us with boundaries and distinctions. Yet to name also empowers us with a concerning leverage, advantage and in some instances, superiority. The distance yielded by othering others is a challenging chasm; in that chasm we feel safer yet we are also devoid of the knowledge that is only obtained by welcoming in the othered. Assumptions and stereotypes form in such places, making the process of decoding the cultural needs, norms and expectations of others difficult at best. The problem is made worse when, in our place of separation, we think we see the 'othered' living up to our ill footed prejudices. So what for Gypsies and Travellers, who after 600+ years are still considered strangers in the land? Do they still move around? Why do they move around? Do Travellers travel? If so, why?

Nomad, or not Nomad? That, is the Question

It's a commonplace practice among media outlets, general public perception and Governmental offices to assume that all Gypsies and Travellers are somewhat nomadic.[134] Such assumptions present a dichotomy where 'traditional Gypsies' and 'Gypsies of yore' travel

[134] Nicolae Gheorghe, along with Jean-Pierre Liégeois, suggest that Gypsies and Travellers who 'no longer live in the traditional conditions which are documented by ethnographers and anthropologists' – such as in the context mentioned, are suspected by differing establishments (political, academic, media etc.) of not being 'true Gypsies' (Gheorghe, 1999, pp. 157 – 158). Also see Taylor, 2008, p. 5.

in bow-topped, horse-pulled vardos (wagons),[135] whilst 'modern Travellers' move from place to place in off-road vehicles and vans, pulling trailers (caravans).[136] Make no mistake, there is a rich historical tradition of nomadism in Gypsy communities extending back into a proto-Romani era and into the emergence into Europe by Roma. However, one should be very cautious when linking physical movement with the intrinsic identity of GRT people. Doing so risks making the mistake of believing that one *must* demonstrate tangible nomadic tendencies – i.e. travelling – in order to identify as a Traveller/Gypsy. Data actually suggests that only a minority of Travellers continue to travel regularly, and that the majority of the UK's Gypsy population are predominantly settled.[137] Additionally, the presence of a perceived social action or trend should not be considered to be wholly conducive to processes of ethnic and racial identification; doing so becomes a form of racial *profiling* – something vastly different and socially damaging.[138]

As alluded to, there are physical nomadic trends among a percentage of GRT people. These movements are usually for the purposes of soliciting work and maintaining employment, or for travelling to events, such as Horse fairs, funerals, and gatherings. However, it is misguided to readily use *permanent* physical travelling as a definitive identifier of Travellers. Liégeois and Gheorghe recognise that Travellers/Gypsies are indeed members of Europe's 'indigenous' ethnic group, whose '*culture* is characterised by ... occupational fluidity, and nomadism'. [139] Whilst that may be true, it all sounds a bit 'lab rat', doesn't it? 'In experiment 54, we found that Gypsy 12 and Gypsy 43 both displayed tendencies to fight when poked.' It's also a little sinister. After approximately 1 million Gypsies were killed

---

[135]   Taylor, 2008, pp. 7 – 9.
[136]   Taylor, 2008, pp. 109 – 111.
[137]   Crawley, 2004, pp. 6 and 8.
[138]   Atkin, 2014, p. 156.
[139]   Liégeois and Gheorghe, 1995, p. 6.

during the Holocaust, being categorised and spoken to and about in clinical forms is, well, concerning. Reclaiming 'occupational fluidity', 'nomadism' and the like from the sterile clutches of certain branches of research for the betterment of GRT culture can be achieved by reimagining and re-understanding GRT nomadism through its own collective religious language.

Gypsy and Traveller nomadism is so much more than the physical acts we see. GRT nomadism was born from collective suffering, it was formed in the mould of Christianity, and it has its grounding in biblical foundations. As such, it is more appropriate and accurate to understand and identify nomadism as a *spiritualised* practice and communal mind-set that operates as a constant in all 'Gypsy' culture and peoples, i.e. Pavees (Irish Travellers), Romanichals (English Romany Gypsies), Kalé (Welsh Gypsies), Nawkins (Scottish Gypsy/Travellers), Roma, Show people, and New Travellers. In reclaiming this 'indigenous' nomadism, our understanding of what it means for GRT people to be nomadic needs to be defined, or at the very least repositioned among its theological foundations. In doing so, we can avoid the dangers and the limitations of stereotyping whilst simultaneously expanding our shared tapestry of Christ-inspired humanity. To begin, we shall look at GRT nomadism in relation to its biblical foundation and the Holy Scriptures. In doing so, we are introduced to the collective term 'sojourner' – or 'stranger in the land'…

INTRODUCING THE SOJOURNER

Jorge Bernal, an Argentinian-Russian Kalderash,[140] is the founder of AICRA[141] – an organisation in Argentina whose specific purpose is to raise awareness of 'Gitano' (Romani/Gypsy/Traveller) culture. What makes Bernal's *Romani Identity Association* so unique, is

---

[140] Kalderash are a subgroup of the Romani people; their distinctiveness comes from a tendency to be involved in and around the metal trade and their strict regulations on hygiene.

[141] The Association Identidad Cultural Romani de la Argentina (AICRA).

that it is potentially the only organisation in Argentina of its kind. Through its work, Bernal has suggested in the past that the Church (with particular reference to the Pentecostal movement) 'constitutes a good alternative to the gorger society because it offers the means for a positive redefinition of Romani/Gypsy identifications … by including the communities in the biblical genealogy'. [142] Bernal identifies attempts at assimilation by the *gorger* society towards Gypsy culture as debilitating, highlighting the specific dangers in parts of South America as an act of 'seduction'.[143] In Europe and the UK, the issue of 'seduction' is less of a threat. As someone living in the UK, it's fair to say that the Blue tie wearing Governments haven't exactly tried that hard to get GRT people on side, let alone try to 'seduce' them through incentives and kind persuasion.

However, the drive to assimilate Gypsies and Travellers *is* happening, albeit through less traditional means, such as TV programmes and other media sources. Such programmes often portray Travellers as primitive people, disengaged with modernity and suspicious of modern practices and values. This in itself is playing into the vulnerabilities of the communities portrayed. Gypsies and Travellers are already overtly conscious of the negative perception many hold against them and desperate to be able to live in peace, and as such there has been a gradual sacrifice of values and cultural norms as a way to reduce demonization. The Bible has the viable facility in which Gypsies can redefine and re-establish their identity. To believe this is not so much radical, 'evangelical', or even original, but is supported by a historical cultural precedent of engagement with Christianity.

Finding the Traveller in the Scriptures

Gypsy and Traveller cultural history and social-structure development has been as much a reaction to an ever-evolving set of external

[142]   Carrizo-Reimann, 2011, p. 172.
[143]   Carrizo-Reimann, 2011, p. 172.

circumstances, as it has to an intentional, culturally collective decision making process in which its members have formed and established its rules. Central to this developmental process has been a primarily Christian narrative. I say 'primarily', as the concepts and practices are not exclusively Christian. For example, Gypsy practices in the area of cultural and community purity originate from what is considered to be typically Hindu-influenced behaviour, whereas ideas surrounding moral codes can be found in Jewish texts (the Pentateuch). Whilst GRT value and purity systems can largely be attributed to, and legitimised by, a number of traceable and historical sources, there are certain core 'identity' narratives, indicative of modern (and historical) Traveller culture, that are not so readily attributable to religious bodies. Some of these narratives include the interrelationships between nomadism, work/career choices and approaches, and intentional separateness from the larger gorger culture. These inter-relational factors make both the unity of GRT communities and the disunity with the 'outside world' much more likely to both happen and stay in place. Some of these factors include a mistrust between the two cultures and *perceived* opposition to certain laws and customs. What may be surprising to you, is that participation in and the maintenance of these factors by Gypsies and Travellers is intentional, despite the proven social and physical repercussions. However, here's the plot twist: the core element at work here is not one of defiance but ultimately one of religious and spiritual pursuit. In this sense, traits of nomadism and intentional segregation can be understood as a form of discipleship; as an act of picking up one's cross.

Annette Merz and Gerd Theissen describe the characteristics of discipleship as self-stigmatisation, as participation in the charisma[144]

---

[144] Merz and Theissen describe the 'charisma' of Jesus as something that can be passed on, and that Jesus owes his own charisma to John the Baptist. However, the central theme to their understanding of Jesus' charisma is that it is something that is participated in by other people; it is not a level of personality but a level of authority (Merz and Theissen, 1999, pp. 213 & 215).

of Christ, and participation in the promise of position.[145] 'Disciples, both men and women, share in Jesus' role as an *outsider*, i.e. their discipleship is *voluntary self-stigmatization*'.[146] Whilst a conversion from gorger to Traveller and vice versa is not a possibility, it could be argued that the *tangible* activities commonly associated with being a Gypsy or Traveller, such as patterns of nomadism and particular customs, are voluntary. Either way, it would seem that very often the physical activities of GRT people serve as an identifier, rather than their own testimony.

As such, whether the actions of GRT are voluntary, involuntary, desired or undesired, they become characteristics of an association towards being a Gypsy or Traveller. In much the same way, the process of being a disciple is distinguishable from that of being a sojourner, despite carrying many similar traits. The sojourner is such because of their position and activities in relation *to* a society; their counter-cultural presence is the primary reason for their *exclusion* from the mainstream. The position of disciple comes not as an escape from persecution but the conscious decision to *enter* into otherness; to become a disciple is to make a statement of difference and separation. This isn't done in order to foster unity and anger towards the larger society but to reposition oneself to be able to produce changing dialogue *in* that culture. The Gypsy thus occupies the contradictive and non-fixed state of 'sojourning disciple'. To operate in such a capacity is, in a Traveller cosmology, a 'true' expression of Christian and Traveller living.

Mainstream society must provide an acceptance of minorities in its parameters in order to gain approval and trust from the minority in question – assimilation, to a certain degree, depends on this. However, for many Travellers the chance to disprove stereotypes and

---

[145] The promise of position primarily refers specifically to the 12 disciples and their place upon thrones, whereupon they will judge the 12 tribes of Israel (1 Corinthians 15:5). Essentially in the context of the sojourner, and indeed the Traveller, the promise of position could be understood to mean an eventual elevation to 'a lofty position... with Jesus' (Merz and Theissen, 1999, pp. 215 – 216).

[146] Merz and Theissen, 1999, p. 215.

negative perceptions is an impossibility that begins from childhood encounters with gorger society. The following statement was made by a Traveller looking back to when he was a seven year-old boy. It indicates typical issues encountered by Traveller children:

> What did I want to go to school for? School was for gorgers. Why should I learn to read and write? No other person I mixed with could … Don't ask me the name of the school … I hated it. Sit still. Sit up straight. Single file. Fold your arms. It was like being in a fucking cage. All silly rules and saying prayers … I couldn't understand why them calling 'Gypsy' or 'Gypo' across the playground was meant to annoy me. After all, that's what I was … Gorger kids seemed to think we didn't like being Travellers for some reason.[147]

One thing to note in this example is the nature of memory. Positive memory experiences are often lineal in nature, nostalgic even. The person recalling the event looks back fondly and somehow misses the trauma that inevitably shaped parts of their adulthood. On the other hand, negative memories feel somewhat like a step towards an edge; the person recalling the event wants to remove themselves from the experience; so much so that often these events become lodged deep within our souls, waiting to appear someday in the form of destructive behaviour or emotional and mental trauma. The problem *we* have is that for GRT people, that past trauma is still here, it's still happening, and it seems unescapable. In the metaphorical sense, Gypsies and Travellers seek to be absent of the social purgatory in which the dominant society affects everything and all others by its actions and intent. Instead, the Traveller's target is to be part of a 'proto-purgatory' in which humanity is operating in its God-given position of freedom and choice yet withheld in the constraints of a divinely inspired moral conscience. This isn't an unrealistic desire for some kind

[147]   Taylor, 2014, p. 215.

of nirvana, but a reaction to a larger society that doesn't see the flaming torch it is holding to the feet of people who think, act and look different. As seen in the above example, differences in relation to the majority are emphasised and thus criticised *by* the majority. This form of 'social exegesis' is incredibly dangerous when left solely to secular structures and systems. Structured systems, unsurprisingly, require structured responses and structured solutions and/or alternatives that speak somehow to the organisational language of these systems. Remember: structured solutions do not have to be complex; in fact, simplicity can and often is the most effective route. So, in this instance that structured approach is achieved by placing the context of the 'stranger in the land' or Gypsy, through a biblical hermeneutic. Doing so, reveals the character of the 'sojourner', primarily (but not exclusively) through the Pentateuch.

How to Understand the Traveller as Sojourner

Before we go any further, two things need to be said: Firstly, this particular section may be a little less 'white-knuckle ride' and a little more 'don't read this if you're tired'. But stick with it; it's necessary. If you want to move from milk to meat, you need to grow some teeth first. The second thing that needs to be said is, we need to get our head into correlation mode. Okay, so technically speaking, there's no such thing as 'correlation mode', but if there was, it would look a little like when you're watching a movie and you start to see yourself in one of the characters. Without dwelling on it you start to empathise with them as you see your own struggles present in their actions and thoughts. You want them to win because in life you need to win. Honestly, if 'correlation mode' was used every time we read the Bible, we'd have a Gospel message with as much tangible impact as one of Tyson Fury's right hooks! I'm sorry, I digress. Let's press on and start by looking at Paul Siu's (1952) brief explanation of the 'sojourner', which helps us appreciate the uncanny resemblance between Traveller and sojourner:

The 'sojourner' is treated as a deviant type of the sociological form of the 'stranger', one who clings to the cultural heritage of his own ethnic group and tends to live in isolation, hindering his assimilation to the society in which he resides, often for many years. The sojourn is conceived by the sojourner as a 'job' which is to be finished in the shortest possible time. As an alternative to that end he travels back to his homeland every few years.[148]

There are varying accounts of sojourners and sojourning in the Old Testament, but not all should be viewed equally due to the context and the time-period in which they are presented. There are different 'stances' on which sojourner can be viewed, and the term itself has had an interesting evolution, moving from something quite embracing to something distinctly nationalistic. Understanding the history of the term sojourner is important because it allows for reflection on our own development in modern (predominantly) Western societies and how that development has either moved towards or away from God's heart for the stranger.

Essentially, the idea of the sojourner takes two approaches: subjective and personal; or objective and relational. These are derived from the Hebrew words – 'ger' and 'ben nekhar'. These words manifested over three time periods: The first time period is pre-exodus. The second, post-exodus, is transitional and biblically can be measured by the formation of the Deuteronomic reformation. The third time period is when Israel was established as a land where the Israelites were in the majority and in control of the land via the implementation of rules, statutes, etc. Although these understandings remain valid, they cannot be retrospectively interpreted with the text. For example, 1 Kings 11:7-8 describes Solomon's wives as foreign – rather than 'alien' or 'sojourner' because of the changed context in which the authority is now placed.

---

[148]   Siu, 1952.

During and shortly after the period of exile, the Hebrew people's conception of the term 'sojourner' changed, in line with their subjugation of 'The Promised Land'. During the Covenant Code and the preceding Decalogue (Exodus 20:1-17; Exodus 20:22 – 23:33), 'sojourner' or 'ger' designates the conquered indigenous population of Palestine rather than the immigrant Hebrew. At this stage the Israelite position towards the sojourner is one that could be considered favourable, given the context and period in which it was set. The Hebrew people are reminded that they were once 'strangers in the land' of Egypt, and as such they are to: accommodate the sojourner; help with food and supplies; do the sojourner no harm (Deuteronomy 10:18; Leviticus 19:33); and special care must be taken to do the 'ger' no judicial detriment (Deuteronomy 1:16; Deuteronomy 27:19). With this taken into consideration, the most significant element of this Deuteronomic reformation was that the criminal legal system was to be applied equally to both native citizen and 'the alien who resides among you' (Leviticus 18:26). Although both, or indeed all the many cultures were enabled and encouraged to co-exist, they did so with the law holding the final word.

Participation in the Hebrew religion meant that the sojourner was able to participate in honouring the Sabbath as well as other celebrations and feasts. However, it also meant that the sojourner was bound and restricted in exactly the same manner as the Israelites. What begins to form in the biblical text is a clear picture of a multicultural society effectively working in the boundaries of a dominant culture. Harold Weiner comments, 'The historical circumstances were such as to render the position of the resident alien important from the first. A "mixed multitude" went up with the Israelites from Egypt, and after the conquest we find Israelites and the races of Palestine living side by side throughout the country'. There are many accounts around this time of identified aliens resident in the land, such as Uriah the Hittite. There was also a census conducted by Solomon which revealed a significant number of non-Hebrews living among the people (2 Chronicles 2:17). Of course, implementing an environment of hospitality was a religious requirement that saw the host protect his 'guest' at any lengths (Genesis 19; Judges 19:24).

The next interpretation of sojourner produces the Hebrew words 'ben nekhar' or 'nokhri' and was brought about in the postexilic period. The application of these terms is far greater in its reach than 'ger'. They remove the specificity of location (i.e. Israel) and thus cover everything that may be considered of foreign character or alien, regardless of the place of residence. The positioning of the ben nekhar meant that the larger society (the Israelites) was now also recognised as the dominant part, whilst the foreigner was now subject to the rules, beliefs and culture of the Israelites. The ben nekhar still enjoyed many of the same privileges as before; however, there were now further restrictions, such as who the Israelites could marry and who could be part of the assembly of the Lord . Despite these factors, the foreigner was still encouraged to worship the Hebrew God. This aspect of availability and inclusion is taken further when the account of Naaman reveals that the ben nekhar was able to worship God in a foreign land. Clearly there are many legal and practical elements actioned toward the sojourner. However, in spite of these, the reasoning behind the integration of the foreigner in the Hebrew's land is ultimately born out of a desire to shape identity through relationship.

There are, potentially, three perspectives that have informed and shaped the laws concerned with the sojourner. The first perspective is a requirement by Israel to remember that she too was once a sojourner in Egypt; God observed her oppression, provided deliverance, and set her up in a fruitful land of her own. The second perspective is reflective of one of God's characteristics; the same God who rescued Israel from bondage is also the God who provides protection for the disinherited, the weak and the poor. As such, the economy of Israel's primary purpose is to meet need, with particular attention being delivered to the welfare of people requiring help. Finally, according to Theodor Mauch, the covenant between God and Israel is dependent on all members participating in not only the advantageous aspects but also in all the requirements. The sojourner is 'almost an Israelite, is entitled to equal justice, is to be judged as the Israelite is judged, but 'must conform as far as possible to the covenant regulations'.

Summary of 'How to Understand the Traveller as Sojourner'

Digging deep within structures that are both theologically significant but seem somewhat disjointed from our contemporary society is interesting, yes, but also a little dry. Let's be honest – if we were to break down the finer definitions of ancient Hebrew interpretations in a Sunday sermon, we might possibly lose the interest of some of our parishioners. However, by bringing about that understanding, we remove the element that feels a little like a Wednesday evening Bible study and we are able to move on with a fresh understanding that has present-day relevance. In this case, we can start to recognise how GRT people and some other minorities (particularly race minorities) are often placed within particular categories by the larger and often more dominant society. We can see how important it is to be able to find sanctity and familiarity within the scriptures. And for those of us who minister to others, we are reminded that when we sit with those who fit the mould of the sojourner, that we sit with the damned. And when we sit with the damned we must do so as Jesus taught us on the Cross; His arms stretched wide, holding us in our moment of pain, with the assurance of unconditional love and the hope of a future.

So what did our initial venture into understanding the Traveller as sojourner produce? Well, to start we learnt that the dominant society is required to recognise that it too has required deliverance and assistance at points but is now in a position of relative favour and control. It is therefore the responsibility of this society to provide this level of assistance and protection for those in its borders who cannot do as such for themselves. But, as the Text shows us, this is a relational agreement. As such, the sojourners among the dominant society are entitled to the same justice, rights and privileges as the larger society, but on the condition that they participate *in* said society, that they contribute *to* that society and that they *conform* as far as reasonably possible to be able to meet said requirements. Instructing that conformity must be done to the level of 'as far as possible' is significant in that it *does not require the sojourner to change*, but to conform in *behaviour* as much as is deemed reasonable and achievable by the sojourner. This appears to be done purely in order to appease the requirements of the larger society. The question of unique and separate identity is not challenged through this structure but rather appears to be given a divine approval of sorts; the many cultures with their unique identities are thus incorporated to assemble *one* collective[149]. All that is required on the part of God, so to speak, is a 'meeting in the middle', where identity is validated through participation.

When applied to Gypsy culture, conformity in this sense is not a dispensation of Gypsy and Traveller life as it has been known, but a necessary adaption to secure its future. This cultural trend can be witnessed in the evolution and adoption of trades in Gypsy communities. From 'hawking' onto other careers such as landscaping and tarmacking, and in changing attitudes in the community towards the otherwise 'historic' rejection of mainstream education practices. The logic of this 'moving towards' (in both physical and cognitive environments) persists throughout the biblical text, and is summarised to some effect in the book of James (4:8); 'Draw near to God and He will draw near to you' (James 4:8). The relational establishment of how the sojourner is to interact with the larger collective and how the larger collective is to support the sojourner, is made apparent in the biblical text. However, contextually the concept of sojourner is with some irony and rather unsurprisingly, not static. Terms and definitions, as presented biblically, often require a synchronicity between the divine and the mortal standard – between religion and

---

[149] The idea of the incorporation of multiple identities into one collective is inspired and taken from Isaiah 44:5 which reads 'This one will say, 'I am the LORD's,' another will call on the name of Jacob, and another will write on his hand, 'The LORD's,' and name himself by the name of Israel'.

politics (Mark 12:16 – 17). The timescale between the Old Testament and the New Testament created yet another development in this dynamic.

As the original Hebrew terms of understanding are no longer present in the Greek words that are translated as 'sojourner' and 'stranger', the use of the term 'sojourner' changes. The Greek word *'xenos'* with its primary meaning of 'guest' is applied for the majority of the text in the New Testament, and as such, 'stranger' is certainly the closest understanding that can be drawn from the translation. So, the sojourner is gradually separated further and further until they are eventually re-categorised as the *stranger*. The liberalistic Mosaic ideas acknowledging strangers, which started around the time of the Babylonish captivity, is notably distinct to the uncompromising exclusivity of early Christian era Jews. This change in approach towards the sojourner could be a natural evolution due to the changing power structure in Israel over that period, or it could be down to political factors such as the Roman influence. Either way, the change could serve as an important factor in determining and interpreting social and political relationships with the 'stranger', with the 'sojourner, with the Traveller and with the refugee.

Having established our new position and reclamation of what it means to be 'Traveller' (in the nomadic sense), we now move forward and begin to see how this plays out, practically speaking. Furthermore, we'll dig deeper into the scriptures and go searching for new narratives of origins, replacing the unhelpful and gorger-ascribed stories of the past, and in doing so, metaphorically ditching our (with some irony) 'Egypt' for a Promised Land. To start, we'll dig straight in, and look at how the motif of sojourner is intrinsically linked to our vocation, and how sojourning is both a fundamental and necessary component in the metanarrative of suffering.

CHAPTER FIVE
NOMADISM AND THE SOJOURNER: PART TWO – I AM SOJOURNER

'The lines have fallen for me in pleasant places; indeed, I have a beautiful inheritance.' (Psalm 16:6)
'And if you are Christ's, then you are Abraham's offspring, heirs according to promise.' (Galatians 3:29)

SOJOURNING IN ACTION
Sojourning as Vocation

The dynamic of the sojourner (rather than just nomadism) is based upon an equation of 'person and identity', as opposed to 'person and location'. It is the removal of attachment to a location that separates those identified as sojourner and those who are not. For example, Abraham is understood as being a nomadic figure whose *settlement* per se was arguably found in his relationship with God and his occupation, rather than any particular geographic location. In that specific example the dynamic of 'person and vocation' rather than 'person and location' is made explicit. As such, the sojourner (Gypsy and Traveller), as with Abraham, cannot be defined simply by their choice to travel or not; the Traveller may with equal reasoning and justification be nomadic, settled, or both.[150] What is common however is the relationship between working and/or deliberate purpose, and the settlement of the person in question. An example can be found in the sojourn (work of the sojourner) of Abraham in Egypt, which is intrinsically linked with his economic settlement as a herdsman rather than an actual location. Likewise, the physical settlement of Isaac in Canaan is partly determined by his seasonal planting of crops and not because of any permanent emotional or trade-related attachment to the area. This is not to suggest that any of the aforementioned people do not have an affiliation with any specific place, but that any concept of a fixed geographical location known as 'home' is located on the periphery of the afore-mentioned dynamic. Please see the image below (Fig.3) for a visual representation of this concept and the linked footnote for an explanation behind the image.

Making explicit this direct link between *Traveller identity* and *sojourner rationality* provides a provisional insight into the operation of the primary relationship between person and vocation. This reveals how such an equation is dependent not only on the resources and offerings of the location, but more importantly, a dynamic relationship with God. Abraham's venture into Egypt is one such account of this formula in action. Many observations about actual location can be raised from this, such as

---

[150]   A contemporary example of this can be found in the Housing (Wales) Act 2014 Part 3 Section 108 (accessible at: http://www.legislation.gov.uk/anaw/2014/7/section/108/enacted). The significant point that has been recognised in this segment of legislation is the understanding that the Traveller cannot be defined by whether he or she is Travelling but by their own choice of identity. Part A (i) of section 108 specifically mentions that the person(s) may have stopped travelling for work, education or health needs, and that these reasons are therefore not reason enough to exclude the Traveller from such an identity. Understanding Isaac in the example given as a sojourner (or Traveller) is possible when positioning the concept of location as secondary to vocation. The notion that to be a Traveller requires travelling is therefore negated. Travelling merely becomes a reliable indicator of a Traveller, and not the benchmark of assessment.

the significance of Israel as a holy and designated land for God's chosen people, and the idea of Heaven or 'Paradise' as a destination. Abraham's sojourn is initiated by him leaving his homeland with family members. Shortly afterwards he is instructed by the Lord to 'Go from your country and your father's house to the land that I will show you' (Genesis 12:1). Home as a concept at this point for Abraham changes. Any attachment he may have held to his nation state is replaced by an instruction requiring faith and the positioning of one's centrality in something other than a known and tangible physical space.

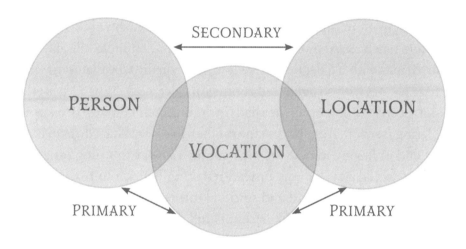

Fig. 2   *Person / Vocation / Location*[151]

[151]   The link between 'Person' and 'Vocation' is representative of an individual and their work or calling – the predominant consumer of their time. This link is primary and holds more immediate value to the person than the location. The link between 'Vocation' and 'Location' is also a primary link. This is due to the dependency of the existence of the work upon the location. The link between 'Person' and 'Location' is secondary because the person is only dependent on location by way of vocation. The Traveller is primarily mobile because of work (and thus, sojourning), i.e. one travels where the work is possible. Although there is almost always a fixed 'home' location, it is the Traveller's trailer/vardo that is to be considered home. For the settled Traveller, the formula is still the same; however, work is local and there may be varying factors that require settlement.

Sojourning as (Self) Affliction: The Birth of Struggle

In our busy and often stressful lives, many of us dream of some kind of escape from the never-ending hamster wheel of emails, bills, advertisements, unkind work schedules and quite frankly, lives that were never intended or designed for us. We medicate the discomfort with TV boxsets and unhealthy habits, and drop out of the loop for a week or two each year to head off to some different destination where work and busyness is very much in the rear view mirror. As such, the idea of a nomadic lifestyle can be extremely appealing, where responsibilities as we currently know them are discarded and where money is a lot further down our hierarchy of needs. And whilst there is some truth in the belief that the removal of attachment to certain factors (such as fixed incomes, clock-watching, multiple bills, and so on) brings with it a degree of freedom, it is equally true that removing these factors with struggle and at times, harder work. When Jesus told his followers to give up all they had (including their families), He wasn't offering freedom from having the mother-in-law over at Christmas or the end of having to take the bins out on a Friday morning (as good as that would be). He was instead restoring balance to the unequal yoking of fleshly comfort and spiritual turmoil. Attachment kept feet warm, heads dry and bank accounts full, but left the Soul famished and the Kingdom far.

However, that was a post-fallen world. In the pre-fallen world, before the link between Creator and created was severed, balance between flesh and spirit were equally yoked. As such, any struggle only served to reward and didn't come with the burden of attachment. For example, working physically hard in the garden (Eden) would have resulted in physical tiredness, which would have resulted in better sleep, which would have resulted in better recovery, which would have resulted in more productive labour, and so on. The process was cyclical, as opposed to lineal. Lineal implied a beginning and an end, of which, at the time, there was none. The imbalance caused by the consuming of the forbidden fruit severed the circle and the circle was laid flat. Now we had lineal lifetimes, lineal processes, and lineal struggles where the end of suffering wasn't quite as certain as it once was. Of course, the result, as many understand it, was 'original sin'. But what for its bastard son, 'Struggle'? Struggle was and is of course, a condition rather than of substance. But much like sin, the offspring of struggle *is* tangible. We would spend millennia struggling against struggle, searching far and wide for something to soothe the burning pain of separation and the void of God-shaped emptiness in souls. We would try to ease uncertainty with our own efforts of perpetual labour, filling our vaults with coins and abating our fears with insurance certificates. Eventually we would grow so desperate for connection that we would create things that would connect us to everyone! But the itch could not be scratched and the pain still remained. So we went further. We shared our lives, our thoughts and images of our flesh, in exchange for some approval, some acceptance, some genuine love. But it never came. Thumbs up, likes and loves, follows and subscribers – and for what? Our freedoms and souls, sold at the altar of artificial acceptance. The God-shaped hole remains.

In the early days after the fall and before the icy sting of death had been first felt, the first indication of suffering was the separation from the Father. With that came struggle, in the form of endless wandering and lack of settlement. The 'condition' would stick and eventually we would call it nomadism. Sin was to be avoided, but what for nomadism? Nomadism was to become our condition until our unification with the Father. It wasn't designed to be comfortable, nor was it designed to kill us. It was designed to remind us that we are preparing for a better place. It was designed to teach us to sever our attachment to anything and everything. However, we have spent a lifetime trying to escape the condition of our sentence and seek the comfort the first of our species once enjoyed. Of course, the terms and conditions of that sentencing has since changed, but the premise still remains: We are trying to create our own little utopian existences to ease our pain, but the only true cure is acceptance of Christ. Physical and spiritual nomadism and the prospect of having some duty of sorts to occupy permanent impermanence is certainly present in the scriptures. Nonetheless, nomadic faith and the roles that accompany it (sojourner, wanderer, etc.) are often treated, hermeneutically speaking, as cameo actors; a side narrative to 'traditional' and more dominant narratives. We want to be wowed by the gruesome Hollywood plagues that strike Egypt and we want to talk about just how good the Promised Land is going to be, but we desperately want to skim over the long, sometimes monotonous, anxiety-ridden sojourn through the desert. The sojourn is the interim; it's the 'I'm in between jobs'; it's the unfamiliar; it's the undesirable; it's the outskirts of the city; it's the Edgelands; it's detachment; it's someone else's story. Except, well, it's not. And it's not just a GRT story – it's everyone's story. The sojourner is a negative position to occupy because it is viewed as 'less than', as a failure, as 'not quite reaching the mark of your peers'. Or, to look at it another way, being Christian is a difficult position to occupy because we live in a fallen world.

Our first indication that to be a sojourner or wanderer was synonymous with negativity, comes by way of Cain – the first-born of Adam and Eve (Genesis 4:1). As punishment by God for killing his brother, Cain is cursed by God; 'You will be a fugitive and a wanderer on the earth (Genesis 4:10 – 12). This issue of displacement had already affected Cain's parents when they were banished from the Garden of Eden, and now a similar, but arguably more explicit, punishment had been administered to Cain. To be a sojourner in this aspect was by no means a 'proud' or pleasurable thing; Cain replied to God, 'My punishment is more than I can bear' (Genesis 4:13) An important aspect to note from the development of this passage is the subsequent account of the lineage of Cain, and that of Seth (Adam's 'replacement' for his murdered son Abel, who died at the hands of Cain) (Genesis 4:25). Seth is included in the line of Adam to Noah; a lineage which would see a blessing to extend territory (Genesis 9:26 – 27) and would result in Abraham – the father of Judaism, Christianity and Islam (Genesis 11:10 – 26). However, Cain's lineage ends after a few short verses with a significant linkage between Cain's curse to be a 'restless wanderer' and that of a specifically mentioned descendant named Jabal, who was dubbed as 'the father of those who live in tents and raise livestock' (Genesis 4:20). The parallel with Gypsies and Travellers – whose genesis emerges from a diaspora spanning centuries, is evident.

The temptation is to view the text with a degree of scepticism and negativity, given that it is the line of the accursed Cain. But as with all exegetical positions, we should always try to consider the full narrative in the context from which it emerges. The verses following Genesis 4:20 speak of Jubal, 'the father of all who play the harp and flute', and Tubal-Cain, 'who forged all kinds of tools out of bronze and iron' (Genesis 4:21-22). These abilities and facilities are qualities and are not simply superfluous and therefore ready to be condemned, but are in fact creations by which God may be worshipped; they can, as John Calvin stated, be 'adapted to the offices of religion'.[152] Although Cain had been cursed, Moses wished to present Cain in a way that showed he was still within the grasp of grace. Further, that although Cain's 'regeneration' or lineage was to be cut short, the Lord would balance his loss with 'gifts of no despicable kind'.[153] The application of grace to those in a seemingly unreachable state creates a tension whereby the initial actions and subsequent pre-eminent endowments would not only make it inexcusable, but would also be categorical evidence of God's goodness. The punishment of being made a sojourner for the sin of murder simply does not make sense. Why would a murderer be punished in this way, when being a stranger in the world is the destiny of all those who follow Christ? The overall impression given for Cain's punishment is that the wandering aspect is implemented to create a sense and state of unsettlement. Likewise, the purgatory-like nature of this 'home' of unsettlement is also a favoured place in which God

[152] Calvin, 1848, p. 218.
[153] Calvin, 1848, p. 218.

is able to demonstrate grace and providence, or as Calvin beautifully says – 'prove most evident testimonies of the divine goodness'.[154]

The place of punishment is therefore a place where restoration and relationship are offered, rather than a place of exclusion. The sin of whatever kind is met with a judgement that seeks reconciliation rather than exclusion, and what the world deems as separation, God deems as a chance for union. As such, the place of unsettlement, of the sojourner, of the wanderer, is revealed, spiritually speaking, as a favourable and preferable place for the faithful. Christians are strangers in the world, however, Christians also benefit from a reposeful yet temporary home. More often than not, necessity limits them, and they move from here to there. However, through tribulation they still keep their peace, until eventually perpetual movement ceases and they leave this world, enjoying the sustenance of the Creator. To the immoral, such sustenance is denied.

Sojourning as (Self) Affliction: Inheritance

Of course, the path laid out for Cain and his descendants whose regeneration was to be cut short, and as such it only represents half the story. What for Seth, whose lineage was to eventually produce Abraham? The text makes it pretty clear that this particular pathway is the favourable path, as evidenced by the eventual unlimited regeneration by way of Abraham (Genesis 26:4), and the inclusion of Noah – a figure to whom God showed favour and trust by using him as the continuation of the human species after the great flood (Genesis 5:32 – 10:1). So how can the position of sojourner still be a place of 'blessed suffering' when one arrives at it from a position of favour, where sojourner and native are presented in equal measure? Could it actually be that to be a wanderer in whatever guise or form is indicative of a model we all should be following? Challenging questions indeed when we so often choose to not see the moth and deny the presence of the thief. We like the idea of a future, but our things, such small things,

[154] Calvin, 1848, p. 218.

keep us here, fixed. Our 'why' is smaller than our 'why not'; and so our faith and our flesh become stagnant like some kind of hibernation that feels so comfortable and makes us unwise to the dwindling oxygen we desperately need. Abraham was comfortable. Yet the God-breathed 'why' in his heart was so great that he ignored the 'why not', he dismissed the 'not possible', and he shook off the 'not now'. Looking through the account of Abraham, we can begin to see how faith becomes key in negotiating impermanence and that faith enacted is faith rewarded. Furthermore, through Abraham we can begin to understand the form that 'suffering' takes in sojourning.

'Now the Lord said to Abram, "Go from your country and your kindred and your father's house to the land that I will show you ..."' (Genesis 12:1). Before this verse, 'Abram' and his barren wife Sarai, are briefly introduced. From here, Abram is spoken to by God in the aforementioned verse in what is entitled *The Call of Abram*. The land that God spoke of was Canaan, however, even when there, the now-called Abraham is referred to as 'an alien' (Genesis 17:8). A consistent theme in Abraham's account is that of movement, travel and unsettlement. Abraham from the outset is truly a sojourner, however, the word 'alien' used by God is as a *descriptor* and not a pejorative accusation. Abraham is in the process of receiving a positive prophecy that is concerned with his procreation and the multitudes of generations that will stem from him; there is no aspect that indicates negative connotations whatsoever. However, despite being described as an alien (and not being condemned as one), Abraham is told that he and his offspring will receive the land as a perpetual holding.

This presents a bit of a dilemma. Is receiving tangible land a hope for all sojourners? That would be nice, and yes, hope is a great driver, but permanently held land for one's offspring is perhaps a little specific. The challenge here is that God's blessing results in an inheritance of the land in which one is a stranger. Obviously this is not the case for everyone; the prophecy given is specifically for Abraham, but it raises the dilemma of where suffering in sojourning, if any, is actually located. Perhaps suffering is caused by deviating from the path we're called to walk upon, or perhaps from not stepping onto the path in the first place. For Abraham the context of settlement means security for his future descendants, and this is enforced by the author's explicit accounts of blessings that concern the future.[155] The nature of our Heavenly Father is not spitefully to withhold good things or to dash our dreams simply because He could. Suffering then, in the sojourning sense, has to become synonymous with the concept of inheritance, with sojourning being the method of travel towards said inheritance and faith being the fuel to drive the journey.

Inheritance is defined as 'the acquisition of a possession, condition, or trait from past generations'; it can also be understood to be an indicator of tradition.[156] A basic exegesis of both the New and Old Testaments, reveals that in multiple instances inheritance is directed or given via the giving or changing of names. Abraham's name was changed from 'Abram' via an experience with the divine, and Abraham's wife Sarah, in a similar instance had her name changed from 'Sarai'. The reason for this was intrinsically linked to the realisation of Abraham's inheritance. The Bible portrays Isaac as Abraham's favourite son – the one upon whom the nation of Israel was built. Incidentally, Isaac was not the first-born; Ishmael was the first-born and logically therefore entitled to rewards that such a position entails. However, owing to the context of the familial relationships, Ishmael was denied this privilege. Ishmael is still blessed by God because of who his father is, but he is simultaneously cursed as well.

From Ishmael, certain nomadic groups are ascribed, one of which is the Kedar; 'a wandering shepherd tribe of the desert to the east of ancient Damascus. They are said to be descended from Ishmael,

---

[155] Specific to Abraham: Genesis 12:3, 13:14-17, 21:10, 25:29-34, 31:14.
[156] Merriam-Webster Inc. (no date/author/page).

the outcast son of Abraham and Hagar'.[157] It is interesting to note the unique tension that arises again in this ascription of Ishmael. He is blessed yet cursed; he is given the promise of land yet his descendants wander; he is looked after by God, yet placed in contention with all mankind *because* of God. The parallels that can be made in the modern sojourner's incarnation i.e. Travellers and Gypsies, is apparent. To be a Traveller and to live as such is both a blessing and a curse, where God's forsakenness and the presence of God seemingly occupy an equal space. In this metaphorical space, however, is an inheritance of *personal and cultural identity* that is passed from one generation to the other. The act of travelling for Abraham and his descendants is normative. Indeed, from after the great fall a nomadic existence *is* the norm. The notion that to be in the position of the wanderer is a curse could not be further from the truth; to be settled is the reward for the many and the inheritance of the few. In a spiritual sense, for the settled, God leads or guides the way; for the sojourner He walks beside. Abraham's third marriage is of particular interest in this dynamic. As we find ourselves caught up in the drama of Abraham post-Sarah, a picture of identity in nomadic and unsettled existence emerges.

KETURAH AND KETURAH'S SONS: THE BIRTH OF GYPSIES IN THE BIBLE

For GRT the world over who seek comfort in the Bible, the path is often restricted to loose comparisons, or readily dismissed modes of living. But within the wandering accounts of Abraham and the motif of inheritance dwells a symbolical ancestral link and a biblical heritage that Gypsies and Travellers can claim. Its existence has been loosely identified before, but strangely a combination of South American politics and dominant religious discourse may have stifled

---

[157] McFarlan, 2003, p. 153. The black Bedouin tents and the flocks of Kedar are referred to several times in the Old Testament. See Genesis 25:13; Psalm 120:5; Song of Solomon 1:5; Isaiah 42:11 and 60:7; and Jeremiah 49:28–9.

its emergence. This is a different platform, ears are open, and hearts are (hopefully) ready to receive. So, are you ready, Church?

'Abraham took another wife, whose name was Keturah. She bore him Zimran, Jokshan, Medan, Midian, Ishbak and Shuah' (Genesis 25:1). After Hagar (his second wife and mother to his first son Ishmael) had been banished and Sarah had died, Abraham took Keturah to be his new (and third) wife, with whom he had six sons. The account proceeds to reveal that Abraham presented them with gifts and eventually sent them away, 'eastward to the east country' (Genesis 25:6). The link is not found in the context but in the detail – more specifically, their names. Much like Abraham and Sarah's name changes were given as a somewhat prophetic indication of heritage, Keturah's son's names also appear to indicate inheritance.

For a moment we have to head back in time and travel across to the East. The world-famous incense trade route has been established for some time, and its snaking roads are busier than ever. The route is extensive, starting from various Mediterranean ports across Egypt and the Levant, moving through Arabia, before finally ending (with some significance to this book) in India. The traders and merchants travelling up and down the seemingly never-ending road do so with scant awareness of the significance of a family who once trod where they now walk. The family in question is of course Keturah and her sons. Starting with Keturah, we find that her name is a descriptive term that means 'incense'; it is not to be understood as suggesting a particular characteristic but rather an item, such as Frankincense.[158] It is thought that her name would have been given because of her family's association with or location on the route. This would then be consistent with the naming of her sons who are identified by the names of various clans and places of significance along the breadth of the road, and who had been sent eastwards by their father, Abraham.

[158] An example of how Keturah's name should be applied can be found in Deuteronomy 33:10 which reads, 'They shall teach Jacob your rules and Israel your law; they shall put incense before you and whole burnt offerings on your altar'.

Furthermore, this naming trait is also consistent with historic traditions of applying names in the context of a setting. Collectively these different elements of biblical 'evidence' paint a picture of a definitive nomadic culture stemming from Abraham himself, which provides us with a Gypsy genesis of sorts. Furthermore, there is consistency in the historical data and therefore a legitimate claim in suggesting that through Keturah, the Roma may have found their biblical ancestry.

In Argentina there are some Gypsy communities that have started to identify themselves with the family line of Keturah, thanks in part to the teachings of an Argentinian and Gypsy Pastor named Ricardo Papadopulos. For Papadopulos, Keturah is 'the mother of the Roma'.[159] In December 2008, Papadopulos was interviewed in Buenos Aires by Agustina Carrizo-Reimann who later published his findings in the journal 'Romani Studies'; Papadopulos was recorded as saying:

> You know, now the Lord wants to reach His forgotten children. We are the descendants of Abraham's third wife and therefore the children of Abraham … We (Christians) are changing the Romani culture. The Pentecostal belief offers us new possibilities, a new self-image and way of living … the marginalised are becoming proud believers.[160]

This statement is of course encouraging. However, Papadopulos' suggestion that such a discovery is an opening to 'a new self-image and way of believing' is a little concerning. It suggests a pulling away from whatever state the Gypsy finds him or herself in, indicating somewhat that Gypsies are not acceptable in their *present* condition. It's clear that Papadopulos' heart is in the right place and that his concern is with his subject's salvation. However, any proposal of 'changing the Romani culture' starts alarm bells ringing, and could be seen as being

[159] Carrizo-Reimann, 2011, p. 171.
[160] Carrizo-Reimann, 2011, p. 171.

sympathetic towards the consensus of the general/settled population. For gorger Ministers, Pastors, Priests and spiritual parents over flocks that include GRT people, there may be a warm feeling when reading Papadopulos' closing statement, 'the marginalised are becoming proud believers'. Being a 'proud believer' within a community indicates both faithfulness and inclusive practices. But the gorger should be aware of the subtleties and tone in such statements. It has a feel about it that wouldn't be very far out of place from the nineteenth-century attempts at conversion by the Church, where those on the edge of society (i.e. Gypsies) were in such a place because of their supposed inferiority and desperate need for salvation from their 'wicked ways'.

By identifying with Keturah, particular GRT ethnic and cultural identities (in this instance, sojourning) become powerfully located in biblical narratives. This allows the Gospel to speak directly into Gypsy and Traveller communities, performing in both the theological narratives of evangelism and liberation. The sojourner, the stranger, the 'impoverished' subject of political whim and historically misguided ecclesiological 'conversion' practice, thus makes a theologically political stance, through a process of gospel (re)appropriation. Ironically, despite the apparent complexity of this process, it's actually the simplicity of Gospel (re)appropriation by those considered impoverished (the outsider, the stranger, the spiritually dead, the sojourner) that is key.

When the 'impoverished' read the Word, their dire circumstances of destitution, ill-health, mental suffering and rejection are reflected back to them; therein dwells the secret to engagement and appropriation of the Scriptures – recognition and relationship, not complex hermeneutics. Our obsession with demythologising the miraculous has unsurprisingly left us with an ordinary faith, for who needs faith when you're happy to turn miracles into intellectual issues rather than believe water can be turned into wine? Miracles, in all their mystery and wonder, offer the possibility for the impoverished to have hope in their own lives. And through such means the stories in the Word become stories in and for communities and cultures. For them, the binding of the Bible and theological discourse in intellectualism is both a luxury they cannot afford and a path they cannot relate to. Instead, *they themselves* are the method by which interpretation of the Word takes place because their reading of the Bible emerges from experience. Because of this, there is no need to move from one social class to another to engage fully; relationship with the story is immediate. In this sense, sojourning does not have to be synonymous with social and religious poverty, because it finds itself in the Word, where *all* can find themselves. For the Traveller, the 'crutches' of sojourning are not an indicator of something broken but a representation of something supportive.

SUMMARY OF NOMADISM AND THE SOJOURNER

'So, do all Travellers travel?' If I had a pound for every time I've been asked that question, I'd have a moderately decent amount of money. It brings us back to the other question of, what's in a name. I have a hoover in my house, except, well, I don't. I have a vacuum cleaner; a Hoover is a brand of vacuum cleaner – not a thing in itself. The problem is, over a long period of time, my family (and many, many others in the UK) have had the name hoover passed down. For us, Hoovers and vacuum cleaners are one and the same, and as such, we expect a hoover to clean in a very particular way. But I'm pretty sure James Dyson wouldn't take too kindly to his premium vacuum cleaners being mistaken for another brand. I digress (again). Look, some Travellers travel, but many don't, and some Gypsies travel, but again, many do not. As such, it's both lazy and grossly negligent to assume *physical* nomadicy does and must form part of GRT identity. However, as we have read, nomadism in *other* constructs do form part of GRT identity. In fact, nomadism and impermanence has been part of the GRT experience for so long that it can be seen in social and work practices, it can be seen in attitudes towards life and religion, and it can be seen in the theologising and exegetical practices of GRT people in all parts of the world.

However, nomadism – both in practice and thought, brings with it challenges of its own – some good, some not so good. The idea of 'sojourner', biblically speaking, is one such challenge. The sojourner occupies both challenge and blessing. It is a position that represents journey – physically, spiritually, and religiously. At times it offers the possibility of exit and rest, however, the journey itself is one that is often made walking alongside God, and as such the call to continually move in our 'walks with God' is one that is as hard to walk away from as it is to stay the course. For Gypsies and Travellers, embodying the concept of sojourner is often without choice, being forced to perpetually occupy the social and religious position of outsider, of alien, and of stranger in the land. Permanent impermanence thus becomes the designated mode for everything. But the blessing dwells in the uncertainty. Stormy seas force us to search for places to anchor. Storms train our eyes to look for the coast and the bright shining lights that both warn and reassure. Storms force us to rely on faith and not ourselves. The storms of sojourning, of permanently moving and testing our Christian faith, is what makes us grow. And that reliance on faith is never unrewarded. For GRT people, part of that reward is an inheritance that sits just beyond the horizon, where the yet-to-be-born reside and hope for a safer future dwell.

Sometimes our inheritance sits right before our eyes, merging between the lines of biblical text, waiting for someone to uncover truths that have been hidden by domineering voices lacking the diversity of the spectrum of human expression and form. Complexity is the name of the game here, where over theologising and an unhealthy obsession with post-enlightenment thinking has resulted in the wonderfully simplistic Gospel message of hope and acceptance being lost to proud peacocks dressed in black. Stories of the miraculous have been shamefully explained away in order to avoid ridicule from a sceptical, atheistic and secular society. But at what cost? The impoverished have relied upon these very stories to find reasoning and hope, yet they have been and are being stripped away by the very people who profess to love and serve them. For GRT people, these stories have been reclaimed. 'If you don't want them, we'll have them!' the voices cry out. Upon these texts new Churches have formed and communities empowered. You sacrificed the greats for modern art, so Gypsies picked up the brush and relearnt Michelangelo. God wants all of his children; if you deny any of them the privilege of knowing Him, don't be surprised when He goes to them Himself.

That brings us on to the question of where does God meet us? It becomes an even more pressing question when that location – tangible or metaphorical, isn't fixed. It forces us to reflect on what our location looks and feels like, and whether it is welcoming to the Creator or not. If God is to be among us, as we so often wish for, is our 'camp' clean? Indeed, is our 'camp' actually a place or is it simply the vessel in which we reside? As a nomadic people, a sojourning people, the answers to these questions begin to reveal the depth of relationship with the Father and the reverence that, much like the stories of the miraculous, is missing from so much of our current climate. Moving onto the next chapter, we pull over the vans and the trailers and we set up camp, heading into the heart of the Traveller's home and finding God among us.

CHAPTER SIX

THE CAMP AND THE CREATOR: GOD AMONG US

'I will put my dwelling place among you, and I will not abhor you.'
(Leviticus 26:11)

NO WORTH OR KNOW WORTH?

'This, once again, is the hottest year on records, say climate scientists.' The once-startling headline being announced by the TV news reporter was in some ways kind of redundant; it was 39 degrees outside and my front room felt like a sauna. This was England but it felt like the Sahara desert, and as such I didn't need the near-on daily reminder from the gloom box that something wasn't right in the world. In the pursuit of more, we as a species had turned our glorious planet against us, and now the Earth was retaliating. The Earth was our gift, but we had become Mother Nature's virus. To make matters worse, the fan was just blowing hot air and we had visitors coming over to see us. I wasn't in the mood for tidying, but then, when are any of us in that mood? Nevertheless, the prospect of visitors is, I believe, the single greatest motivator for house cleaning. Honestly, I have never cleaned my house more quickly and effectively than when I've known people are coming over. Despite the crazy temperature and the ineffective fan, I blitzed the house, took out the household waste, and tidied up. My visitors, their comfort, and indeed their potential judgement of my abode were factors that were way more important than my temporal discomfort. The thing that bugs me most about those situations though, is the five minutes between finishing cleaning and the arrival of the guests. It's during that time that I sit and look at my presentable and clean dwelling, and think, 'Why don't I have it like this for me?'.

Our visitors, however, are not always what we expect or whom we were expecting. When God first 'entered' the world, He hovered above the waters. The second time, He physically walked into political and civil unrest. If we're not careful, the third time He turns up, it'll be to a combination of the two! When did we lose our reverence for the Creator's creation? The same question can sometimes be asked for where we reside. Sometimes the same question can also be asked for the bodies in which we dwell. It's true that all creation belongs to God, but it is equally true that we have been charged with looking after creation (Genesis 1:26). As such, there is often a high degree of frustration among many believers at their seeming lack of ability to influence climate policy and bring about necessary changes. However, in the meantime there is always fruit in doing what we *can* do, rather than focusing on that which we *cannot* do. When we begin to draw the focus of our stewardship a bit closer to home and the temple in which God has placed our spirit, we feel both blessed and convicted. A Church is a sacred place, but a Church that is filthy or has been neglected is often considered desecrated. Why then do we view our bodies less favourably than mere buildings? And why do we look upon the places we rest our head at night as something secondary? Don't misunderstand me; I'm not advocating getting unessential cosmetic surgery or taking out loans to decorate our homes. I am however suggesting that there is a necessary principle of care and stewardship at play that has to start with ourselves.

Care and stewardship isn't just a factor for priestly ministry; it is also an element of preparation and accommodation. If we care and lead, it is ultimately to convey authentic love and set beneficial direction. When we apply those principles to where *we* reside – even temporal accommodation, then we exercise reverence not just for those who share our bed and sit beneath our shelter, but reverence and appreciation is shown to the gifted bodies in which we dwell and to the Father that provided both the pillow to lay our heads on and the head that lays on the pillow! Gypsy and Traveller homes and sites are in many ways practical demonstrations of this reverence. With family at its heart and Christ as its heartbeat, the home, is for many, sacred. Cleanliness ensures purity as well as reducing ammo for those who would condemn Gypsies and Travellers as dirty. Expensive, inordinate and often extravagant decoration ensures often modest accommodation is fit for both the Creator and His children. Gypsy homes are not 'proud as a peacock' – they *are* the peacock, and that is why they are proud.

NOMADISM AS IMPERMANENT PERMANENCE: INTRODUCING THE CAMP

Enter Stage, Left

A couple of years ago, I undertook some field research for my PhD. During that time, I had the privilege to stay with several Gypsy and Traveller families around the UK. The families were diverse, in that they 'presented' very differently to each other; some lived in trailers on official sites, some lived in fixed accommodation (i.e. houses), whilst others were technically homeless, living in caravans that were constantly being moved on by local authorities (Councils) and the police. Two families in particular were helpful and open enough that they became case studies for my thesis. The families lived almost at opposite ends of England, and the settings in which they lived were markedly different. One dwelling was in an officially registered 'camp', comprising of plots or 'pitches' where mobile homes and trailers were (mostly) permanently positioned. The other dwelling was a brick-built house, located in a predominantly gorger-occupied street. Interestingly, both properties were fixed and stationary and thus incapable of fulfilling either the gorger's stereotypical perception of Gypsies as 'nomadic' or the GRT self-conceptualisation of unrestrained. However, the unique presentations of both properties suggested otherwise.

External decorations of large wagon/cartwheels, an unused trap (small carriage) and various 'horse' ornaments and accessories inside the windows adorned the abodes. For the most part, they were decorative, symbolic even. There was a hint of nostalgia; an indication of remembrance, maybe even a longing for some past-generational 'traditional' Gypsy living. More importantly however, their narration shouted out that in many ways Gypsy *fixed* abodes were *impermanent*. These external spaces were deliberate, intentional, and representative; setting the stage for the beliefs of its inhabitants to be expressed as both a welcome and a barrier to those wanting to enter. If one were to look a little deeper, one would see there was more to what some unfavourable media outlets had called 'kitsch'.

Between the lines of these decorative statements was movement among the stationary; like fixed clock hands among the moving cogs of time. The cold hard permanence of brick coexisted with the temporal indeterminate destination of the wagons. Indeed, theologically speaking, what was at play here was the eschatological 'hoped for' and the redemptive 'past' residing in an unstable present. Yes, it was performance. These objects were not going anywhere. But even for the Gypsies and Travellers who had real horses and still pulled vardos, their existence was blurred among the past and the contemporary. Such existences were powerful, at least for their symbolic qualities. However, there were no Gypsies or Travellers that I knew who were still dependant on a horse to pull their plough or whose bow-top was their only dwelling.

As such, performance was not secondary. *Performance – the cleaning of the home, the preparation of the property, the dressing of the entrance and garden, the exuberant dress; these were and are performances of Christian-Traveller symbolism and where, at least in its contemporary guise, the motif of nomadism is best found.*

The embodiment of nomadism as a performative identifier has, as suggested previously, been one of the measurements by which *gorger* culture has assessed or imagined Gypsy and Traveller culture. As such, the presence of these public decorations that are representative of a nomadic or itinerant nature, serve as appeasements to the expectations of gorgers. They solidify gorger-created stereotypes, which in turn permeates collective thinking – not just in our streets but in our Churches too. And when Gypsies, Travellers – indeed, most minority groups – fail to live up to externally given stereotypes, or when minorities dare to break the glass ceilings of industries or simply live 'conventional' lives, they are abused, feared, or given sickening congratulations as if to say their apparent lower form shouldn't be capable of such successes. Or, rather than simply practising acceptance, they will say 'Here, have a day, no, a month in honour of your race'. Why? So you can gawp at us a little longer? Spotlights on differences, unsurprisingly, highlight differences.

When our genuine curiosity about difference is replaced with dedicated days, support badges, photo filters and meaningless gestures, we run a risk that the only thing that might change is the hateful get more infuriated and the so-called supportive feel better about themselves. True altruism and genuine Christian love can be enacted by allowing space in society for our varied expressions and cultures, where explanations flourish and defences are not needed. This is not multiculturalism – it is a blended culturalism; an expansion of the tapestry of our societies. When we apply this principle to our theologising, we do not dilute or compromise existing messages – we simply add to the rich tapestry of our ecclesiological and theological world. Of course, fight fires where you need to; you're always going to get bad eggs in society. But by making all of a society feel like criminals and racists whilst simultaneously highlighting the suffering of certain minority groups, dangerous situations and hate evolves where once no such intentions dwelt. Besides which, by holding groups such as GRT people to the standards of certain stereotypes, such as nomadism, a kind of 'Perform for me, monkey' situation arises. In this instance, looking at Gypsy and Traveller usage of space or style of dress from an outside perspective with some form of nostalgia or expectation is at best informatively limiting, and at worst culturally insensitive. The meanings and significance of such space and 'performances' are esoteric, privy to Travellers and Gypsies, and are not for 'external' examination and interpretation. This 'performance ground' is sacred and clean (and therefore capable of becoming polluted) to the Traveller. Allow space for dialogue and expression. This book, for example, is one such space.

We can begin to recognise that our homely decorations are, even at both the subtle and subconscious level, extensions of our innermost identities stretching forth. At times such decorations are like dances, designed to be noticed and to draw the viewer in and to allow the personality out. At other times, these decorations are symbolic and ritualistic, engaging the area in which they dwell like some kind of holy space. The home, the camp, the site; these are the performance spaces in which the identity-laden decorations undertake their function. In reference to Indigenous Australians, Richard Schechner (2006) describes such a relationship between the person (in this instance, the Traveller) and the performative space. He suggests that '[o]nly the initiated know the relationship between the ordinary geography and the sacred geography'.[161] It makes sense then that Gypsies and Travellers are both symbolic gate keepers to their culture (as are every other minority or marginalised group), and they are directors of how and what operates in that space – be it tangibly or metaphysically. As such, it's probably a good time to remind everyone again that traditional nomadism in Traveller communities is not always a readily observable activity – and thus is not always an identifier of Travellers and Gypsies. However, nomadism *is* an institution in Traveller and Gypsy culture and a motif in the performative realm of a Traveller theology. The nomadic camp setting creates a platform whereby the indigenous nature of Gypsy Traveller culture is most explicitly revealed. The following comment from an Irish Traveller named Martin, gives an insight into when his camp received a visiting party:

[161]   Schechner, 2006, p. 36.

What was actually cool was around this time some Native Americans were travelling through Ireland and they came to visit our camp. They told us how we shared traditions such as building and lighting fires and everyone gathers around the campfire to chat and share stories. Like the Romany travellers the elders drank and also chatted with each other around the fire. I loved that day with the Native Americans, we had so much fun. It was great being around people who understood our ways of life. I don't recall their names but I do remember dressing up in their traditional dress.[162]

Home is where the ~~heart~~ God is

The dwelling place for Gypsies and Travellers becomes the performative area whereby nomadism is played out. Whether in honour of historical cultural traditions, in remembrance of ancestors or for affiliation to the community as a whole, GRT art and presentation of publicised space is sacred and honourable. It is not a 'trend' or a 'statement' aimed towards those outside of the community. Travelling or nomadism, as spiritual and cultural practice, takes a form. If the idea of a place of residence (particularly a mobile camp) being sacred is ringing any bells, then it's probably safe to say your mind's eye is heading back into the Pentateuch. Moses, under the instruction of God, creates the template for this very model when he begins moving around a people with no land to call their own.

So, in the instance of the *dwelling place*, the 'travelling space' can be seen as the 'Mosaic camp'. In this scenario, the Trailer or house (the Tabernacle) is located at the centre – an honorary and sacred nomadic form that is both fixed and impermanent. Theologically, the rationale is underpinned by the logical understanding that God is Lord of everything – both His creation (the property) and His people. Since both are open to defilement or 'pollution', they must be separate from that which can defile

---

[162] G4S/HMPS, 2016, p. 9.

(gorgers and gorger culture). As Creation belongs to God, its occupiers are temporal – as is everything else; therefore, the pattern of movement – or nomadism (physical, mental, or spiritual) is divinely sanctioned. This, as we have seen already, is exegetically supported through numerous examples in the biblical text (with particular reference to Abraham, Sarah, Hagar, and their sons and daughters), where nomadism is not exceptional but is the normative mode of being.

We see an almost mirrored theological underpinning utilised in the Levitical 'idealistic institutions', such as the 'Sabbatical Year' – or 'Land's Sabbath', and 'The Jubilee'. Creation was and is in the Creator's ownership; as such, Israel belonged to the Creator. Legally speaking the Israelites were, in this respect, tenants and not landowners. Tenants do not determine terms of tenancy – owners do; 'The land shall not be sold permanently, for the land is Mine' (Leviticus 25:23). Intriguingly, this instruction is issued by God, with the following rationale; '...for you are strangers and sojourners with me' (Leviticus 25:23). In an arguably complementarily interpretation, the Amplified Bible replaces 'sojourner' with 'temporary residents with Me'. In this way, God is making it clear that (1) there is a deliberate and intentional separateness between the Father and His creation, and (2) that the reasoning behind the separateness is to maintain purity. Leviticus 26:1-2 drives this point home, showing that reverence in these spaces is key; to achieve that reverence we must avoid the things that pollute, that corrupt, that contaminate. Doing so enables an inner-cultural demonstration of reverence for what can be considered the sacred space of the presence of God. Key to this approach, is that this isn't some futile effort by humans to appease the Father, as if divine grace doesn't exist. No, it is simply obedience to a mode and model of being that God has appointed.

THE CAMP
Stage One: Maintaining Separation
Outside of the (actual and metaphorical) camp are those considered polluted (gorgers) and physical waste. On occasions this divisional

area is immediately recognisable upon approaching some camps and Gypsy/Traveller houses (large collections of dumped refuse; tall metal gates and walls). See the following images:

Fig. 3   *Dale Farm Site, England*[163]

Fig. 4   *St Syrus Site, Scotland*[164]

---

[163]   Note that the border of the camp is marked by barbed wire on fence (Fagge, 2011).
[164]   Note the tall border fence surrounding the camp, and individual plots with high walls and gates (Dingwall, 2015).

Fig. 5   *Cardiff: House Gates*[165]

The space is often divided into three areas/stages (or two for fixed accommodation, such as a house), with the first stage reserved for bodily waste, cleaning – both personal and clothing, and general waste. These are kept outside of the primary dwelling area[166] to avoid contamination in the actual home/house. Sometimes waste is left on unauthorised sites when Travellers have left, but it must be understood that despite the belief that taking waste back into the residence (trailer/ vardo) would cause pollution, the waste is only ever left because of practical reasons such as no facilities to dispose of waste, or the lack of access to waste tips (which require fixed addresses or waste licenses to attend). Modern residences – mobile or otherwise, *are* capable of

[165]   Imposing gates and substantial brick columns mark the border between 'gorger' and 'Traveller' space. Also, note the decorative stone horses (on pathway to house) (Tomlinson, 2012).
[166]   On a camp or mobile home park, the washing and toilet facilities are kept separate to the living quarters, in an external building or structure. The 'dwelling area' should be considered anywhere inside the fenced or walled areas. As such, it may contain vehicles, other trailers, vardos, caravans and possibly animals.

accommodating these 'normal' pollutants, and the fear of spreading disease or disposing of the dead is not a ready concern in UK homes. As such, the practice of maintaining these stringent, deeply ritualistic and spiritual boundaries is withdrawn from an enigmatic state, and placed firmly in a single synergistic state in which the usage of space for the Gypsy or Traveller is much more straightforward: that of maintaining purity, and that of removing pollution. Once again, through deliberate and intentional practice, we see how (Gypsy and Traveller) Christianity can and does operate as a 'lived religion'.

Before we move on to the 'camp' itself, we can't simply bypass the soteriological elephant in the room. If our spaces can, for some, be considered as sacred, performative and representative of a Christian core, then can it be that these spaces are as impactful to our salvation as our own personal actions are? In some GRT environments, this can certainly be the case. There is a consistency and a relationship between space and the aforementioned areas of purity and ownership of sin. You'll recall that some causes of sin are considered to be separate to the person; i.e. an object or event is responsible for the wrongdoing and not the person. Furthermore, 'pollution' is often linked to tangible objects. It stands to reason then that space – particularly that in which some dwell, can become a component in the salvific process of Traveller faith. It is of course a theoretical concept, but one that shouldn't seem surprising, controversial or even remotely original.

As a species, we've had sacred spaces pretty much since day dot. Our ancestors recognised the power in certain places, going so far as to drag giant stones across entire lands and raising impressive structures. We have created separated spaces for males and females, we have places for books, for purchasing, for entertainment, and for worship. Our places are intentional, deliberate, often purposeful and separate. If I confused the bookshelf in my local bookstore for that of a library, I'd commit a sin if I walked out with an unpaid object. Consequently then, this suggests that in some circles Traveller salvation, in much the same way as contemporary African Christianity, has a 'solid, material context'.[167] Its success is thus partially dependent upon the physical, social, and metaphorical separateness of the Traveller and their property from pollutants – both physical and spiritual.

During critical periods of their development, both Eastern and Western Christianity were dramatically affected by processes of thought originating from indigenous elements, in which the material – including the body – were equated with evil.[168] This perspective has been challenged through theologies that find their roots in the liberal institution of the Enlightenment. These liberal approaches include (but are not limited to) certain feminist branches of theology and queer theology.[169] Some of these theologies (namely, Queer theology) adopt ecclesiological narratives when it comes to situations of (un)intentional social, spiritual, and theological boundaries and divisions. In these situations, symbolism in the LGBT space such as the 'pride marches' and the rainbow flag, are understood to 'dissolve boundaries based on traditional identity markers'.[170] Compare these to the divisional walls of the Traveller camps and the images of nomadic culture such as the stone horses (see *Fig. 5*). These 'walls' operate conversely in an identical framework function to *maintain* boundaries. Clearly the dissolution of boundaries and the reinforcement of firm boundaries dwell on the same spectrum, albeit at opposite ends. However, what is clear in both is that there is a direct correlation between non-determined space and its usage (such as the rainbow flag or the Traveller's 'waste area') and that of a theological agenda. As such, despite its abstruse and esoteric composition, the simple act of keeping pollution outside of the 'camp' (unknowingly and unwittingly) becomes both a political act and a theological standpoint.

In neo-orthodoxical style, the Travellers' theology becomes less of a response to human questions and more of a response to God (and

167 Walls, 1998, p. 148.
168 Walls, 1998, p. 157.
169 Watson, 2003, p. 59.
170 Cheng, 2011, p. 106.

his Word).[171] This tension is not a new one. There has always been an observable and constant tension between the forces that streamline Christianity to a relationship between God and man, between act and response, and 'those which universalise it' – that is to say, those who liberalise Christianity with an emphasis on a human-centred story.[172] However, this dichotomy can be unified to some extent when applied to the instance of the Traveller and the salvific properties or pathways found in the use of space. The human condition is such that we need to be able to lean on a myriad of materials from nearly every realm of culture, allowing the idea that God can meet us anywhere and at any stage He chooses. Furthermore, if we are to serve God in this life, we are to do so in the form in which the Creator has made us. It makes sense then that we should not so readily dismiss the validity of human expression, understanding and form in our pursuit of relationship with the Father. Indeed, we may be at the centre of the Father's story, but it is still the Father's story and not ours. He must always be the focus, for it is only through Him that our own story makes sense.

Stage Two: Within the Camp Walls

We've stepped off the main path from where we glimpsed the images, objects and decoration that spoke of a different life to our own. We have passed the entrance, and made our way through the gate. The Edgelands that once appeared like a distant fog has cleared, and what we now see around us is form, structure, something deliberate. In some ways you're already there, having got through the first couple of chapters of this book, where you approached the edgelands of your own thinking and waded through the unwanted wasteland of traumatic pasts and historic stereotypes. Looking around, you're struck with both the sense of normality and the awareness of difference; a bit like when you arrive at your foreign holiday, where the familiarity of shops, restaurants, roads and people are offset against the noise

171   McGrath, 2011, p. 86.
172   Walls, 1998, pp. 156 – 157.

of unknown languages and the sight of unusual gestures. For those outside of our faith in this present age, this is their reality when we speak of a loving God and a fellowship of believers.

With that in mind, never lose sight of the absurdity of the Christian customs we practise and the language we speak. To the uninitiated, we are, quite frankly, bonkers. This, more so than ever, is one of the reasons that we must always be aware of the challenges people could be experiencing when entering our Churches. And those challenges aren't limited to buildings and institutions. More so than ever, we need to be conscious of how we are the church, and not just the places we frequent on Sundays. Scary thought, but an interaction on social media with you may be the closest one of your friends has ever come to knowing God. Keep your 'place' clean, keep it sacred, make it always welcoming, and speak to all and not just those familiar to you – for you are 'under obligation both to Greeks and to barbarians, both to the wise and to the foolish' (Romans 1:14). With that in mind, we can relax our shoulders and take a walk inside the camp walls.

Like the decoration and the equipment we've seen, nothing in the camp is without purpose or reasoning. Inside our camps we find an escalation of deliberateness and very particular usages of space. A quick Pentateuchal exploration gives us evidence that God is involved in creating such order, and has been for some time. Located in the Levitical text is the inception of the Deuteronomic model of instruction, given by Moses to and for the benefit of the camp. The model maintains a theme of purity, intentionally presenting it as divinely preferable to its oppositional narrative – pollution. However, the focus is realigned from one that draws a response towards polluting and sinful activities (and peoples), to one that in an idealistic manoeuvre seeks 'traditional' concepts of purity[173] (Deuteronomy 23:1–14). There still appears to exist a tension of sorts; after all, in the arena of our homes where we spend much of our time is where both prayers are offered

---

[173]   Mays, 1988, p. 229.

to God and sins are frequently committed. Likewise, the spirits in our flesh are clean whilst our flesh is often contaminated with sin. To deal with this, we have to remember both the impermanence of where we are, the bodies in which we dwell, and the lives in which we live. The inevitable tensions between contestable acts (or pollution) and principles of worship (or purity) might be better understood when we understand that our place of worship and our 'war camp' are *integrated in and as one area*. This integrated area is an environment that is a permanent fluidity in the impermanence of the camp as a whole. The cross-tensions of permanence and impermanence, and of war and worship, are symbolised via a transition from the impurity of the camp walls and beyond, to the purity of the camp home, the trailer, the house – the 'tent of meeting'.

In this area 'war' or fights for honour and settling disputes[174] are not considered polluting but are 'honourable' methods, or at the very least *acceptable* in which to settle issues and conflict[175] (Deuteronomy 23:14). Conversely, this 'middle ground' is also considered to be a 'safe' ground where Gypsies and Travellers are essentially free citizens in their own land – even if that land is not his or her own (i.e. an illegal or temporary stopping ground). Unless under a specific and particular invitation, gorgers who are unknown may be considered to be unwelcome or even prevented from gaining entry[176]. This is not an intentionally conflictual manner of conducting oneself but simply a method in which potential pollution is prevented from entering a 'pure' area. After all, you don't accept every 'friend request'…

The religious nature and spiritual value of this temporal, 'undecided' middle-ground, operates between the poles of impure

---

[174]   See *Chapter Two – Conflict: People*

[175]   'For the Lord your God walks in the midst of your camp to deliver you and to give up your enemies before you. Therefore shall your camp be holy, that He may see nothing indecent among you and turn away from you'.

[176]   This cultural trend – whilst not universal, is documented as happening through varying means, and often with varying reasons being given for such exclusions. See Hancock, 2013, pp. 58 – 59; Cullen et al, 2008, p. 11.

and pure. It initially appears to be related to some form of reductive theism, which in some ways is reflective of the contemporary sense of a vague spirituality expressed by some in the modern era. This 'sense' comes from our ever-connected, expansive yet disillusioned world that ridicules both public religion and private belief in a transcendent and immanent God. Critically however, despite the temptation, positioning Gypsies and Travellers in this same category of 'vague spirituality' is in fact contrary to the biblically-based impermanence of the Traveller camp. The camp is where Traveller and Gypsy Christian spirituality is representative of an 'ordered universe in which the theological baseline is deliberate, discriminating divine providence'.[177]

The question of the sovereignty of God or 'Creator' over the nomadic camp is unchallenged. However, to find how those in the camp relate to the nature of God, we have to start by acknowledging the subscription to values and worldviews that are based on narratives clearly originating from Pentateuchal sources. There is, through certain cultural practices and preferences, the implied suggestion that the Creator who dwells in the midst of the Traveller's 'Mosaic' camp is the same Creator that was revealed as 'the LORD' (YHWH) to the nation of Israel. Key to this point however is that this 'LORD' is the same Lord whose just and responsive support of humankind is often expressed in the New Testament with the metaphor 'Father'. As such, scriptural propositions that can offer explanation as to how such a relationship operates, must also be concerned with the attributes, purposes, activities, and accessibility of this providential celestial being. Of course, that means any GRT hermeneutic that entertains *literal* translations of the biblical text runs the risk of welcoming into the camp a murderer of children and a bringer of genocide. Indeed, that's the risk of any unregulated ministry born from oppression. We've seen it before in its extremes: from liberating theologies that have found themselves in the hearts of people prepared to hold guns,

[177] McBride, 2012, p. 434.

142

to the placards being waved high and proud calling for 'death to fags'. However, in this instance 'Father' is the emphasis. Moreover, any focus on suffering or crying out to the Father is done *alongside* with and *in replication* of Jesus in His crucifixion.

To reiterate, the sovereignty and governance of God over the Gypsy's cosmos (or camp) and the Gypsies themselves is certain. However, in this environment of intentional separateness, when looking at the nature of the Father we have to ask, does God dispense benefactions and justice in relation to the maintenance (and conversely the neglect) of pollution related practices, *primarily* or *exclusively* from a transcendental distance?[178] Or, as circumstances may support, does God also choose to draw near to Gypsies in an impendent capacity, responding to human needs 'in our midst[179]? Witnesses from biblical text often attest to such impendence. This forces a shift in the criticality towards 'works'[180] for the pursuit of purity. In turn, this seeks to further open up the relational dynamic between the Gypsy and God, asking how God's closeness is perceived and manifested. Additionally, given the fragility and sinful state of the human condition, are there any assurances of the divine presence being reliably efficacious, especially given the often attested to historically tormentous existence of the Gypsy? Such questions are perhaps ineffectually answered through observation and critical engagement with the 'perimeters' and 'inner boundaries' of the camp. However, progressing towards the centre of the camp – the living quarters, facilitates more engagement with the 'pure', as the impure is left firmly behind. This developing 'Traveller doctrine of God', in the face of intentional but purposeful isolation/separation by Travellers (by proxy of an enforced 'barrier' between cultures), begins to raise further questions about the impassibility of

---

[178] Exodus 2:25; 1 Kings 8:27–30; Psalm 93; Matthew 6:9–10; Revelation 4.

[179] Zephaniah 3:17; Hebrew 13:2.

[180] 'Works' in this sense, should be understood as being as being one half of a dichotomy, with its biblical opposite being 'grace'. It should be noted that I interpret the 'works versus grace' equation to be markers at opposite ends of a spectrum, rather than opposing binary propositions.

God and the Traveller's participation in what appears to be a voluntary mode of suffering.

Stage Three: The Centre of the Camp

God is interested in our hearts. Without the Father, our hearts and our bodily homes may be ours, but they are also corrupt (Jeremiah 17:9). However, when we submit our hearts to the Father (Proverbs 23:26), we acknowledge God as Lord over and through us. Still, there are times when we find other contenders to the throne of our heart attempting to edge their way in. For some, it may be money; for others, it may be their careers. We know that 'man cannot serve two masters' (Matthew 6:24). However, the truth is life is fluid, unpredictable and often distracting. So, no matter how sincere our submission to God, there will always be temptations and usurpers seeking to dethrone the Father from the seat of our hearts. So then, it makes sense that we should be prepared and ready to accommodate Him in the midst of our dwelling place (physical and spiritually).

Moses knew this. He kept the centre of his camp sacred, using it as the location for the tent of meeting, the tent of the congregation, the tabernacle – the earthly dwelling place for the Creator. This area was once again separated from the last; this time by huge boards mounted in gold, held in place by silver mounts. Leaving the 'second stage' of the Gypsy camp, we are greeted with the boundaries for individual plots. In place of 15-foot high glimmering boards are brick walls, elaborate metal railings and decorative but strong fencing. The trailer (or, caravan, house, etc.) is the tent of meeting. In this centre of the camp (the home) the manifestation of God is made apparent through abstract forms, which among other things include: art works; ornaments; and in some instances a sterner, more illiberal and puritanical application of the *mokhhadi* code.[181] There is a biblical precedent for this philosophical dualism of mind and matter, and

[181]   Clark and Greenfields, 2006, pp. 40 – 45.

unsurprisingly it's found in the Pentateuchal-Israelite narrative. On several occasions in Scripture, God appears in and through various forms.[182] In the Gypsy home (and sometimes, vehicles), the power of the 'Spirit' or 'divine presence' can be invoked in several ways, including through the touching of crucifixes, ornaments of Christ and Mary,[183] rosaries, and images of saints.

Ecclesiological ears may be twitching at the sound of this, and rightfully so. The influence of common and 'recommended' Catholic (big 'C') practices are evident, demonstrating the powerful influence of: Anglo-Catholic Christian missionaries; the broad spread of 'high Church' C of E weekly worship; governmental policies; assimilation; acculturalisation; and education, all dating back to the mid-nineteenth century onwards. Given the monumental rise of Pentecostal-led and non-specific denominational Evangelism among the UK Gypsy and Traveller community over the past 30 to 40 years, the application of Catholic style Spirit invocation seems, at first, relatively out of place. This is not to suggest that Gypsies and Travellers are not identifying as Catholic in the UK. But it does suggest that Gypsies and Travellers are practising another mode of Christianity – albeit a syncretistic Christian practice that, as many other (former) Indigenous collectives have experienced, is heavily tainted with the effects of colonialism. For clarity, Catholicism in this sense is not synonymous with Colonialism, nor is Catholicism underrepresented. However, the misinterpretation of the Traveller's nomadic 'trailer' or 'home' and the practical application of a Gypsy Christianity undertaken therein as

---

[182]   'The Angel of the Lord appeared to him in a flame of fire out of the midst of a bush...' – Exodus 3:2. Also see; Exodus 13:21 – Pillar of cloud; Exodus 13:21 – Pillar of fire; Exodus 19:16-19 & Exodus 20:18-22 – Thunder, lighting and a thick darkness; Exodus 24:9-11, Deuteronomy 4: 11,12 & 15, & John 5:37 – Unclear form, with a voice, hands and feet; Job 38:1 – Whirlwind; Genesis 3:8 – Possibly the form of a man.
[183]   Ian Hancock remarks on how Romani-Indian heritage has maintained elements of Hinduism in its spiritual and religious practice – including instances of recognising spiritual power in objects / items (Hancock, 2013, p. 74).

any form of Christianity other than a *Gypsy Christianity*, is simply a continuation of Colonialist practice and evidence of the appropriation of Gypsy religious practice by dominant Western denominations. It is also a gross devaluing of the sanctity and relevance of the Gypsy or Traveller's dwelling place, ignoring the spiritual, historical, and cultural value and significance of artwork and decoration.

Not all spaces are created equal, and the centre of 'the camp' – the home – is certainly not equal to the environment outside. Clearly then, devaluing Gypsy spaces is troublesome. A significant issue here is that Gypsy spaces are persistently devalued by others. Camps are placed at the margins of cities and towns, in disused car parks, and in remote areas. The gorger message of 'We don't want to see you' is loud and clear. I remember speaking to a newly retired gorger couple living in a village in the Midlands. They seemed reasonable but were furious and outspoken about the recent appearance of a permanent mobile home appearing next to an old barn on a small private plot of land a few hundred metres away from their house. 'It's put the value of our property down by at least thirty grand', I was told. 'Have you had any issues with the new family living there?' I enquired. 'No, no. They've waved most days when they've gone past, and to be fair, we've not really seen or heard them.' The issue at hand was not the Gypsy family themselves but the perception of who they were and the (social and physical) value of both them and their property. Merely the idea of a Gypsy residence nearby was enough for local estate agents to reduce the value of what was a stunning eighteenth-century property by tens of thousands of pounds, and instil a bitter resentment in a seemingly lovely couple for a Gypsy family who were barely seen or heard. Imagine how much worse the situation would have been if a refugee family from the Middle East with an expectant mother had turned up, and opted to forsake the trailer and make home in the disused barn on the property instead! Barns, trailers, even remote homes for cattle in Bethlehem – all have value when their residents are seen as God created.

146

Stepping up into Rosie's trailer, I was immediately greeted with the glimmering reflection of the sun, bouncing off the plastic covers placed over every seat. The same could be said for the marble flooring (yes, marble flooring in a mobile home), which had sparkles throughout and was etched along the sides with 'Louis Vuitton'. Crystal cut glass cabinets filled the living space and were a million miles away from the mud-filled lanes I'd travelled through to get to Rosie's home. The family's dogs were, as expected, for the most part outside the trailer. (Dogs, like cats, are impure because they can clean themselves. Technically horses are pure because they can't clean themselves, but try fitting a 17 hand cob into a caravan!) I didn't need to ask if there was a toilet inside – I'd already walked past the ablutions and toilet block when I parked up my car. To the untrained eye, this was an expression of opulence; to those in the know, this was the understanding of one's worth as a person, it was cultural pride, it was a demonstration of blessing, and it was the recognition that our space is God's space and it should be treated accordingly.

We don't always have the option or opportunity to alter our surroundings in such a way as described above, nor do we have to. Gucci wallpaper and silver cutlery are thankfully not prerequisites for God to consider dwelling among us. To drive home a point here, God is after our hearts and our minds. Our possessions are, in the eyes of God, worthless. However, if hearts express honour, gratitude and respect to the Father through physical means, then those physical forms adopt new values that eyes cannot appreciate or comprehend. As we sing of the old rugged cross with such passion, do we consider its splinters and knots as barriers to the love that was shed on it? Or when we look at the detailed architecture and decoration of our Cathedrals, are our thoughts more occupied with the cost of upkeep than with the faith of investment that keeps unchurched folks walking in God's presence? Of course, we are not bound by single options of thought, but we are bound by our faith in the Creator to acknowledge that He can and does occupy all of His creation. If all of creation has been made by Him, through Him and for Him (Romans 11:36; Colossians 1:16), then we have to acknowledge that God may be present in the places that we choose to not see; those places on the margins of cities and towns, in disused car parks, and in remote areas. God dwells in houses and He dwells in caravans. He does not dwell in hate.

Within Rosie's 'Tent of Meeting' was authenticity; not necessarily when I was there to visit her and her family, but when Rosie and her husband are alone, when Rosie and her husband are sitting with their children, when Rosie is sat by herself. The expectations of both the gorger and Traveller world are left behind and authentic human expression manifests. When Jesus instructs us to go into our room, shut the door and pray (Matthew 6:6), He does so because it's our true nature He wants to build relationship with – not the Christian who wants to assure their peers that they are most holy, nor the businessperson who wants to demonstrate to others their competence and success. When we welcome the Father into our midst, the burden of our self-ascribed labels and expectations vanish as He reminds us that we are called 'child of God'. In the Tent of Meeting, we rest – physically, mentally, and spiritually. Rosie's home enabled her to rest and heal without judgement or condemnation. Furthermore, her use of religious decoration enabled her to enjoy her home as both a place of dwelling and a place of prayer.

Rosie's somewhat reappropriation of what is typically understood to be Catholic imagery and symbolism is reasonably commonplace. In many ways, this distinctive decoration of the home is simply another arm to Gypsy Christian 'performance', including its many examples of 'oub' nuances (purity; nomadism; use of space; etc.). The deliberateness of expression on display here is often overlooked, seen in some ways as a very 'un-British' bolshiness that could do with a little more decorum and a little less pizzazz. However, the trick here is to remind ourselves that if we are to see God we have to look for God. So, in this instance we must seek to understand the *deliberateness* (or intention) of the expression. What is it that Rosie is trying to achieve by decorating her modest home with the finest furnishings money can buy and filling her cabinets and shelves with many exquisite ornaments and icons depicting Christ, Mary and crucifixes? Every penny Rosie owned had been invested into her home. When we truly understand who we serve, then washing feet with tears and anointing them with the finest oils begins to make sense.

Rosie had, in many ways, immersed herself and her family into the scriptures, enacting principles that she recognised others doing in the Bible. This process of contextualisation should come of no surprise; typical Gypsy biblical hermeneutics that I've examined have often been based upon a literal interpretation of Scripture. Indeed, I would suggest that to truly understand Gypsy Christianity, we must place Gypsies and Gypsy social narratives into the exegetical process, as I have done through this chapter; the primary example being the direct comparisons of the Traveller and the nomadic camp with the Israelite camp and the Pentateuchal motif of purity. Through this method, Gypsies and Travellers are able to re-appropriate Christian denominations for and through their own individual or family preferences. This goes some way to explain the intense unity on display between the varying denominations during my visits to Appleby Fair. The denominations who, whilst having vastly differing modes of operation, also had an evident shared 'missional' and cultural bond that went beyond its 'Christian' baseline, making any distinctions between the groups onerous.

This is important, as it reveals a nomadic nature in Gypsy and Traveller culture that is present in not only the social sense, but also the religious sense. It's clear that there is a certain 'fluidity' of Christian positioning (i.e. denominational preference) among GRT communities. However, there remains a lack of transparency as to what orthodoxical and theological consequences (if any) such a fluidity may entail. Take the example of the aforementioned symbolic objects and pictures (iconography, etc.) in the Traveller home Unlike certain Catholic understandings, there appears to be no explicit indications that such items in the Traveller home are considered to be tangible *representations* (rather than *manifestations*) of the divine presence. This contextual difference is marginally seen in the Israelite camp motif when Moses is confronted with the cult of the golden bull-calf (created in some ways as a consequence of a desire for the substantiation of the Lord, but undertaken in violation of the covenantal agreement between the people and God [Exodus 32:1 – 35]). And whilst there is an acknowledgment that spiritual power can reside (or manifest) in certain objects,[184] there is no clarification or certainty as to what degree these objects go beyond their symbolistic properties and blessed status, and are thus treated as the 'golden calf'. Arguably, and in defence of the Traveller position, these 'concerns' may be more symbolistic of a colonial indoctrination. Such indoctrination affects both those *outside* and *in* the Gypsy community. Those outside aim to ensure orthodoxy in the Christian faith and subsequent presentation of that faith, whilst those operating *in* the Gypsy community seek to achieve a critical self-awareness in an environment that has been consumed by its colonial masters of past and present.

SUMMARY

We once thought of God as distant, whose interest in us was somewhat akin to the tales of Greek gods, playing with our mortal lives like chess pieces and toys. However, the love of the Father thought much differently. For millennia, God's love interacted with us, giving hope, saving people, building nations. We once welcomed God into our temples, then one day, we welcomed God to our streets and to our homes, He walked among us. Since then, whilst fleshly divinity was absent, the Spirit of the Lord was not. And so in the centuries that followed, the scarcity of temples were replaced with an abundance of Churches and Cathedrals. We welcomed God everywhere we worshipped, and gave Him homes that we and the Creator could meet

---

[184] Examples include Moses' (serpent) staff – Exodus 4:2; and Paul's cloth or handkerchief – Acts 19:12.

in. Our innate human instinct to build shelter and to then improve on that build, was in full swing. But behind all of this was the reality that God had first met us in the lowliest of environments – a cattle shed in a small, dusty middle-eastern town called Bethlehem. From there, Jesus moved from town to town, village to village; all His worldly possessions kept upon his person, as He dwelt in humble abodes (I don't recall any accounts of Jesus living it up in mansions or making appearances on MTV's 'Cribs'). Yes, Jesus would head to the temple, and yes He would get annoyed when the temple was polluted with greed and corruption. Still, Jesus only visited temples and synagogues; He lived in our homes.

We realise our worth when we realise that the King of Kings wishes to reside with us. When we realise that we're children of God, we realise that He already resides with us. So we respond accordingly. We decorate our 'temples' (homes and bodies), we prepare our 'temples' (cleaning and praying), and we set apart our 'temples' through boundaries – both physical (walls, fences, etc.) and spiritual (avoiding sin, receiving the sacraments). For some Gypsies and Travellers, these elements have, as a result of multiple social and religious historical factors, taken on new and tangible meanings. The significance of cultural and spiritual separation, and the preparation of home and body, has meant that the interplay between scripture and lived experience is both fluid and experiential. Making sense of this 'lived Christianity' when so much of your experience originates from a philosophy and theology of movement can be challenging. This is especially true when all around you much of the larger culture often signifies their success by pursuing stability (through income, housing, pension plans, etc.), as if they can predict with near certainty what tomorrow may bring. The reality is there is no one right answer; we were made as individuals by God and placed in various tribes for a reason. The proposal then, as opposed to an 'answer', is that we strike a balance between the practices of our people groups and the acceptance of those outside of our groups. In this instance, those groups are separated by physical and metaphorical boundaries that surround the permanently impermanent camp. However, for a moment let's put on our scientific and critical self-awareness hats on so we can summarise this from another angle.

We see that there remains a tension of sorts residing somewhere between the nature of the religious experience happening in the entire camp system (boundaries, inner realm, home or 'tabernacle'), and that of theological and ecclesiological reasoning. Even so, this experience could still be stripped of any and all theological value and simply reclassified as a phenomenological experience. We could be a little less harsh and give it more credence by suggesting that the Gypsy and Traveller's religious experience is a 'religious one' (in the sense that Durkheim suggests that 'religion is a well-founded illusion'[185]). However, one would still be presented with a tangible and measurable effect and outcome as a direct result of the 'lived religion' being exercised in and beyond the camp borders. Essentially, the nature of this kind of reasoning is *deconstructive*. Deconstructive reasoning creates a process whereby social physics moves into social phenomenology, resulting in what Pierre Bourdieu describes as 'social reality'.[186] In this social reality, perceived or tangible 'folk' narratives and perceptions acquire a 'truly real power of construction'.[187] For Gypsies and Travellers, this 'social reality' consists of a performative – or 'lived out' Christian narrative, in which an interplay of ethnic identity and a language of discipleship is formed. The Christian narrative enables the institution (in this case, GRT culture and community) to be fully realised, meaning that the property (the camp) with all its features and modes of operation, commandeers its owners and embeds itself into the structures and rules, seamlessly observing with its logic. In short, the nomadic camp model that I have proposed and utilised is not simply an act of cultural practice. As a motif of Gypsy ethnic and

[185] Pickering, 2009, pp. 336 – 338.
[186] Bourdieu, 1989, p. 18.
[187] Bourdieu, 1989, pp. 18 – 19.

religious identity and as an act of intentional discipleship, the 'Mosaic' camp model of nomadism and dwelling is at the least a measurable and observable act of politicised theology.

With that said, we've seen how God is welcomed into our midst and the importance of making that space: (1) Worthy of hosting God; and (2) Ensuring that through various divisions, that space is separated both from external sin and from internal issues. But like any home, we have ideas, rules, practices and even ideologies that govern it. A quick example of this in practice could be back from when I was a boy. The rule for returning home after playing all day with my friends was 'be home before it's dark'; the rationale behind the rule was it was dangerous after dark; and the authority behind the action was my mother! So, in understanding how our relationship with how the present God operates and any associated themes of rules, rationale and beliefs, we need to explore Traveller Theologising in a cosmological sense; i.e. what does a Traveller belief system look like in a collective way and how does that relate to God? To do this, we will look at ideas of space, time, language and the core of our distinctiveness – our bloodlines. We've seen the construct of the camp, now let's see life in the camp...

CHAPTER SEVEN

LIFE IN THE CAMP: A TRAVELLER COSMOLOGY – PART ONE

'Yes, just as you can identify a tree by its fruit, so you can identify people by their actions.' (Matthew 7:20)

HE'S GOT THE WHOLE WORLD, IN HIS HANDS

'Mate, where's the long pad that goes on the bar?' asked the confident young guy with the bright kit bag and white Apple ear dummies. 'Ah', I thought; 'he's not been here before'. 'Erm, I'm not sure they have one. You could ask at the reception, but if I were you, I'd just wrap a towel around the bar, assuming you're going to be squatting?'. 'Sure. Thanks', he hesitantly replied. The young man in question had inadvertently revealed his outsider status at my local gym – a place predominantly filled with world-class bodybuilders and physiques that make Marvel superheroes look like regular folks. The pad in question is a commonly-found item in many 'high street' gyms and fitness centres, and is placed over a weighted bar to prevent the metal rubbing on a person's neck and back. However, in strength and bodybuilding gyms, these items are usually non-existent, often being referred to as a 'sissy pad' or worse. In such gyms, the regular activity of picking up heavy iron and putting it down again doesn't just create bigger muscles – it creates callouses on hands that like the changing physique, cannot be bought but must be earned. The young guy didn't do anything wrong; he simply went about his gym routine in a gym environment that wasn't his, and as a result he stood out. In his own gym, no one would have thought any different of him. However, on this day you could see the cogs turning in his mind as he realised he was in a place that not only did things differently but that the people in this place had a different mind-set and ethos. Square pegs in round holes, comes to mind.

In the previous chapter, we saw how the 'camp' is staged in such a way as to support the social and religious ideologies of its inhabitants and not necessarily those outside of its walls. The same can be said for all of our homes, for our social clubs, for the corporations we work at, for the teams we play in, and for the distinct congregations we worship with. We choose one over another because they mostly and often fit with *our* beliefs and *our* values. Like the visitor to my gym, we all behave more naturally – mentally, physically, and spiritually in environments suited to *our* ideologies. Quite often, these ideologies become most evident through our actions, as the fruits of our intentions are made manifest in the world around us. Personal service announcement: This isn't a moment for alarm bells to begin ringing as we critically examine ourselves in light of the text, asking 'Should my ideologies, my intentions, my heart even, should they be more broad and encompassing of the world and others?'. However, this is a moment that we can be thankful, knowing it's perfectly acceptable to be simultaneously interested in both others and their paths whilst also protecting our own path. In the process of Creation, the Father sanctioned order and distinction – day from night, male from female, 'every animal according to its kind' (Genesis 1:25).[188] Through the

---

[188]   'And God said, "Let the earth bring forth living creatures according to their kinds: livestock, land crawlers, and beasts of the earth according to their kinds." And it was so. God made the beasts of the earth according to their kinds, the livestock according to their kinds, and everything that crawls upon the earth according to its kind. And God saw that it was good. Then God said, "Let Us make man in Our image, after Our likeness, to rule over the fish of the sea and the birds of the air, over the livestock, and over all the earth itself and every creature that crawls upon it." (Genesis 1:24-26)

Camp model, a metaphorical landscape is imagined that demonstrates deliberate structures designed to keep order and distinction.

The truth is, no matter how 'inclusive' we think we are or we intend to be, we can only ever achieve so much through efforts, initiatives, and good intentions. If we truly wish to practise inclusion, we can start by sharing the divine love of our spiritual order. Meanwhile, difference should be celebrated and seen as an ongoing expansion of the tapestry of God's Creation. In recent decades, it seems that the peak of human science is to create clones of itself; man-made man. Yet, whether you subscribe to a literal translation of Genesis, the Big Bang theory, or the theory of Evolution, the outcome is the same: unlimited difference and distinction in all creation. As such, God-breathed creation (in whatever form or theory of origin you prefer) is the greatest act of inclusion we can ever witness. So, protecting that creation – be it the Earth, nature or our fellow humans, is our moral Christian duty. Surely then, understanding the inner works of that creation should be our passion? As the old song tells us, *He's got the whole world, in His hands* – each and every one of us. The whole world is our world – our bodies, our lives, our families, our thoughts, our pains, our desires, our hearts, our pasts and our futures. Everything. Our worlds (including our words and our thoughts) are like the tides of the sea, moving toward or away from the shores of the Father, bringing with them the power of life or death (Proverbs 18:21). When we understand this, there comes a little more gravitas to the instruction of doing everything unto the Lord (Colossians 3:23-24). Therefore, as part of the process of Traveller theologising (much like any other theologising), an understanding should be sought in and through all areas of our existence. Doing so is not just helpful, it can also be an act of worship, as we seek to understand God in us – His creation.

As we remain in the camp, this chapter will seek to find God among the phenomena of the collective GRT body, as we look towards patterns of understanding and modes of operation from a diverse

157

selection of areas (language, space and symbolism, and time). By doing so, a Traveller 'cosmology' of sorts can begin to emerge. It's important to point out that there are of course many other possible areas of exploration beyond language, space, symbolism and time. However, it is these areas in particular that help us to begin making sense of the world immediately around us and how we communicate with that world – both inside our walls and outside of them. Furthermore, it's important that when we theologise, that we do so both in the material and abstract realms. It's not often you'll find a discussion (or chapter) that simultaneously speaks about how people use language whilst also exploring how the concept of time is understood; and that's usually for a good reason (it can be very confusing). However, God is in all the elements of our existence, and so when we seek to understand the diversity *of* creation, we have to also understand the diversity *in* creation. If it still sounds a little bit leftfield for your liking, try rephrasing it in the following questions: Does my life honour God? Does my life resemble a 'godly' life? How is my self-talk today – positive, affirmative, negative, or destructive? What are my thoughts on death and how is that affecting my life and my thinking right now? Is church found in my house as well as in a stone building with fancy windows? Am I living my life with purpose – if so, what is that purpose; if not, why not? You see, at best we see the overtly familiar and the seemingly abstract as separate – at worse, we leave them alone. To prod and poke these areas requires effort, and can sometimes seem pointless. However, I encourage you to apply this self-examination to your own life, because it will always result in fruit. Fruits of new direction, fruits of new understanding, fruits of confirmation, fruits of revelation. When you begin to harvest these fruits, you will begin to know yourself.

TRAVELLER TALK

Language, more specifically, spoken language, is the medium by which our thoughts, feelings, beliefs and ideas are often expressed in their most raw form; usually unfiltered, tone and emphasis take naked words and immediately clothe them in meaning. Our spoken language can create life and can take away life, it can bless and it can curse, it can set free and it can bind. In many ways, our spoken word often forms the bridge between the physical and the spiritual worlds, as prayers are made manifest and healings brought into being by the invocation of Christ's name. With that in mind, this part of the chapter is focused upon the *use* and presentation of Traveller language in a theo-logical context. This section is *not* an investigation into Romani linguistics – a subject which has been discussed and examined in great length by a number of academics. On that note, it is worth mentioning (for the uninformed reader) the primary narrative emerging from the academics and linguistic experts suggests that the dialect evolved over several centuries from its Indian origins into something unique (partly owing to the transition into Europe by Travellers);[189] and that during the twentieth century there were numerous investigations into the original 'Gypsy' language of *Romani*. However, many aspects of Romani have been lost or become obsolete in the UK over time, and the language itself is seldom used as a complete dialect. Rather, certain words or phrases are used in a complimentary or slang context in amongst a 'normal' use of English. The Romani term '*poggerdi jib*' is a direct reference to the language of British Travellers and can be translated as 'broken tongue/language'. Whilst the origins and identifying nature of Gypsy language is contestable, it can be argued that at a minimum Gypsy language is functional, universally present, and, as current research would suggest, is related to a wider discourse. As with all aspects of GRT culture, intentionality is also part of the structure of Gypsy language. Further to this, British Gypsy language is also functional.

The functional use of the language often takes three distinct forms or themes: a consistent theme of preservation for the cultural lineage of the society (i.e. maintaining a 'pure' Gypsy or Traveller

---

[189]   Richardson and Ryder, 2012, p. 143.

blood); an intentional separation between Gypsy and gorger cultures and peoples;[190] and a form of identity – in that, there are particular terms that are only used (and possibly only understood) in Gypsy and Traveller circles.[191] This last element also extends to certain GRT dialects which can make accessing or relating to some Gypsy and Traveller communities challenging for outsiders. Furthermore, the directness, intentionality and occasionally explicit nature of the language and dialect is sometimes interpreted as an act of aggression or inappropriateness.[192] Indeed, the 'direct' nature of Gypsy language is often characterised by a contractual intentionality consisting of definitive borders and unassuming positions where a yes is a yes and a no is a no.[193] ('Let what you say be simply "Yes" or "No"; anything more than this comes from the evil one' [Matthew 5:37].) I know of many bartenders and pub managers who have gotten nervous when the Travellers in their establishment have started getting loud or 'direct'. The reality, especially more so in England, is that we live in a culture that favours so-called decorum over excitement and filtered speech over unbridled passion. Life in Gypsy circles is, to reference the great British movie *This is Spinal Tap*, usually turned up to 11. However, listen a little closer and you'll notice that this affirmative approach is often balanced out with a kind, generous and somewhat vulnerable side. The combination of these distinct natures show how there is a knowing and intentional sacrificial action of choosing to remain in a personal position of suffering; an 'I'm hurt but I still give

---

[190] Hancock, 2013, p. 139.

[191] Hancock, 2013, p. 139.

[192] The perception that Travellers are showing aggression or hostility through language often emerges from sources such as media representation and historic narratives. For examples see the following: Liégeois, 1994, p. 244; Mayall, 1988, pp. 79 – 82; Knapton, 2015.

[193] Scripturally this approach is explicitly dealt with in Matthew 5:37. However, the rationale and theological underpinning is primarily located in the Deuteronomic instruction (Deuteronomy 23: 21 – 23) pertaining to making good on one's word, so that any statement made is integral and contractual (v.23). A refrainment from such an agreement would be shameful – and therefore polluting (v. 21).

and need love' kind of vibe. This state of contradictory vulnerability acknowledges that the language used is necessary in order to preserve one's identity and culture but can at times can be detrimental, drawing unwanted external opinions and perceptions. However, it is in the contradiction that, with some surprise perhaps, we are met with the revelation that GRT speech is quite possibly Christologically orientated. The contradiction is found in the rigidness of the speech and in the fluidity of the vulnerability that that speech creates. On one side we have rigidity, on the other we have fluidity; the result in between these is a Christ-centred stability in the uncertainty of the Gypsy and Traveller's environment.

Traveller Language as Christian Expression

Traveller and Gypsy language can and should be recognised beyond its *basic* context of communication, and understood to be a reflection of the Traveller's permanent unsettlement. Trying, however, to draw clarity from a situation in which gorger societal norms and interpretations can offer no reasonable explanations or support is, at best, challenging. But we *all* face these dynamics in life, sometimes on a regular basis. Our beliefs dictate our tone, our words, and our actions, and there are moments when we press onward with those beliefs, even when the world around us cannot fathom why. However, the 'understood' has to make way for the absurdity of Christ. Absolute absurdity. In our darkest moments, we are called and comforted by Christ. When all seems lost, Christ is there, guiding us. Through heartbreak and abandonment, the outstretched arms of Christ welcome us. In amongst the rigidity of our prideful self-assurance and the fluidity of vulnerability, there sits Christ, absurdly and unconditionally supporting and loving us whilst the world burns away. As such, keeping Christ at the centre and as the foundation behind the perpetual discomfort of a defended and (arguably) self-imposed suffering, is a logical alternative to a world which cannot understand our condition. Contrary to the common belief that safety

161

is found within the majority, intentional separateness serves as a form of empowerment by the excluded. Key to this principle is a shared centrality or point of belief. In this instance that centrality is Christ.

In Christ, Gypsy language and the application of it is neither condoned nor condemned, but is given space in which to exist. This dynamic can also be understood as the contradiction of the Traveller's language finding solace in the contradiction of Christ's own language and proposition – to have life in abundance but to also pick up the Cross daily (Matthew 10:38; Matthew 16:24; Mark 8:34; Luke 9:23; Luke 14:27). By embracing this state of limbo that avoids the comforts of acceptance and the conveniences of assimilation, a state of 'joint (liberative) suffering' is made with Christ – in both His comfort and His moment of suffering. Pursuing this avenue draws the Traveller, knowingly or unknowingly, into what Jürgen Moltmann would present as a 'theology of the cross'. This 'human way of life and practice chosen by this congregation of weak, lowly and despised persons' becomes a 'way of life which takes away the power of social circumstances which bring about the aggression of dehumanised man, and endeavours to overcome it'.[194] To put it another way, the core of the spirit is not an immutable thing found below the residue of one's culture, history or economic status. The core is Jesus Christ killed and raised to life who is constituent to the spirit. Or, to simplify it even further, Christ is the absolute centrality and functionality in this 'being of otherness'.

Understanding language in this manner is helpful and progressive but it is not without its difficulties. As mentioned, Gypsy and Traveller language is at times challenging for those outside of the community because of its spectrum of applications; sometimes it is blunt and direct, other times it can be obscure and hard to engage with (often during periods of negotiation or because of particular dialects). Consequently, the common response by gorger ministries has been to 'cut to the chase' so to speak, and enter into conversations with

---

[194]   Moltmann, 2015, pp. 66 – 67.

Gypsy and Traveller communities through channels of *syncretism*, whereby contrasting perceptions, i.e. 'good and evil', are used. Mostly, this is fine, but it's worth remembering that this kind of discourse is rooted in Western epistemology, and with that, there are certain risks for marginalised groups. How so? I hear you asking. Well, Western hegemonies are typically, biblically speaking, grounded in the desire to see the lost converted. Syncretism creates a threat because it advances the saving message of the gospel by separating heaven from hell, good from evil, blessed from cursed, and for the GRT community – gorger from Gypsy. The problem here is that this understanding is part and parcel of Western thinking and Western Christianity – it's not getting undone in any of our lifetimes, and perhaps, for many reasons, it shouldn't. Theologically speaking, its nature is political. Even so, where the gospel resides there's always space to include, support and reflect. This can be achieved by acknowledging and expanding the conversation's context within these existing theological parameters. By doing so, the demonising power towards and in the marginalised communities can be reduced. Thus, what was once dismissed as alien, in both secular and religious circles, becomes humanised and worthy of acknowledgement.

By examining and exploring the concept of 'spirit' in this expanding and widening context, those whose identities are found or drawn from a state of 'otherness' (such as Gypsies and Travellers) can be better understood. However, there is an absolutely crucial caveat to this understanding; the core of the individual's spirit (or their 'self'), is incorrectly centred – their innermost identity is naturally, inherently, and unavoidably misbalanced and off kilter. This incorrectly centred self requires Christ. To do this, the human spirit needs to be crucified with Christ, in order to de-centre the self from its 'human' centre into its 'Christ' centre. Paul understood this concept to his core, declaring 'I have been crucified with Christ' (Galatians 2:20). In this way, Christ acts as a balance or a permanent contradictory tension, allowing the options of free will and salvation to operate freely and in a syncretistic fashion. As such, the outsider (whomever that may be) is able to construct and reform themselves by finding common ground with others and rejecting others, by creating foes and by suffering hostilities, and by loving and loathing. This element of contradictory presentation in the application and perceived application of Traveller speech transcends beyond just the element of language. Whilst the idea of a contradictory nature (in the sense stated above) is not by any means exclusive to Gypsies and Travellers, it is *consistent* in Gypsy and Traveller communities. Traveller dialect (and not the structure/grammar of language) therefore, is something that once acknowledged as much more than merely speech or an accent, can reveal a greater depth – a history even, of a people-group that have suffered oppression and embraced Christian grace. Beyond the immediacy of being a cultural identifier, language in Gypsy and Traveller communities exposes an unsettlement – a characteristic present in many other encompassing areas of GRT culture. And whilst arguably more culturally protective than theologically engaging, language, for Gypsy culture, indicates an underlying Christian experience. Importantly for this book, it is through the direct, vulnerable, functional and shared (or universal) structure of Gypsy language that a particular and wider discourse of Christological centring is revealed.

SPACE AND SYMBOLISM

As Jesus sat by the well, he asked an unnamed Samaritan woman for a drink as she drew water (John 4:7). Whilst the well could have been seen as simply incidental, it was in fact a giver of life – much like the man that sat before the woman. Contextually of course, Jesus' analogous point was about Him being the water of life, and about the demonstration of His position as Messiah, Son of God, and bringer of redemption. But let's look a little deeper at some of the details. It was midday and the woman was drawing water by herself. We know that culturally the process of getting water from the well was done both in the morning and socially, and as a group. This suggests that the woman was a social outcast; the details that emerge about her marital status confirm this (John 4:18). Yet astonishingly, despite the woman's marital status, her gender, and the historical ethnic tensions (Jesus was Jew, the woman was a Samaritan), this lowly setting and outcast woman become elements in the longest and arguably most revealing engagement Jesus has with anyone in the Gospel of John. The symbolism of the well becomes key, as Jesus uses the metaphor of water to reveal how He is the water of life (John 4:14). Equally so, the space becomes key, as it not only hosts the symbolic elements but also accommodates the meeting between the two. But let's go a little deeper still… It's the woman, for all the aforementioned reasons, that is the space where redemption happens. Redemption doesn't happen to or in the well, but in the heart of the person touched by the words and spirit of God. Conviction and belief doesn't change the physical nature of the water from the well nor the place where Jesus sat, but conviction does change the heart, and belief does change the mind. When conviction occurs and belief is ignited, witness is born. Witness is contagious and energetic. Witness is the fire that spreads and the joy that infects. When the woman at the well experienced conviction and belief through encounter with Jesus, she ran off to tell everyone[195] (John 4:39). However, witness requires conviction and belief, and conviction and belief require hosts; hosts that speak through words, text, images, objects and actions – all of which require a space and setting to occupy. The words that we speak have the power to breathe life and death; so too is the power and potential of the spaces we occupy and the symbolism (both physical and metaphysical) that fill those spaces.

Space and Symbolism: Common Motifs

It's quite clear from the previous chapter on the camp, that space, the decoration of space, and the usage of space are fundamental factors

[195] 'Many Samaritans from that town believed in him because of the woman's testimony…'

to both the facilitation of beliefs and the perpetual power of beliefs. We can of course attempt to take away one or more of these factors (space or symbolism), but when we do, we are simply left with a new equation of faith and practice. Even looking upon the vast emptiness of the space of Space, we are greeted with unlimited opportunities for faith to tell its story. Where one person will see nothingness and an absence of life, for another they will see hope, promise and inheritance (Genesis 15:5).[196] The combination of our environments and our interpretations of those environments often work in a synergistic fashion, becoming as Aristotle once famously theorised, 'greater than the sum of its parts'. Some would like to say that as believers we are all in some ways experiencing our own unique religious Aristotelian holisms, but this term would be doing a disservice to the deeply spiritual, relational, and often bizarrely collective experience we have of God in our lives. The experience we are privy to, if only we would open our eyes and see it, is an experience that transcends time, space, peoples and history. As tangible beings we crave tangibility; this is completely understandable. But we are also spiritual beings, and until we are reunited with the same force that once sent us out into material existence, we must also learn to see and crave spiritually. This tension is the crossover between the physical and the spiritual, the meeting place between material and metaphysical, the ethereal plane, the unbreakable relationship between space and symbolism. When our mortal hands cannot grasp that which is in front of us, and our minds are seeking structure to understand these ideas, we have several tools at our disposal. Perhaps one of the most accessible tools for working on the immaterial is the immaterial concept of motifs. Motifs allow us to organise and categorise, to separate and to understand. Motifs are much like theology; except motifs predominantly work on the miniscule and are often encompassed *in* theology. Within GRT circles

---

[196] 'He (God) took him (Abraham) outside and said, "Look up at the sky and count the stars—if indeed you can count them." Then he said to him, "So shall your offspring be".'

we can lay out the DNA of Traveller theologising by looking at the individual elements/themes – or motifs. In this scenario, we might see a Purity and Pollution motif, and another for Supernatural and Superstitious.

Understanding Gypsy spaces and the symbolism in and of those spaces, can be approached in much the same way that we would seek to understand the usage and function of Churches or even sacraments. We begin with a synchronistic approach, understanding that the parameters of both 'areas' require accommodation by the other. Taking the cup or the bread by itself is of no purpose or value, until that is we firstly recognise its (symbolic) value and meaning, and secondly, we physically act upon our beliefs associated with said meaning. Synchronism in faith and an awareness of it is a crucial indication of maturity in our Christian walk – a sure sign we have moved from milk to meat. Synchronism in faith is praying for someone to be well and warm and fed, and then actually feeding and clothing them (James 2:16). After all, as James (2:17) says, 'faith by itself, if it is not accompanied by action, is dead'. What we're talking about in this instance is purpose and intent – a principle ingrained within the collective GRT psyche. Synchronism thus becomes a practice of purpose and intent, but with the distinct marker that it is done to honour and worship God, to uphold and respect tradition and cultural practice, and to give out of one's self. This of course raises questions of soteriology, which in turn gives us an indication as to why the structures that are in our lives are there at all.

Through the motif of purity, the temptation is to understand the pollution code simply as a matter of 'pure' and 'impure'. However, as we've established, none of these concepts sit alone; they occupy spaces and places, minds and motives. With our theological tool belt of theology, hermeneutics and synchronism, our translation of purity is expanded to include the *physical* 'impurity' elements and its *immaterial* theological equivalents of 'sin' and 'forgiveness', 'grace' and 'judgement'. In this unsurprising twist, it appears that searching for God, results in, well, finding God. It's almost as if (cue sarcastic tone) He's at the beginning, middle and end of creation, and that when we start knocking, He answers. The theological responses we receive from looking at the seemingly mundane through faith-filled lenses are much more than clues to our queries of soteriology. They are signposts, guiding us; they are lamps, lighting our path; they are beacons, calling us. Like the expectant open-armed father awaiting the prodigal son's return, when we raise our head, we will see God. When we run towards Him, there He is. Is it any wonder then that we cannot remain still? It is our condition, for every ounce of our being and psyche, to seek the Father. All of creation yearns to be reunited with its creator; from cradle to grave. Just as all creation rotates around the *Sun*, all of life rotates around the *Son*. And whether or not we choose to pursue the Father, we and everything around us will one day be reunited with Him in one capacity or another. For from the Creator the created shall return. Dust to dust. Movement is thus inevitable.

Everyone – GRT or otherwise, is permanently impermanent, being moved in their own spaces and transitioning to new ones. In GRT communities, we witness this most explicitly and tangibly through nomadism. However, as we saw previously with the 'sojourner', nomadism is in some ways more than physical movement; for physically it occupies the space of lanes, fields, roads and lands, but spiritually it forms a new narrative – nomadism, an element of 'being' Christian. Sojourning, in the space of nomadism, is the modus operandi; the facilitation of a politically theological intentionality and method of servitude. When given a platform on which to operate (in this instance, the 'Camp' model), nomadism, in addition to being understood as a spiritual process, also becomes a sacramental undertaking directed by an oral and socially inherited liturgy. This seems to contrast the commonly perceived 'freedom' of nomadism; a romanticist imagery that in some minds is the pinnacle of rejecting rules and governance. And to be fair, in some ways it is. After all, God beckons us into freedom – not captivity. But it is equally true, however, that the parameters of the seemingly *free* nomadic tradition reveal a *definitive* and *intentional* system that is constructed with the following properties: a functionality around an inherent purity code; something extraordinarily ecologically sensitive and aware; and something theologically interwoven with a cultural narrative and perception on time, finality, and cosmological positioning (both personal and that of the divine/God/'Creator'). The hermeneutic of nomadism is not incidental, nor is it without forethought. It is hope and faith lived out. It is choosing to worship as Paul and Silas, resisting captivity through deliberate and intentional praise.

The spaces we occupy are fluid, yet, with enough effort we can define them. Sometimes those defining points look like borders; tangible, tactile, deliberate. Other times those defining points look like beliefs and practices; mindful, emotional, spiritual. Still, it is the symbols we place between those defining points that govern our responses. If we seek to fill a romantic relationship space with commitment, we might introduce the symbol of an engagement or wedding ring. If we seek to fill a home with God, we might introduce symbols of a physical nature, such as altars, ornaments and pictures, or we might introduce symbols of a mindful nature, such as 'purity' codes or regular prayer. Performative elements (e.g. language, nomadism, and sacraments) are given a tangible functionality. The result, much like the woman at the well, is witness. What message of witness will you have? Will it be of Christ's goodness and mercy or will it be of the pain that you refused to let go of, all in the name of success, prestige, pride and bitterness? For in truth, ultimately everything is meaningless – 'a chasing of the wind' (Ecclesiastes 2:11). Everything that is, except for the space in your heart and the territory of your soul. In such places, which one day will encounter the living God, let our witness be forgiveness and love.

CHAPTER EIGHT

LIFE IN THE CAMP: A TRAVELLER COSMOLOGY – PART TWO

'Jesus Christ is the same yesterday and today and forever.'
(Hebrews 13:8)

TIME

The kettle is boiling. The promise of a hot tea in a few minutes is a welcome relief from the bitterly cold air. As I breathe out, it looks as if cotton-like clouds are forming in front of me; a reminder, as if I needed one, that I am sitting by a fire in the woods during the bitterest winter I can remember. Looking up, the clear, blackened sky is full of glimmering stars dancing around a moon hiding half its face. Burning embers scurry upwards, flickering for one final moment before being lost forever to the night. The sound of crackling wood tempts my gaze back down again. Lost in the beauty of dancing flames, I forget for one moment the dreadful reason that I am sitting here. For whilst the lure of an open fire in the woods is a primal indulgence that I partake in often, the reasoning for this fire is different. I'm sitting alongside a family who have lost a loved one in the most tragic of circumstances. And in a moment, a father will begin to tell us a story; a story of loss and a story of success. A story of this generation and a story of generations past. This isn't history retold. This is history revived and relived …

Our personal stories are so much more than fairy tales or memories. They are alive, they are powerful, and they erase the disconnect of lineal time. For centuries, GRT people have told stories; sometimes within their own communities, sometimes to a public audience. Some Gypsies have even secured fame and finance from their verbal artistry. With all that said, the tradition of storytelling in such communities serves greater purposes than mere entertainment. There are of course the obvious purposes: a reconnection with the past; a reminder of traditions; conformations of important social, cultural and familial events; pure nostalgia; and, as in the story above, remembering the dead. However, our stories – and not just within the GRT community, have the power to transform our relationship with time and our movement through it. To some degree, every sermon you've ever sat through or perhaps even given is such a story. Through our words (language), we are transported back, sometimes thousands of years, through biblical accounts – some mythical, some grounded in fact. In those moments of recollection, our spirits are stirred in the present, our skin tingles, and we develop faith.

As faith grows, we experience change, and the trajectory of our own stories (and that of generations to come) is tangibly altered. How can our lives be radically affected by messages of God so loving the world that He gave His only begotten son,[197] if such messages are merely recollections of the past? Could it be that Jesus is still taking our sins upon Himself on the Cross whilst also living now as our resurrected and salvation-bringing King? Yes, is the short answer! Jesus didn't just take the sins from the lucky few who happened to be both alive at the time of His crucifixion and present at said event. Nor did Christ merely set up a new constitutional law that day, whereupon all before and after Him would be granted the forgiveness of their sins, the healing of their ailments, and everlasting life (*if terms and conditions are met). When we suffer, our comfort comes from

---

[197]   John 3:16

knowing that Jesus is there, with us in our suffering. As He hangs from the Cross, we cling to it, for whilst we know that joy comes in the morning, He continues to protect us from the terror and pestilence of the night. We are together in both His suffering and His resurrection. God is alive in both our stories – past and present, demonstrating that events in our lives are not played out on some finite timeline but are instead deliberately placed chess pieces on an unending board. Jesus' crucifixion still has power because it still remains in play.

Time and Free Will

It's understandable that at times we doubt the presence of God in our stories; the sometimes chaotic nature of our lives can at first glance look as if they are open to the whim of the wind. Such a route of thought ultimately can only end in nihilism, as we see no intention in our origin and nothing but darkness in our end. However, as Christians we are blessed with seeing the full equation. If the opposite to God's absence and chaos in nihilism, is God's presence and structure in belief, then what we are faced with is not a question of belief but a debate of free will. The fact that we can all choose differing paths in life shows that there remains a nondeterministic nature in play, demonstrating that in spite of appearances, a rationale of sorts *is* operating in our lives. From the physical determinates such as gravity and breathing, to the metaphysical determinates such as time, we are structured souls in a structured universe – chaos is simply free will without belief. Of course, the determinates of free will, have been discussed extensively in one way or another for as long as humans have existed. Often those discussions have taken the shape of questions, such as '*What is the meaning of life*'? Even so, it is the parameters of free will that are most often overlooked. Parameters, in this equation, are a little more intriguing than the context ...

The *context* of free will is God has given you a life and you can pretty much do what you want with it (but ideally you should use it to draw closer to Him because that's how you find true happiness, contentment, meaning and salvation). But the primary *parameter* of free will is time. You might have free will but you only have 'X' amount of time in which to exercise free will. With free will, you can make choices about who you follow or do not follow, and what you do or do not believe, but you only have a short period in which to make those choices. Time and its finite properties set the boundaries for everything we value and love in our human experience. Like in a gameshow where the timer is counting down, our limited period for our freedom to operate, is set in excitement and (sometimes) fear. Unfortunately, Louis Armstrong was incorrect when he famously sung, 'we have all the time in the world'. Much of the time in our worlds are given over to family, to raising children, to working a job, to attending meetings, to answering emails and texts and messages, to checking social media, to attending sports events and theatre shows and music concerts, to more meetings and more messages, to hobbies, to fixing cars and repairing houses, to deciding what to wear and what go get rid of, to our relationships and to our worries and fears. We do not have all the time in the world. The world has all of our time. I think that sometimes we are truly out of touch with what it genuinely means to give God our lives. Perhaps giving God our lives would be better read as 'giving God our time'.

Asking ourselves what does giving God our time look like, is a fair and necessary question. But it's also a deeply subjective question. A more interesting question is 'What is time?' In a Christian context, asking about the nature of time raises the importance of this life whilst simultaneously kicking into gear our eschatology engines, forcing us to think about the next life. Time doesn't stand still, and nor do we. In this form, we are temporal. Time is both the marker and measure of this fact. However, we are also spirit. Salvation through Christ transcends these planes and transports us from temporal life to eternal life. We have a coexisting nature of permanence and temporal, and time is the link between these two. Make no mistake – these concepts are not merely abstract, nor do they only reside in our minds and imagination. Looking at the nomadic nature of some Gypsies (and the Gypsy camp), we can see a deliberate embrace of permanence and temporality. For example, look at the distinction between the Gypsies' 'Mosaic' camp and that of a non-nomadic people's 'settlement'; it's not just the impermanent nature of the camp – there is a specific and intentional design for the camp to move at a designated time. It's a structured approach but it's far from complex. In fact, this 'simple nature' of permanently dwelling in the temporal form – both physically and spiritually, is probably the aspect that many people think of when they yearn for freedom in their lives and/ or when they experience wanderlust.

This narrative of time and purpose can be seen in the book of Numbers (Numbers 10:11 – 36), as the climactic movement from Sinai and the Wilderness toward the 'promised land' begins (Numbers 10:13). In the preparation phase of the journey, there is a meticulous and elaborate maintenance of both the camp's holiness and its purity. The process of deconstructing and reconstructing the camp is an act of faith and, with God leading His people through the wilderness, the 'march' or movement from camp to the next destination, it is also liturgical in nature. The faith posited in the liturgical process of nomadism is drawn from a particular perception and engagement with time. In this understanding of time the eschatological 'hoped for' and the redemptive (past) 'Cross event' dwell simultaneously in an unstable and often contradictory 'lived out' present. Crudely speaking, in a social sense this could be understood as 'living in/for the moment'. Exegetically speaking, it is an application and amalgamation of both the Proverb(ial) warning to refrain from dwelling in the future (or being in an anxious state) (Proverbs 27:1), and the assertion made by Jesus of His alternative purpose for humanity to 'have life and have it abundantly' (John 10:10).

Where and what is Time?

We've seen how a Traveller 'cosmology' is actively engaged with time (i.e. living in the present). We've also seen how a Traveller cosmology is culturally aware of the scope and impermanent nature of time (i.e. a preference for nomadism; and a sojourner exegesis). What we haven't looked at is the actual nature of time. Understanding how we think of time allows us to mentally position both ourselves and God. This in turn opens up our thinking to be able to understand important doctrines and themes such as the Kingdom of God, in new and radical ways. Typically we understand time as something linear; our history laid out as a series of events and moments. As we've already seen, our natural instincts are somewhat predicated on creating and enforcing barriers (some rigid, some permeable) to both protect us and our kin, and to define ourselves more readily. A linear understanding of time can support this way of thinking by creating the start and end points of our narratives; like book ends on the stories of our individual and collective lives. Often, in the contemporary age, when we recount the past we call it 'history' and mentally categorise it as something that once happened but is no longer happening – its power has gone but it is still possibly effecting the present in some capacity. However, within GRT communities, we see a degree of permeability in time. The clearest (and arguably, broadest) example of this is through the recounting of the past via 'storytelling'.

Recounting the past in this purposeful manner is distinctive, in that there is an inferred 'temporal' that exhibits the nature and qualities of something moving 'towards' (perhaps a 'promised land' or otherwise). We see a similar purposeful method being used in multiple instances in the Bible, where past events, doctrine and texts are recounted to tangibly achieve something (as opposed to simply recounting for remembrance sake). The 'sign of Jonah' passages demonstrate this quite nicely, as Jesus makes comparisons and crossovers between Himself and Jonah to bring a new understanding to those around Him of His soon-to-happen resurrection (Matthew 12:40). It seems that Matthew understood this concept well. A few chapters earlier (Matthew 4:1-11), we see an interaction between Jesus and the Devil, whereupon a series of scriptures are recounted and quoted by both sides in a battle of temptation and rebuke. If this sounds a little familiar, it's because it is familiar. In the Christian world, we commonly refer to this as preaching; however, it appears in numerous other expressions as well, such as praise and worship (singing), Bible study groups/home groups, and prayer. Indeed, treating time as something alive rather than static is to invite the Holy Spirit into all of our existence – past, present and perhaps most importantly, our future. In this way, the somewhat liturgical action of storytelling in Gypsy circles should be considered more prophetic rather than entertainment.

Entering into our near and distant past, in its many forms and guises, creates a link between the temporal present and the yet-to-be future or destination. We begin to see a nomadic nature (or 'purposeful movement') in the idea of a past combined with a seemingly determined future. To reference pop culture movie references – that (the seemingly determined future) is an Easter egg! It gives us a clue as to what is coming next, revealing much of the plot. The eternal God, God of the eternal, through His limitless grace, is wholly committed to our being with Him in eternity. So much so, that He entered into our temporality. Meanwhile, our focus remains upon the condition of human temporality. Our allotted time is much like another piece upon the chess board of existence, wherein human life attempts to discover its limits. In this scenario, God is, to quote Karl Barth, 'the one in relation to whom our life has its limit and our time is allotted'.[198] This is certainly compatible with a God whose activity among and relationship to His people (the Gypsies and among the Camp), is based upon consequential and measurable outcomes in relation to eschatological and salvific beliefs. Of course, God is not limited in or bound by this linear narrative. The eternal nature of divine understanding has no limitations whatsoever. Instead, God draws our gaze from the now to the not-yet – a place where Kingdom has come; where salvation has been fulfilled; where limitations are

[198] Webster, 1995, p. 73.

forever limited; where life is eternal; and where the grave is redundant.

Time is irreversibly interwoven in the interrelatedness of the Divine and humanity, and of humanity's place in the temporal and eternity. Indeed, upon this framework the unstable and indeterminate nature of the Travellers 'condition' (Camp and personal) develops permanence. It is in the uncertainty (and therefore the instability) of time that God is known. As such, time cannot be an absolute, and to some degree, it cannot even be real (in that it is not subject to any other factors or conditions). Even from a (relatively recent) scientific view, the post enlightenment idea that time is unbending and untouchable is incorrect. The idea of time as an absolute is both excluding of science and God. So, in response to time, as a minimum, we can begin to gain an explanation and an understanding of the 'permeability' and transcendent nature of our *Creator*. Rejecting the idea of an 'absolute' time serves as an apophatic[199] translator when applied to the Gypsy time narrative. However, what is key is the reason *why* the Creator is transcendent and why He has made both His creation and time permeable to His presence. That reason is, of course, Christ.

If we are to speak of God in the same sentence and context as humanity's determinates of 'now' and 'moving towards', then we can only be speaking of the yet-to-be-realised work of Christ. Christ isn't confined to our parameters; Christ is imminent in every sense and in every time – our past, present and future. Without Christ, our life is measured between book ends. With Christ, the tension between the 'now' and 'not yet' does not exist. Instead, the focus is between our time (past, present and what is yet to come) and eternity – time without time. Both the imminence of Jesus' Kingdom and His declaration that He 'makes all things new' (Revelation 21:5) are not temporal, coming-from-the-future elements; they are heaven here on earth, right now. The Kingdom is at hand.

How does that play out when on one hand we put in place things related to our salvation, such as 'purity/pollution' practices

[199] Sometimes referred to as 'Negative Theology'.

or sacraments, and on the other hand we draw on the past through stories, preaching and prophecy in relation to our eschaton moment? Well, the truth is, it doesn't play out at all if these things aren't acted upon. For sure, they don't have to look or sound like the examples I've just given, but they do have to look like *something*. Our choice is to, using a previous example, remain bookended, *or*, become intense and intentional. You have to ask yourself, would you prefer living in the 'Kingdom has come' or 'Kingdom may come'? The great thing is, intentionally living Kingdom minded in the present doesn't require monumental faith or impeccable Christian upstanding. It requires conviction, a belief (the size of a mustard seed), and love. For example, it could be argued that there is a lack of certainty (or assured salvific grace) in the Traveller's *eschatological* moment, hence the continual application of *mokhhadi*. The same could be said for certain (big 'C') *Catholic* traditions, in which continual and public sacramental 'removal of sins' is arguably a key narrative in the process of liturgical worship. Furthermore, whilst Christianity is complete (in the sense that it offers both 'promise' and 'fulfilment' by way of the messianic covenant), in light of Christianity's Jewish roots, there has been a response by some Christian theologians to charges of triumphalism by a shuffling of the overtly obliging classifications of 'now' and 'not yet' in which Christian eschatology is placed in a never-ending Groundhog Day. However, we would do well to avoid doing a '*doubting Thomas*' or a '*darn, I denied I knew Him 3 times Peter*' and being too hard on ourselves and others with regards to the assurance of our salvation. For whilst Christianity, through promise and fulfilment, is complete, it would benefit us to remember that a promise from the Creator is not like a promise from man; with man our yet-to-be promises are unfulfilled, but with the Creator such promises are assured and as such are as good as complete.

However, let's be fair and accurate; the rawness and inherent social disadvantage of Gypsy society, with its embrace of explicit expression,[200] warrants an escalation of the time narrative that is more reflective of the Gypsy's 'dramatised' norm. Indeed, this same principle applies to all who are marginalised, ostracised, abandoned and kept to the margins. This escalation should be understood as apocalyptic rather than eschatological, based upon its more 'radical' connotations. Such an escalation in terms is not without precedent. A quick exegesis of John reveals the simultaneous glorification and fleshly crucifixion (John 3:14 and 12:32) – the moment of permeability between the spiritual and the physical; the moment of simultaneous purity and pollution; a process set in linearity but above conventional proleptic Christian understandings. Through Jesus, we directly and at once encounter the end-times via God's love and judgement. Furthermore, John's dissatisfaction with the linear eschatology of the Christologies in the synoptic Gospels sets about this shared 'apocalyptical' experience with Christ. John's presentation of our time (past, present and future) are still key; not for the common purpose of looking ahead to the upcoming Kingdom of God but to demonstrate that in and through Jesus, the Kingdom and the last days are here already.

SUMMARY OF LIFE IN THE CAMP: A TRAVELLER COSMOLOGY

Independently the differing themes we've seen (language, space, symbolism, and time) produce specific outcomes. Meanwhile, it's the amalgamation and synchronisation of these themes that produce a more directed, intentional, and coherent landscape of the theological positioning of Gypsies and Travellers as a collective. Our own languages are constantly expressed through diverse means, which makes understanding ourselves challenging at times. Yet, when we

---

[200] One example of this 'explicit expression' is highlighted by Bhopal and Myers (2008, pp. 32 – 33), who present the situation of Gypsy weddings and the potential for such an occasion to be an arena where 'long-standing rivalries may resurface and be resolved through fighting' (p.32). Also see, *Chapter Seven: Traveller Talk.*

interpret our innermost expressions through theological lenses, we are gifted with an opportunity to re-evaluate how we communicate and understand communication – in both ourselves and others. Our language, through Christ, allows us to speak life. But it also enables us to reveal our cards and the sometimes contradictory conditions we find ourselves in, such as wanting to be loved but keeping love at arm's length through intentional isolation. When we understand that we hurt, we can appreciate that our neighbour also hurts. Furthermore, it is the freedom of Christ in our communication that brings life and possibility to the spaces we occupy and the symbols with which we fill those spaces.

The spaces we occupy are fluid and in constant transition. What we do in those spaces is determined by how we understand those spaces. And whether we are talking about physical realms or the environment of our minds and soul, the rules remain the same: we have been designed to move, transition, evolve and relocate. The seasons of our life demonstrate this movement, from the spring of youth to the winter of old age. How we speak and communicate in those spaces is one thing; how we live and operate is another. Our thoughts and deeds produce witness, and it is our witness which is ultimately the truest language and symbol of our faith. As temporal and fleshly beings, our witness is *timely*. Through understanding our own ideas on time, we are presented with the opportunity to resist fear and reassure faith.

Gypsy and Traveller engagement with and interpretation of time is undertaken through and with Christ. This is done in such a way that the present becomes an escalation of the eschatological. The juxtaposition of the nomadic camp narrative and all it entails provides a clear example of this 'now' and 'not yet', of living presently but with mind, heart and faith set in the future state. As such, Christ rightfully (at least with regards to orthodox belief) assumes His position as mediator and enabler. For Gypsies, Christ operates as a mode by which all rules – including those of time, are not applicable, for the simple understanding that, as John Yoder proposes – Christ *is* the rule.[201] To live 'in the now' is to live in Christ; to live 'in the now' is to live as a Gypsy. Time, in the way we've looked at it, is both measurable and a theological construct in which ontological and eschatological narratives (personal and collective) dwell. We saw an example of this through the rich Gypsy tradition of storytelling, which serves as a method of intentionally relocating the past into an immediate setting. Meanwhile, the eschatological narrative with its dissatisfaction of a 'next life' resolution (conversely witnessed through a 'joy' in confronting suffering in the present),[202] is violently implemented into the present. Doing this produces an escalation and urgency in our eschaton. The result of this 'apocalyptic' scenario is the introduction of a linear time narrative that is of a dualistic nature – human and supernatural. It's fair to say that the Gospel of John goes some way in contextualising and grounding our understanding of the permeability and relationship between the two natures. For it is by Christ, through Christ, and for Christ that all things exist – including time. To reiterate what was said above; Christ is the rule. It is Christ that is the answer to our question of time.

As always, questions and answers produce more questions and answers. If Christ is the answer to our question *of* time, surely Christ must be the answer to the question of what is *after* time. And what for *us*? If Christ is the answer to our time, to time after time, to our language and to our worlds – both physical and metaphysical, then who are we? What are our origins? This last question is particularly poignant for a people whose history and identity has for so long been penned by the hands of others. The following chapter will complete this picture we are painting by examining the origins of the person, in addition to dissecting their antagonistic and dichotomous

---

[201]   Barber, 2007, pp. 63 – 65.

[202]   This specific approach of confronting suffering in and through what Gustavo Gutiérrez describes as 'joy' (Farmer, 2013, p. 179), locates its precedent in the Liberation Theology narrative. Also see; Moschella, 2016, p. 213.

alternatives of death and the afterlife. In doing so, a more complete image will emerge that will demonstrate that beyond Christ being 'the rule' for our lives, that Christ is also at the epicentre of our entire condition – from bloodlines, race and identity, to life, death and beyond.

CHAPTER NINE

TOWARDS A TRAVELLER CHRISTOLOGY – CHRIST IN US

'Therefore, if anyone is in Christ, he is a new creation. The old has passed away; behold, the new has come.' (2 Corinthians 5:17)

BEGINNINGS, MIDDLES AND ENDS

My mother pointed to a seat near the back of the bus; 'Sit on that one', she said, 'and mind that lady's bags'. The bus was busy. It was a Saturday and this was the No.2 'Stanhope to Town Centre' line. At the time, Stanhope was the largest and arguably most notorious Council housing estate in the south of England. Poverty was rife and not many owned a car. Heck, we didn't even own our TV. Fun fact: my mother was the last person in our town to still be renting a TV set from Granada before they shut down. I remember the day they took her final payment and thanked her for her years of loyal custom. As she handed over the cash, the manager placed a piece of paper in her hand. It was a receipt for ownership; they had gifted her the television. As she tried to conceal her tears of happiness, my small 8 year-old fist punched the air in joy, knowing that I'd still be able to get my Saturday morning fix of *He-Man*, *ThunderCats*, and *Ghostbusters*.

Anyway, back to the bus. As the morning condensation dripped down the inside of the bus window and the raised seat rumbled from the large diesel engine beneath us, I couldn't wipe the smile off my face. In my hands was a practically brand-new 'Transformers' puzzle. We'd just been to the town's market and stopped by a 'jumble sale' being held by a local Church. My mum knew that getting to these places early was key to being able to barter for cheaper fruit and veg, which for us meant the difference between having a hungry week or a starving week. On this occasion, whilst mum looked for school shoes at the jumble sale, I happened upon the aforementioned puzzle. I had to have it. Thankfully, the people manning the stalls knew my mother, which meant the puzzle found its way into my ownership for a matter of pennies. Sitting down an hour later at the dining table, I frantically started sorting the pieces into piles using the universally-agreed method of edges in one pile and 'middle bits' in another, with the puzzle box picture face up. As I excitedly began placing the pieces into their positions, I grew confused. What I was seeing didn't match the picture on the box. It was still *Transformers*, but Optimus Prime and Megatron were looking markedly different. I called my mother over. We quickly established that the puzzle was not the same as the cover. 'Oh well, never mind', she said. 'It looks like they've put the wrong one in the box. You'll get a surprise when it's finished.' 'How can I get excited when I don't know what it'll be?' I thought to myself. But as the puzzle developed, mum was right. The picture was great, perhaps even better than what it was *supposed* to look like.

In one single morning I'd experienced a complexity of emotions and feelings, as elation turned to excitement, excitement turned to confusion, confusion turned to frustration, and frustration turned to joy. My expectations and understanding of what I believed things should be like did not match reality. Those beliefs were not far from being correct. (I still had a *Transformers* puzzle of some sort.) However, the process of making the puzzle revealed that sometimes the beginning part of a process isn't always reflective of the true form. We're not talking about future potential here, but certainty and assurance. I don't buy a flat-pack set of drawers with the expectation that by the time I finish building it, it'll be a wardrobe. Likewise, I don't accept that in its flat-pack form, the set of drawers is reflective of its true or final nature. What I do expect and accept is that in the first instance my foundations have to be right; whether that's something inconsequential like a puzzle or a piece of furniture, or something much more profound such as how I understand myself. Ensuring the activity I'm partaking in or the political party I'm voting for is what *I think it is*, is crucial, if I am to see the ending I'm expecting.

Secondly, I have to understand the *why*, *what* and/or *who* behind the process; puzzles are done for pleasure and relaxation – otherwise they're just oddly shaped cardboard pieces placed next to each other on a flat surface. In the same vein, purity practices, for example, are mostly unessential practices in the modern age. But because we understand the why, what and who behind purity practices, we understand both their necessity and, to some degree so far, their hoped-for ending. And thirdly, even in the flux of the temporality we enjoy and endure – whether a challenging *Transformers* puzzle or the daily grind of a job, we have to pursue the outcome we set out for. Thankfully, through Christ we do not have to do this in our own strength or with the fear that the outcome will not be a positive one. We are reminded in the scriptures how God is not in the business of jumping out and scaring folks (unless of course, your name is Saul of Tarsus – Acts 9:3), Instead, God wants to reassure us that when He is given the reins, the outcome is certain, beneficial, intentional, and full of life. 'For I know the plans I have for you,' declares the Lord, 'plans to prosper you and not to harm you, plans to give you hope and a future (Jeremiah 29:11).'

However, so often we believe down to our very core that the narratives we see in our lives are immovable, true and concrete. Paul's 'Damascus' experience (Acts 9:1-22) tells us otherwise. Paul, then referred to as 'Saul', believed his zealous and murderous persecution of Christians – or 'followers of the Way', was not only entirely justified but the right thing to do. Paul's foundational understanding of who he was, the world in which he dwelt, and things he had been told, were the very things that shaped his perception of the who, what and where of his life journey. At his core, Saul/Paul wasn't a bad person. He had many admirable qualities and strengths. The problem was, Paul's understanding of God at the time was off kilter and incomplete, and as such, Paul's life could never follow a 'true North'. Aiming in the wrong direction by a fraction isn't a problem over a short distance. But when that distance is eternity, being out by just one degree will result in a very different outcome. Paul didn't know the Son, how could he ever conceptualise God as 'Father'? Paul's conversion is, excuse the attempted verse 18 pun, eye-opening for many reasons. Not least because the direction and nature of Paul's life is so radically altered, but because of the grace shown to someone who, even in their own understanding, didn't deserve such a response. The grace of Christ facilitated the conversion; the grace of Christ provided hope and the possibility of a new outcome; and the grace of Christ retrospectively altered the start of Paul's journey. For whilst Paul had murdered, he was no longer a murderer. Paul, like all of us, had sinned, but his sins were remembered no more. The 'new' Paul was still every bit as tenacious, as intellectual, wise and quick thinking. The difference however, is that Paul was now all of these things because through God's grace, Christ now steered the ship. Christ had rewritten Paul's past. Truly, Christ was now the author and finisher of Paul's life.

When, like Paul, we give over our life to Christ, He doesn't just take our sins and infirmities; Christ adds to our lives. We are more, in every way, because of Jesus. Our past, our future, our flesh, our heritage, and our identity – all are in His hands. Nothing is beyond His reach. Nothing. What man has claimed, the creator of man can reclaim. For those who have historically faced persecution and marginalisation, these are key points to wrestle with. So many of our origin stories or past accounts have been skewed or defiled by triumphant armies and poisonous practices. Christ and His grace are the answer in redefining and rewriting our origins.

For many collectives and races on the margins, this is important. Unsurprisingly, the story is the same for Gypsies and Travellers. As we have seen so far, through Christ we are able reclaim our histories, our practices, our languages, and even the places where we live. However, like Paul, more often than not our unique understanding and practices of faith are intrinsically woven into the fabric of our culture. When this is the case, we must enter a process of voluntary and unhindered deconstruction, in order that Christ is rightfully given what is His – our life. *Saul* held the belief that Jew and Gentile were separated by purity of religion; that was his origin story. *Paul* on the other hand, held the belief that there was 'neither Jew nor Gentile, neither slave nor free … nor male and female, for you are all one in Christ Jesus' (Galatians 3:28). When, like Paul, we allow Christ in, we begin to ask of ourselves questions of a cultural, theological, and potentially ecclesiological nature. In this instance and with the explicit belief of purity in GRT circles (most notably through a belief in a Gypsy race), we must ask questions such: What is the formulation and location of a Traveller purity or Traveller bloodline – in the flesh, as a soul, both, or neither? At what juncture does 'purity' or a 'pure bloodline/pure Traveller/Gypsy' begin? These questions can, among other things, pave the way for other areas to open up, such as eschatology.

Questions of this nature are on one hand the produce of a theological crux. However, on the other hand, they potentially represent what Professor Charles Taylor describes as a 'semantic innovation'. This is where the complexity of an originally existing set of ideas, often expressed through Christian text, practice, and philosophy, are initially introduced as simplistic (academically speaking) and then redefined through a process and combination of *semantic* logic and *enacted* logic.[203] Odd place to drop a little methodology bomb, I know. But theology isn't passive – at times

---

[203]   University of Nottingham (2014a & 2014b).

it's a multipronged tool, like a Swiss army knife, and it's quite nice sometimes to know how tools can work. So, for anyone wondering why a section of the book dealing with 'beginnings' has turned up at this late stage, well, wonder no more. So often our beginnings have been decided by someone or something else: the area you grew up in; your parents' and grandparents' life choices; the actions of your government; and a million and one things besides. For some, their theological response has been one of liberation. But 'liberation', in that sense, doesn't work for communities who aren't willing to escape or run, or who don't feel the need to break free.

We don't run from the foot of the Cross – we cling to the foot of the Cross; and in doing so, we reclaim our stories through Christ, just as Jesus reclaims a narrative of glory from the horrors of the Cross. Who wants liberation with the proviso of compromise, when you can have reclamation with the promise of a future? Reclamation, however, requires courage. So, be courageous! 'Have I not commanded you? Be strong and courageous. Do not be frightened, and do not be dismayed, for the Lord your God is with you wherever you go' (Joshua 1:9). The idea of purity in GRT history finds its roots in the ideologically based 'inherent' condition of Traveller lineage, also known as 'pure bloodline'. If any foundational ideas need challenging in any of our cultures and races around the world, then it is the idea that we are separated by blood. Cultural and racial uniqueness is one thing,[204] but regardless of our origin stories, there can be no denying that at the point of human inception we all share the same source. As such, dismantling ideas of racial purity and letting Christ reclaim them, is not something that weakens us – whoever 'us' is – but is something that transforms our Kingdom living into His Kingdom living. His Kingdom come, not ours. His will be done, not ours. On Earth, here, now, as it is in Heaven.

[204] '... a great multitude that no one could number, from every nation, from all tribes and peoples and languages...' (Revelation 7:9).

ORIGINS

The Construct of a Pure Gypsy Lineage: Dismantling Myths

The application of the purity (or *mokhhadi*) code, regardless of motive, is by its very nature exclusionary. However, in this instance that 'exclusion' is very particular because it doesn't result in the loss of something, but rather creates an opposite (and excluded) option. If we want to get technical, in the academic world it's more commonly understood as 'dialectical reasoning'. Dialectical reasoning is drawn from Hegelian logic, whereby the presence of one thing means the exclusion of the other, resulting in a series of antithetical stipulations. So, if for example we have light, then light can only exist because of its opposite – dark; if we choose light, we exclude dark. In *mokhhadi*, to maintain purity, pollution must be either dealt with or avoided. Likewise, to achieve holiness, godlessness must be eliminated. And finally, to maintain Gypsy or Traveller lineage, gorger lineage is not an option. This raises a plethora of issues, both in a sociological and theological sense. However, in the first instance the concern for 'separateness' can be summarised in two elements: firstly, there is a fear of (sinful) contamination; secondly, there is a desire to maintain (sinless) purity. Consequences of a cultural and soteriological nature are both directly and *inherently* attached to the observance of these elements. In the *immanent* Gypsy and Traveller setting, social acceptance and standing among the community, peers, and family is at stake. This directly correlates with the *transcendent* Gypsy and Traveller setting, where the ramifications are extended to including and maintaining an exclusively GRT lineage.[205]

The concept of the *literal* 'pure blooded' Gypsy or Traveller, or a literal 'pure bloodline', is troublesome. Not just because of the fallibility of Traveller and Gypsy communities in subscribing to such concepts, but primarily because of the origins of the idea of a pure bloodline. Surprisingly, the idea didn't come from Roma, Gypsies or Travellers,

---

[205]   Bhopal and Myers, 2008, pp. 13 – 21; Clark and Greenfields, 2006, pp. 36 – 38.

but was adapted off the back of late-nineteenth and early-twentieth-century eugenics studies, primarily in Germany. An unlikely bed pair of romanticist ideas and skewed science, led to an overt racialisation of Gypsies, resulting in a number of quite frankly bizarre and (in the modern context) offensive articles and books. A couple of decades later we'd see a plethora of novels and images, depicting 'down to earth' folk and pretty bow-top wagons travelling down country lanes. Gypsy romanticism was born! But it was the historical racialisation of Gypsies and Travellers by Gypsiologists and social scientists[206] that created two primary issues.

The first was a scenario in which the proposal of a 'pure Gypsy bloodline' meant that by default there existed the possibility for an impure bloodline. 'Pure' Romany Gypsies/Travellers were situated at the top of this racial hierarchy, followed by 'didikais' (half-Travellers), and then by those of 'questionable Gypsy blood' – also known as 'Pikeys'. The rhetoric emanating from the Gypsiologists stated that the 'half-breeds' (or, those less than 'pure' Gypsy) had 'inherited all the vices of the Romany and the Gaujo (gorgers) but none of their virtues'.[207] The second issue was that stereotypes and 'popular imagination' created by the Gypsiologists now formed part of the Gypsy's own narrative. The purity code which had for centuries formed the inherent core of Gypsy culture had been 'repackaged' by the Gypsiologists and social scientists and 'sold' to Gypsies and Travellers, replacing a Christian value with 'fleshly' connotations that held a secularised *social* value, formulated on a created and artificial concept of race.

The repackaging of 'Gypsy purity' allowed for an undermining of GRT culture through a gorger-led process of relocating the inception point and genesis of Gypsy and Traveller purity. This subsequently created a tool for the state to legitimise oppression policies and actions. Thomas Acton notes that whilst Gypsiologists were 'fortunate in almost never meeting a Gypsy who is not "true", "the authorities"

206   Taylor, 2008, pp. 8 – 9.
207   Taylor, 2008, p. 9.

tend to claim they never meet one who is.'[208] If a *critical* Traveller theology is to emerge, elements beyond that of a physical purity bloodline must also be considered. This is owing to the combination of an explicit appropriation of the purity bloodline narrative by a gorger contingent, and of an immersive Gypsy acquisition of the gorger-created eugenically orientated narrative. Furthermore, Acton's comments (1974) highlight the undermining and troublesome nature of clinging to physical genetics as the benchmark of being Gypsy or Traveller.

So where do we go from here? Carrying on as if we didn't just hear or realise something damaging isn't an option. Continuing in blind ignorance with oppressive narratives for racial issues is in some ways like the abused victim returning to their partner in the belief that 'it'll be different this time'. It won't. Unfortunately, restarting the discussion at a location situated before the aforementioned interception of GRT culture would at best be a speculative process. Furthermore, it would also be disjointed from the spiritual and social struggle of the *contemporary* Gypsy and Traveller. Conversely, Black Theologian Edward Antonio, suggests that in the instance of the Black struggle any *post*colonial discussion can 'only speak through its parasitic relationship on the colonial'.[209] Gypsy and Traveller 'blood' must therefore remain in the present but be refashioned in the mould of its pre 'Gypsiologist' Christian experience. Doing so, Gypsy purity takes on a form of theological 'postcoloniality', in what Antonio would refer to as a 'practice of resistance'.[210] As such, to negate all the elements of the gorger interjection in the bloodline narrative, even if they are incorrect, would be to steal from the Gypsy and Traveller hermeneutic itself. Remember – reclamation over liberation! Moving on then, the premise of the question at hand ceases to ask *if* a 'pure' Gypsy bloodline exists, instead challenging the concept of *how* a Gypsy bloodline exists.

[208]   Acton, 1974, p. 84.
[209]   Antonio, 2012, p. 299.
[210]   Antonio, 2012, pp. 299 – 302.

The Construct of a Pure Gypsy Lineage: Rebuilding Truths

The temptation of course, is to simply ignore and rewrite the Gypsiologists' 40-50 year long 'bait and switch' bloodline myth. But true strength and courage, and as we've seen, is found in the resistance of misinterpretations – not in the destruction of uncomfortable pasts. So we have to exegetically relocate the bloodline account *in* the narrative, rather than allowing it to continue being a *narrator*. If we return our issues to biblical sources, we enable the text to contextualise our grief. This can be a much healthier method than letting our grief run wild. If we apply that principle to ideas of a tangible Gypsy bloodline, that bloodline becomes an internal *phase* rather than being an external *driver*. In this instance, we look to the Mosaic narratives. What we can see is what could be interpreted as a series of intentional dehumanising and 'othering' actions by the 'Egyptian political authorities' – our equivalent of those original Gypsiologists (Exodus 1:11; 1:13; 1:16; 1:22). Pharaoh's intentionality in the systematic and methodical eradication of the Israelites (Exodus 1:16 – 22) originates from his (and his people's) anxieties over elements pertaining to the physicality of another ethnicity and race to his own. These anxieties are enacted through a policy of increased labour and servitude;[211] 'He said to his people, behold, the Israelites are too many and too mighty for us. Come, let us deal shrewdly with them, lest they multiply more...' (Exodus 1:9 – 10). The response by the Hebrew midwives to the external pressures is to enact a physical manifestation of their faith, and is explicitly and directly linked to their confessed reverence and fear of God (Exodus 1:17 and 21).

This raises two key comparable factors with the Gypsy and Traveller response to both historical and present-day manifestations of societal oppression. Firstly, the *spiritual* response is one and the same with the *physical* response – an active, measurable, and intentional demonstration of a 'lived-out' religion. Secondly, that by employing a

---

[211]   Mays, 1988, pp. 132 – 133.

specific systematic exegesis, we can see that the locale of the Israelites' identity is in the *religious* ideology of being a chosen and separated people that belong to God (Deuteronomy 7:6). Here's the crunch: The bloodline (or collective identity) obtained its value through an identity grounded in God, and was not determined by geographical locations or societal expectations. God's 'chosen' people placed their value not in who they perceived they were, but in who they believed God to be. Compared to elements of the Gypsy 'condition', such as nomadism and the Sojourner narrative, it is evident that *Traveller and Gypsy 'blood' is first and foremost a spiritual concept*, synergistically located in and operating through the purity code. Indeed, it's possible that the ideological centring of the purity narrative is worthless without the inclusion of the 'pure blood' aspect. This doesn't entirely do away with the physical 'bloodline', as this is still clearly evidenced through *ethnic* means. In short, Traveller and Gypsy 'blood' is located in the ideological, supported and constructed by its relation with God, and evidenced through practical means. This second definition, sociologically speaking, warrants further investigation beyond the parameters of this book.

However, for now, such definitions invoke theological challenges and require attention as questions pertaining to the origin and makeup of this quasi-Christian ethnicity emerge. For as with the Israelites, the Traveller's identity – their 'Gypsy' blood, is not always one that is focused *towards* Creator (Exodus 32:1 – 35; Nehemiah 9:16 – 21) but is permanently hopeful *in* said Creator (Jeremiah 14:8; 17:13; and Psalm 33:20 – 22); spiritual permanence anchors physical and ideological nomadism. The seemingly contradictive state of 'permanent impermanence' that both the Traveller and Israelite occupy reveals in great detail the suffering, the history and the reasoning of a people group (as detailed in the Pentateuch and indeed this book thus far). This challenges the contextual positioning of the 'story', from a people in *relation to* their God to that of the relationship *between* Creator and his people. The dynamic of dependence *upon*

God rather than being independent *of* God, suggests that divine justice (present in the process of adhering – or not adhering - to the purity code) or 'grace'[212] is a significant factor in the enablement, existence and thus the genesis of any Gypsy bloodline. Again, the emphasis is a withdrawal from a subscription to a racial element, and instead a move towards an ethnic-religio construct. As such, the determining factor of maintaining true Gypsy and Traveller identity lies not in the physical reproduction of the human form but in the provision of grace originating from the divine.

IT WAS ALWAYS THE CROSS
Grace as Lineage Enabler

It would appear that grace, not blood, serves as a lineage enabler. Grace in this context is characterised by 'the God of the biblical traditions' and is described with some proviso by Miroslav Volf as 'a profound injustice'.[213] This highlights two aspects of the involvement of God in the arrangement (or relationship) that must be considered – God's interest and God's partiality. Volf's description of the justice administered by God as 'profoundly [unjust]', originates from a comparison to the judicial motif and image of Justitia, the somewhat angelic-looking, blindfold-wearing goddess of justice who holds sword in one hand and scales in the other. This legal representation and administration of justice operates outside of any personal relationship and is applied without any pursuit of personal *interest*. Importantly, it does this entirely in ignorance – something wholly opposite to God's vested interest and concern for the personal and the collective (in this instance, the Israelites).

We can see this in action when we recount the biblical record of the history of Israel which presents itself in the form of a continual

---

[212] 'Grace' is primarily being defined using Aquinas' proposal of 'Actual grace' (*gratia gratis data* – "grace which is freely given"), meaning 'a series of divine actions or influences upon human nature' (McGrath, 2011, pp. 356 – 357).
[213] Volf, 1996, p. 221.

theme or pattern. Broadly speaking the pattern is as follows: a collective suffering; a petition to the Lord; a hearing by God of said petition or 'crying out'; and finally, a response of deliverance by God. The cynic in us would rightfully assume that the repetition of suffering (as a result of sinful actions [Judges 4:1]) is the focal point of God's interest, but we'd be wrong. Instead, it is the Israelites' welfare that is the cynosure of God. God's attention, indeed, God's justice, never seeks detached objectivity, but constantly pursues the salvific option for its intended target. As such, there is an interweaving between the salvation and righteousness of God (Isaiah 45:21) and the kindness and justice of God (Psalm 145:17). The actions of God's salvation and God's justice are one and the same. In comparison to the objective motif of Justitia, the subjective presentation of justice that God delivers is, in the judicial sense, unjust. By considering the partiality shown by God towards those marginalised, ostracised and oppressed (both individually and collectively), the perspicacity of God's 'unjust justice' is facilitated. In the instance of the biblical representation of the *Traveller* – the *Sojourner*, we can turn to Volf again, who proposes that:

> [w]hen God looks at a sojourner, God does not see simply a human being, but a stranger ... subject to prejudice and scapegoating. How does the God who executes justice for the oppressed act toward widows and strangers? Just as God acts toward any other human being? No. God is partial to them. God watches over the strangers...[214]

The divine partiality shown towards Gypsies, Travellers and the marginalised, forms a statement of faith from inside 'the camp' itself. Furthermore, it also operates as a supporting narrative from God (alongside God's 'interest') in the functionality of grace in both

---

[214] Volf, 1996, pp. 221 – 222. Also see Psalm 146:7 – 9.

the formation and continuation of identity (or 'Traveller blood'). Read alone, Romans 2:11 appears to contradict this statement, as Paul claims that there is no partiality shown by God. However, impartiality presents itself in verses 9-10 as a *characteristic*.[215] As Paul understands, the priority of the Jewish people entails God's impartiality. The paradox we're faced with isn't an unpleasant one - God is, it would seem, impartially partial. This is exactly the response we should expect from the God who gave His life for His beloved. After all, impartiality is very much a human measure that addresses the balance between the shortfall of our limited concern and the bribability of our emotions. Conversely then, the paradox of the divine's impartial partialness towards Gypsy blood indicates that God must and does show partiality to those *beyond* those whom he has indicated favour towards (the widow, the stranger, the Israelites, the Gypsies, etc.). God's partiality is for everyone. Because *all* people are treated *differently*, everyone is treated justly.

Christ: The Heart of Grace

'If you give me a call when you get there, I can come pick you up if you want.' As I put my coat and woolly hat on, the shout from my wife was a tempting offer. 'No, it's okay. I want to walk', I shouted back. I didn't want to walk. Well, my body didn't want to walk. More specifically, my body didn't want to go out into the freezing winter afternoon and the heavy snow. However, I've never outgrown going on adventures, and the prospect of heading out for a 4 to 5 hour trek to the hills and woods in what looked like a blizzard, was far too tempting. Besides which, I've kept myself fit since I was a boy and tried to do something physical every day of my life (gym, long walks, building something in the garden, etc.), and putting my body through this would benefit my mind, body and spirit! Snow, woods, hills, empty streets and roads,

[215] 'There will be tribulation and distress for every human being who does evil, the Jew first and also the Greek, but glory and honour and peace for everyone who does good, the Jew first and also the Greek' (Romans 2:9 – 10).

adventure – this was too good to miss. Did I have to do it? No. Would it make any difference to my health if I just sat this one out and curled up on the sofa like every other sane person in my town? No. So why do it? Because as well as being fun, it was going to benefit me in a myriad of ways! There are many things in our lives that we do that aren't always necessary. However, being both physical and spiritual beings, our heart language shouldn't be considered to be any less valuable, impactful, and necessary than the physical forms of our expressions and intentions. Take for example the application of the purity code (or righteous acts). Pressing on with purity (*mokhhadi*) actions, behaviours and thought processes is, in many ways, an attempt to secure grace, lineage, and ultimately salvation. However, in the process of doing so, there is an acknowledgment (consciously or subconsciously) of the dynamic that one is intentionally partaking in sacrificial efforts in spite of the acceptance of an all-embracing and invitational grace.

We all do it, all the time; things like trying to secure the affection or forgiveness of loved ones through gift giving, or obtaining favours by giving favours – these are all understandable and very much well-intended human responses, but often they are unnecessary. Quick disclaimer: if you've upset your partner, do still buy the flowers; I don't want any complaints that I've ruined someone's relationship! Resolution, forgiveness, progress, understanding; many of these things can be accomplished through better and more regular communication. However, when it comes to matters of a spiritual nature, our confidence and reassurance can at times be challenged when we call out to the seemingly empty void of nothingness and plead with a creator that we so often fail to see. But, nevertheless, we are reassured of our position – through scriptures, through nature, through other people, through divine intervention, and through the answering of prayers. As such, and specifically with the application of religious practices in mind (such as *mokhhadi*), we as individuals or collectives are forced to contend with the apparent irrationality

199

of a purposeful decision to remain positioned in what appears to be unnecessary suffering. Or, in other words, all of us in a number of ways for a number of considered reasons choose discomfort, rejection, possibly even ostracisation, even when we don't have to.

Unless we have some deeply troubling issues, it's fair to say that most people choose to willingly participate in the aforementioned discomfort for positive reasons. Much like my long trek in the snow, the perceived benefits and my good intentions far outweighed the consequences of cold snow and tired legs. Assuming a similar logic exists in acts of purity, nomadism and separation from the larger society, it is better then to consider that efforts made in such circumstances are not simply 'works' but instead are *sacramental* acts, made willingly, consciously, and lovingly. Jesus, in the Gospel according to Luke, makes a charge to His followers, stating that; 'If anyone would come after me, let him deny himself and take up his cross daily and follow me' (Luke 9: 23). Reimagining Luke 9:23 not as a march towards inevitable suffering but instead as an action of voluntary sacramental living enables two important distinctions. Firstly, the unavoidable *absence* of said comforts becomes the voluntary *denial* of comforts. Secondly, the positive move towards that which is *sacrificial* (i.e. the taking-up of one's cross), instead becomes a move towards the *source of divine love and grace*. Indeed, the statement by Jesus to his followers that 'my yoke is easy, and my burden is light' (Matthew 11:30) suggests that whilst Jesus is aware that the charge to follow him is burdensome (John 15:20 – 21; 2 Corinthians 4:17), it is cushioned somewhat with the same grace that enables one to 'take up [their] cross' in the first instance.

However, the participation in salvation and the receiving of atonement in this context assumes both a giver of salvation (Christ) and a location from which salvation and thus atonement (again, Christ) draws humanity. It also rightly assumes a participant in salvation and a receiver of atonement. So what for Gypsies and Travellers, and indeed anyone who knowingly or unknowingly chooses not to participate in this equation? Participation in Christian sacraments is widely adopted by Gypsies and Travellers but is not always consistently extended to that of an application of faith or belief in the atonement, the 'Cross event'[216] or even Jesus himself (as the Christ; as God).

Whilst this can initially appear troublesome, participation in a predominantly sacramental Christianity which extends beyond human 'good will and intentions' and ventures into liturgical and ceremonial expressions (including Christian weddings and funerals, etc.) is both possible and theologically viable. If Christ and the Cross are to be the genesis and the cornerstone of experiencing God (and all that that entails), then it is possible that experience informs faith, followed by faith informing experience. This cyclical pattern supersedes both doctrinal understanding and denominational commitments, rejecting (if only for a short while) intellectualism in exchange for participation in Christ's proleptic promise that 'while we were still sinners, Christ died for us' (Romans 5:8). Even so, this does not dismiss the necessity of faith in the divinity and crucifixion/resurrection of Christ. It does however allow for a *spectrum* of Christianity (rather than a fixed denominational narrative) to be implemented – a fluidity of faith and works; not stretching as far as to be considered Pelagian, where arguably salvation is achieved through the imitation of Christ, and not settling for a purely Augustinian position of justification by grace. Instead, there is a position of flexible negotiation between both the imitation of Christ and having life made possible through Christ (including the continuation of lineage). For Gypsies and Travellers, the nature of this Christological centring, or more precisely – the Cross event, is and must be greater than something purely theoretical or incomprehensibly abstract.

Christ: The Grace of the Cross

Justification, sanctification and salvation require the *movement* of our minds and our spirits, a *stirring* of our emotions, and at times the *application* of our flesh through the partaking in sacraments and

---

[216]   Bultmann & Ogden, 1989, p. 39.

cultural nuances. Among these 'journeying' elements can be found a willingness of participation in a 'suffering' context. This calling that so many hear is not without fruit, for it comes with eschatological promises and the hope for a journey beyond this journey – time beyond time. With that in mind, Christian and cultural identity (and the continuation of said identity) is not only present in the affectionate character of grace and salvation but is also participating in the brutality of the crucifixion and the process of atonement. The violent nature of the salvific process through the image of the crucified Christ is paradoxical in that it becomes the beneficial means of the community's transformation via a refocusing of the community's 'violence'. Christ, as well as the *means* of salvation, also serves as the *scapegoat* for the price of said salvation. Both Christ's sacrifice and the violent process He endures are sacred and necessary, as humanity is protected from its own inhumanity.

Christ's eventual sacrifice (i.e. the crucifixion of Jesus) is both the 'death' of God and of (the old) human life (Ephesians 4:17- 24; Acts 17:11; Romans 6:1 – 23), in a move that invites consideration of Jesus' death both in its salvific efficacy, but more strikingly, in the very nature of the event. Violence, more specifically – redemptive violence, becomes necessary. Our challenge here is to strike a balance. On one hand we have the relatable and the relational dynamic we hold with Christ, namely the hypostatic union. Here we are faced with the person of Christ in the crucifixion event, where our attention is upon the two states of Christ – namely the *humiliation* and *exaltation* of Jesus. On the other hand, we have the full Trinitarian picture. Here we have the somewhat challenging-to-grasp magnitude of the entire Godhead participating in the most important event of what we believe to be 'human' history. However, Trinitarian contextualisation is necessary in formulating a complete understanding of the cross event. Furthermore, by refocusing the narrative upon the tangible event of the crucifixion, a more particular and complex presentation of God is forced to emerge. It is one that begins to assemble the

Traveller's moderately disjointed narratives of the Godhead into a Trinitarian image, with the person of Christ and the Cross event being the method by which any understanding of God, the triune complex, and the culture is to be interpreted.

SUMMARY
New Beginnings, True Beginnings

If the Cross has taught us anything, it's that we were never meant nor designed to carry the burdens that we possess. But, as we have seen, sometimes in life we voluntarily hold on to certain things that challenge and change us for the better. Still, at other times we find ourselves somewhere in-between, not knowing if the weight we hold is a tool or a shackle. If we are to avoid being at the mercy of these stormy seas, then we have to seize control and be assertive. It is not enough to do nothing. As we remind the seas of the one who commands them (Luke 8:25), these points in life become check marks, new chapters, starting points.

This chapter took the same initiative by deconstructing existing myths and narratives concerned with the purity of a Gypsy race. The proposition was altered accordingly, from 'if a Gypsy bloodline exists' to 'how a Gypsy bloodline exists'. This (and an exegetical exploration) revealed the co-dependent and synergistic nature of the purity code along with the idea of a 'pure' Gypsy lineage. The conclusion? *Any* Gypsy bloodline in the first instance should be understood primarily as a unified spiritual and ideological construct. The reasoning for this mostly centred on the idea that an aspect of divine grace facilitated the participation (or conversely, the abstention) in the purity code whilst simultaneously being the subject of that purity. Therefore, that same grace could remove itself from this 'grace-filled' equation at any moment. Paradoxically, it is because of the very nature of this 'grace' that the removal never happens, lest God denies God's own self. This places grace – *not blood*, as the foundation of any Gypsy, Roma or Traveller 'bloodline'. Thus the emphasis is and must be a withdrawal from a subscription to a racial element, and instead a move towards an ethnic-religio construct.

Grace in this manner is wholly unwarranted when based upon a human standard of justice. However, Gypsy blood, purity, and spiritual certainty (i.e. salvation) is dependent upon divine grace, and as such it stands to reason that it must therefore be wholly subject to divine justice. It's the continual sacramental life that sees Gypsies and Travellers actively participate in the equation of divine grace and justice, and it is this equation that results in the judicial decision of salvation. And as we saw, participation in salvation and the 'giving' of atonement (in this context) assumes Christ is both the giver of salvation and the location from which salvation – and thus atonement (again, Christ) draws humanity. Christ is the beginning; Christ is the bloodline; Christ is the facilitator; Christ is our grace; Christ is our justice; Christ is our rule; Christ is our middle; Christ is our journey; Christ *was*, *is* and *will be* our destination. Now we will continue our journey beyond our beginnings, beyond our present and to the next stopping place; the one beyond the now and tomorrow where every tear will be wiped from our eyes, 'where there shall be no more death, nor sorrow, nor crying. There shall be no more pain' (Revelation 21.4). It's time to approach the end, to examine planes beyond our mortal coil, and to look for the lay of the land in time beyond our time.

CHAPTER TEN
TRAVELLING ALONE: DEATH, MYSTICISM AND ESCHATOLOGY

'A good name is better than precious ointment, and the day of death than the day of birth.' (Ecclesiastes 7:1)

'So we are always of good courage. We know that while we are at home in the body we are away from the Lord, for we walk by faith, not by sight. Yes, we are of good courage, and we would rather be away from the body and at home with the Lord.' (2 Corinthians 5:6-8)

THE MOST IMPORTANT JOURNEY

The normally busy road stood still. There hadn't been a car pass for at least a minute; they must be close. The uncomfortableness of anticipation was momentarily lost as the piercing early morning summer sun broke through the scattering clouds. A deep breath in filled the lungs with fresh, chilled air, whilst sunrays warmed closed eyes. A long breath out, opening the eyes, a temporary calmness filled the mind. A rustling among those gathered began, as more and more people stood on tiptoes to get the first glance. Something was happening; you could feel it. The sound arrived before the sight. The unmistakable noise of hooves hitting the road signalled that the next phase of the funeral had begun. The procession approached. A horse-drawn carriage carrying a coffin was being led by four beautiful and well-groomed horses, followed by vehicles, ponies and traps, and a procession of people as far as the eye could see. This wasn't just about remembering; this was about ensuring the recently departed successfully and comfortably moved from this plane to the next. And despite how the procession looked, it wasn't about image; it was about absolute respect for the dead and avoiding agitating their spirit. It was about ensuring that the body that had given so much in this life could rest in peace in the next.

At the Church, only a handful of the nearest and dearest would go inside. More could fit in, but most chose to stay outside, ready to deal with what would come next. The service finished and the burial began. For some Gypsies and Travellers, it's important for the coffin to avoid contamination, and so graves are occasionally inlaid with bricks or other materials. For this service, an ornate 'blanket' lined the grave. The coffin began to lower. Then the wailing began. Tough, hardened men who for much of their lives understood the expression of emotions to be akin to a badge of shame wept with heart-wrenching cries. At times, the public mourning of some seemed to be fabricated, over the top. But that didn't matter – it wasn't about the living, it was about the dead. And then it fell silent. Some left the graveside whilst a number of chosen men stayed behind. A couple of them went to their open-back work van, which had been part of the procession. They returned with several shovels. The discretely distanced grave digging team sitting in their vehicle, hidden somewhat by hedgerows, looked flummoxed and redundant. The men with the shovels took their ties and jackets off and began to infill the grave, at times working in tandem where there wasn't enough shovels; everyone wanted to show their respect. Within hours, tears turned to song and stories, as drinks flowed heavily into the night. The morning had begun with mourning; the day would end with hope and reflection.

What had been clear that day, and indeed in any Gypsy or Traveller funeral, is that there was a plethora of customs, rituals, beliefs, and liturgical moments that turned the all-too common feeling of finality in death, into a journey where the only thing that stopped moving was the living. And as much as there had been a rainbow of emotions shed that day, what was noticeable was the presence and broad spectrum of fear among a number of attendees. Of course, there was 'conventional' fear – or anxiety, in wanting the day and service, etc. to run smoothly and according to plan. But there was also the presence of less obvious fears, such as fear of the deceased not completing their journey to the other side; fear that the deceased wouldn't 'find' their loved ones because of where their grave was positioned; fear that the deceased would be angry or holding a grudge against some of the living; fear that the deceased would return to haunt the people talking about them; and fear that whilst a 'door' from this realm to the next was open, that someone or something could come through from the other side. Whilst some would hastily dismiss many of these concerns as mere superstition, centuries of experience and a reverence for not just the sanctity of this life but of the next and all that that entailed, meant that for a number of people attending that day, 'superstition' was an authentic and experienced element of the Christian experience.

We all at times have fears of the unknown and the unfamiliar. It's perfectly natural; in fact, to some degree we're supposed to have fears of the unknown – it's biologically hardwired into us; it's the difference between touching a naked flame and avoiding the fire, or walking across a train line instead of waiting to see what the distant noise is. However, fear should only ever be a prompt, an advisor of caution; fear should never be in command nor should the voice of fear be magnified; 'For God gave us a spirit not of fear but of power and love and self-control' (2 Timothy 1:7). The fears that were present during the funeral arose from the unfamiliarity of temporarily having to pause 'the journey'; of transitioning from sojourning to blissful movement. The fleshly journey for one member of the community had ended, and it was the responsibility of those who remained, to ensure the journey of the deceased could continue elsewhere. After all, this wasn't the end but a *transition*. A little like one would change trains midway through an expedition. The difference here was that this transition had to be made alone. However, for all this talk of transition, of movement, of journeying from one place to another, the real focus is on the present, on being present, on recognising the value and importance of now. When we become caught up in the fallacies of linearity it's then that we fear the future rather than anticipate it. When we devalue and misunderstand the incredible imminence of God, it's then that we choose to wait for God rather than see Him here, now, in us and everyone and everything around us. And when we think of invoking the Spirit of God and calling for Him to come down to us, it's then that we have already dismissed the idea that the Holy Spirit is always here – in us and among us.

That last point is key for this chapter: if we do not 'see' the Spirit in this world, then why do we yearn for the next world, which with our spiritual blindness will be alien at best? When we profess that we are mind, body and spirit, how many of us truly believe that we are what we profess – spirit? When you experience God, your spirit experiences His Spirit. Being 'present' in our journey here is much more than simply being mindful of the activity or situation you are currently occupied with; it is also being aware (or seeking to develop awareness) of the permeation between this world and the next. Permeability between this world and that which we don't see makes itself known every time we engage in the sacraments. Why then do we sometimes hesitate to believe the spirit(ual) world can exist beyond our own (sacramental) actions? Are we really that prideful? Did the Creator have to wait for our permission to engage with humanity, to send fallen angels to Earth, to baptise us in the Spirit? Of course, the answer is no; before flesh and form even existed, there was spirit (Genesis 1:2; John 1:1-3). How, when and if we should engage with that world is another topic for another day. For now, our task is to temporarily and confidently sit in the sometimes uncomfortable realm of death, knowing that it is nothing in and of itself but a transition; a transition that has been reclaimed, repurposed and ultimately defeated by Christ. Our destination is a better understanding of both this side and the next – a 'Traveller eschatology' if you will. To begin this final journey, we will now take a brief venture into Gypsy mysticism and meet a wonderful lady called Mary. From heartache and endings to limitless hope and eternal promise, let's once more pack up the camp and head out on the most important journey of all.

MYSTICISM, SUPERSTITIONS AND SPIRITS

Spiritual commerce isn't something many consider when thinking about death. However, it's been around in many forms for most of human history, including in Christian circles. For those looking for faults in the global church, eyes might turn to certain unscrupulous individuals who parade on television, selling promises of healings and abundant wealth, all in exchange for a 'love gift', arguably more accurately described as incremental sums of cash. Such 'gifts' offer the potential to possibly postpone a creeping death by securing healing. In the late middle ages, the Church wasn't quite as bold as to promise you wouldn't die; the seemingly never-ending presence of plagues and wars made the certainty of a prolonged life a tad challenging. However, there were 'indulgences'; essentially a process whereby you could pay for certain privileges, such as getting out of Purgatory a little quicker, making it into Heaven, and other things that conveniently weren't going to take place in this life. Your purchase was certain, at least, you thought it was until a certain Martin Luther took exception to the situation, 'Tweeting' and posting his objections sixteenth-century style – by pinning his 'Ninety-Five Theses' to the door of the All Saints Church in Wittenberg, Germany. Importantly, even with the rising resistance towards all things purgatory and a brief objection to acknowledging the existence of the supernatural (namely, ghosts, in England, late-sixteenth/early-seventeenth century), there still remained across much of the European church unwavering belief in the Holy Spirit, intercession by the Saints, and divine presence in the sacraments. Spiritual activity, regardless of man's futile and sickening attempts to commodify it, was and still is very much, well, alive!

Despite the coming and going of religious trends in Europe,

Gypsies and Roma continued to hold very distinctive and at times quite incredible beliefs, both in the supernatural and the potential for interaction with and from the supernatural world. These, like any beliefs, would evolve and change overtime, with many eventually disappearing entirely. However, two distinct strands that were present from day one in Europe, would remain to this day. The first strand would be a series of 'superstitious' beliefs and practices that were present in every area of life, from ideas about procreation and marriage, to the avoidance of saying certain words (such as diseases, like 'Ca*cer'), to creating entire elaborate and detailed funeral 'liturgies'. For most of these practices, they were performed in the context of the purity code. As such, it would arguably be a disservice to refer to some of them as superstitions when in fact many were more akin to an element of mysticism within GRT Christianity. The second strand would be the practice of palmistry and the ability of clairvoyance.

Palmistry originated in India. Unsurprisingly when the Roma left India and made their way to Europe, palmistry travelled with them. Still, to some degree 'fortune telling' and psychic communication only remained a relevant factor out of necessity. Excluded from most avenues of work, simply for the 'crime' of being a Gypsy, incomes were hard to come by, and as such, Gypsies had to get inventive. Many already perceived Gypsies to be exotic; that perception, coupled with a mysterious culture thrown into the mix made getting one's palm read by a Gypsy a must-do and somewhat taboo activity. A number of Gypsies – predominantly women, cashed in on the venture. Some were genuine, many were not. Either way, whether the practising Gypsy believed in their abilities as a clairvoyant or not, the collective cultural belief in the inherited spiritual power of seeing the future and communing with the dead was certain. At the time, many Gypsies would not perform readings and the like with fellow Gypsies. It was too dangerous. Furthermore, engaging with Spirits and divining had the potential to be spiritually unclean, and, as the biblical text and church would make clear, it was forbidden. Practising such crafts for gorgers though was more acceptable and on the whole less dangerous, as any spirits making the leap into this realm would hopefully be leaving the tent or vardo with the gorger!

Old Habits Die Hard: Appleby Horse Fair

Context is key, hence the brief history lesson above. To understand where we might end up – either in this life or the next, in our spiritual walk or our physical trek, or even in our relationships and in our faith, we must get a grasp on the foundations of how we got to where we are and what elements might influence our future. Christ is calling all of us. If we are to respond faithfully and fully, we must understand both what it is we are leaving and what things we have put in place to help us achieve that journey. In this instance, our context is that in reaching Christ, humans have for millennia both knowingly and unknowingly partook in practices that have sought to bridge the ethereal plane between flesh and spirit, between Earth and Heaven. It's easy to dismiss the necessity, importance and relevance of this area, more so in the current period when religious identity and belief in super-natural activity has largely been pressed aside for en vogue atheism and theology so dry, dead and detached from reality that even Ezekiel couldn't revive it. But the reality is, most of us engage with practices that attempt to reach the spiritual every single day. Whether by prayer or by reading the living Word of God, on the most basic level, humans – and not just Christians, try to connect with Spirit every day. Our return journey to our source, to *the* source, much like time, is not lineal but is a steady ebbing away from our temporary form back to our eternal form. As such, we would do well, if we ever find ourselves sneering at the 'primal' beliefs of others, to remember that it was the established church that introduced the bizarre concept of paying actual money to engage and influence the spiritual realm. If, when and where people pay money these days for divination services, the church should be intervening – not with judgement, but with love and education. People use these services to seek refuge from unending grief and to quench the fire of anxiety. And whilst money is still an initiative for many who provide such services, there are some that do so out of a desire to help those who suffer.

Fig. 6 – *Appleby Horse Fair: Palmist offering psychic-related services*

Let's be clear – Gypsy churches do condemn palmistry practices and the like. However, because of the historical and familiar symbolism of palmists and clairvoyants at annual horse and trade fayres, such as Appleby, divination services remain in the community. During a (excuse the pun) spell at Appleby Horse Fair, I encountered a number of these services. Some were actively seeking business, displaying signage and advertising boards outside their caravans and trailers, whilst others gave little or no indication of any activities (spiritual or otherwise) taking place inside them. In this instance, the proprietors were 'known' by certain people and were found by word of mouth. The advertising and notices on the other trailers were bold in colour and design and perhaps more befitting of a carnival environment. One trailer, in particular (pictured above) had a board with a list of former clients who are (or were) considered to be celebrities.

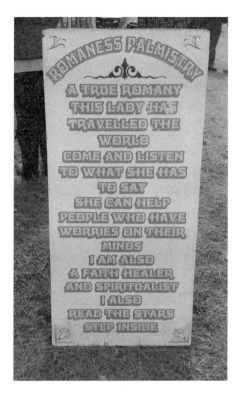

Fig. 7 – *Appleby Horse Fair: Advertising board for psychic services*

These advertising boards were used as a way of enticing more trade and to provide credibility and grandeur to the proprietor's claims of psychic abilities, however, it's fair to say that in this instance the psychic's advertising appeared outdated and potentially misleading. The names of celebrities on the boards were mostly 'character' names rather than the actual actor or performer's name – many of whom were only considered 'famous' from the 1970s to the early 1990s. It's evident that palmistry is entering its final days in the community. And whilst this may be a cause for some celebration, given the potential dangers of incorporating spiritualism within Christianity, it reminds us of two things:

First, that behind every request of a psychic reading or attempt to communicate with the dead is someone who is hurting, concerned and loved by God. As these needs are met less and less, people (and in this instance, mostly gorgers) will turn elsewhere to heal these wounds. Ecclesiologically speaking, the church must be positioned to take more seriously the concerns people hold for what comes next after this life and for their loved ones who have already made that transition. Gypsies tried to carry this message for centuries but were met with continual savagery from religious authorities that should have known and been better; from being burned as witches during the 1600s to open ridicule in the twentieth century – the response by the church and others was simply wrong.

Secondly, behind every attempted reading and communication with the dead is: someone who is in need of money and can see no other way of earning; someone who recognises the dangers but doesn't fully understand the consequences of their actions; and/or someone who genuinely means well and fully believes in their abilities and powers. Either way, in light of God, all of these reasons can be stripped away and we can simply say that behind all of these actions is a person; a person with a story; a person made in the image of God; a person just trying to figure their way through life and back to the source – just like you. I met and spoke to one of these people. A wonderful old lady named Mary whose account reminded me that behind every face is a story. Sitting down with Mary, I travelled through her life, through her pain and through her faith and her walk with God. When we condemn homeless Travellers who park their caravans on public space and village greens, we actually condemn entire families. Mary is a reminder that when we condemn those who seek comfort through different avenues, we actually condemn those who need the loving touch of God the most. Here is a snippet of my encounter with Mary.

Mary

Mary was in her late 60s. On the day we met, she wore a long detailed skirt that came to her feet, a light-coloured cardigan and large gold earrings – several in each ear. Her trailer stood out from many of the others nearby; not because it was ornate or colourful but because it was quite the opposite. Mary owned a conventional modern caravan – albeit an older model (around 20 to 30 years old), and it was showing excessive signs of wear and tear. Appleby was in some ways an opportunity for Gypsies and Travellers young and old to show off their horses, traps, trailers and vehicles. Mary appeared to intentionally buck this trend. She invited me into her trailer, asked me to take my shoes off, and then offered me a drink. As I sat listening to her talk about the weather and the 'bloody noisy kids', I took in my surroundings. Mary's caravan was fairly dark, with little by way of lighting, and drawn curtains. There were small trinkets and ornaments everywhere; many were of the Virgin Mary and some were of Christ as an infant. On the walls were pictures of Jesus, numerous crucifixes, and several mirrors – all with ornate dark cloths over them. On the table in front of me was two sets of cards, two small boxes (one about the size of a matchbox and the other big enough to fit a watch inside), and in the centre of the table was a crystal ball, perched on a black flat stand.

We started by talking about what she did (or had done) for a living. Mary explained that she no longer actively promoted her business of giving psychic readings and reading palms, but still provided the service for a charge when required. 'I got the gift from my mum. She used to read palms when my father was working away on the farms. She taught me what to see and how to listen.' 'How to listen?' I asked. 'To the dead. They talk back, you know,' she replied. Trying to be as respectful as possible, I asked if she thought such practices contradicted her Christian beliefs. Pointing over her shoulder at an ornament of the Virgin Mary, she said, 'I've prayed to Mary my whole life, and the Saints – they're dead ain't they? Praying is just talking son, it's no different with other people.' Mary explained how her late husband had always insisted that when she worked that she did so outside of the home. 'He'd say to me "I don't want none of those ghosts in here I say", and then he'd get all bothered and go out for a while.' Mary chuckled. She continued, telling me how her husband had been absent on and off for many years, before he died in a road accident.

He was a loyal man in some ways. I know he was seeing other lasses when he was on the road, but we wouldn't talk about it. I got angry one day and we had a row. I mentioned it and he answered with his fists. It happened a lot but I didn't say anything. I couldn't, could I? I wasn't able to have children. He stuck with me cos we were married and he believed there was a chance one day it might happen and he might carry on his name. It never did.

Mary's honesty surprised me. In my naivety I was expecting a spiritual show of some sort, but instead I was told about her experience of domestic abuse, married life, and the hope and disappointment in the desire to continue the family line. The old, dishevelled caravan and simple furnishings began to make sense. Mary was a widow, but she was also a Gypsy without children. She had lived alone for many years with very little family around her and as such she did not have adequate financial stability. Mary had experienced difficulty securing accommodation on officially recognised sites due to her lack of family ties, and she was too old to travel and maintain a vehicle to tow her trailer. As a result, she had been forced to settle 15 years previously and was living in social accommodation. 'My neighbours don't like me, I know they don't, because I'm a Gypsy. And I can't get onto a site. For a start there's no plots. And even if there was, unless you're known or family, you've got no chance.' 'Does anyone take care of you? Meet with you?' I asked. 'My Church does. They're wonderful people. They've been my family for a long time now. But they ain't blood. Are they? So it's not the same.'

Mary's conservative Christian core had shaped her approach and conduct through her entire life. She was able to mentally separate Church and Gypsy but not Christian and Gypsy. Her dedication to her husband was reflective of her character and beliefs. Conversely and contextually, it must be remembered that the option to leave an abusive relationship in the era when Mary was married was not as straightforward as it is currently. Additionally, there is a fundamental belief amongst many Gypsies and Travellers to honour the contract of marriage by refusing divorce at any cost. As Mary revealed, to leave a marriage is to be ostracised from the community; 'you either put up with it or leave – you might as well commit suicide'. Regarding her faith, Mary had found no contradiction between her Christian outlook and that of others. Her practice of consulting spirits was to her no different than when she prayed to Mary or the Saints. When I questioned her about aspects of reading the future through her preferred methods of the crystal ball and tarot cards, she responded by likening it to how a weatherman gives the forecast; he or she uses tools, devices or items and couples it with experience of working with probability, and then gives a prediction based upon the combination or results. Mary insisted that she was operating in the same way, albeit with assistance from 'the spirit'. 'If it was science-like, like the weatherman and his computer, then the church wouldn't have a problem would they?' I decided not to challenge her on the theological issues with that last statement. Instead, we laughed and joked a little longer, shared another tea, said a prayer, then I left.

Death and Funerals

Mary and I had discussed the nature of her trailer's decoration and her understanding of how it related to deaths and funerals in Gypsy communities. The significance of such events for GRT people cannot be overstated. Gypsy funerals draw upon a number of unique cultural sacraments, involve many symbolic elements – Christian and otherwise, and often draw relatives and friends from many parts of the country to the family in question. In the main there is a 'traditional' method of practice and course of actions.[217] At the news of a death a fire is often lit – known as a 'pit'. This fire will be tended to continuously by family members until the body is buried. Stories about the dead person will be told around the pit, informally starting the (often lengthy) 'wake', which itself will continue until a day or two after the funeral. The purpose of the pit is to simultaneously provide a light and a comfort to the spirit of the dead individual whilst also

---

[217] Dawson, 2000, pp. 14 – 22; Clark & Greenfields, 2006, pp. 45 – 48; Horne, 2014, pp. 9 – 10; Bhopal & Myers, 2008, p. 36.

serving as a method of purifying or 'cleansing' the spirit, to make it 'clean' to enter the next life.

Meanwhile, candles will be lit in the vardo (trailer, caravan) of the deceased, initially for the same purpose as the pit. The 'wake' element serves as a facility by which family and friends can gather to honour the dead, and pass on their respects (and sometimes gifts) to the family of the deceased. In a move that is sometimes deemed to be contentious by local health authorities, the body of the deceased is expected to be kept in his or her living quarters during the evening and night before the funeral. In a ritual known as a 'sitting', the deceased will be dressed in their finest clothes and jewellery, and kept in an open casket. The room in which they are kept will be dressed in white sheets, with lit candles surrounding the body. Any mirrors will be covered, and photos of the deceased will be turned away from the dead person. All family will be expected to spend some time with the deceased (even if it is only for a short moment) to pay their respects and say a few words. The purpose of the candles is both to guide the spirit of the dead person into the next life and to act as a method of purification for the spirit. The covering of mirrors and photos is a preventative tool, used to keep spirits (dead persons, malevolent spirits) from entering the physical realm. As with the pit outside, family will stay with the deceased continuously until the funeral process begins.

The funeral service usually sees otherwise conservative and 'private' members of the community express their grief in a public display of loud wailing and seemingly uncontrolled crying. This is perhaps more striking because such grief is also displayed by the men in attendance, who would otherwise find it dishonourable to cry in public. At the funeral (which is usually marked by a large procession of people and vehicles, including vans and lorries), the deceased is often buried with their valuable possessions. Traditionally their vardo would have been burnt along with their remaining possessions, but in the current era, these items are usually sold by the family. It should be noted that the deceased's items are never sold to Travellers or Gypsies, as in many instances they are considered to be both polluted and a possible conduit between the dead and the living. Keeping the dead content is a priority after the funeral, and this is marked by having elaborate and decorative gravestones and grave sites. The graves will be visited by family on a regular basis, with emphasis placed on Easter, Christmas, the deceased's birthday, and the anniversary of the death. Additionally, to prevent an arousal of the spirit (which could cause the spirit to become malevolent), often the name of the deceased will not be mentioned anymore after a day or two of the funeral; they will thusly only ever be referred to indirectly and with a prefixed condition of their name; for example, 'my poor blessed mum', or 'blessed Tony', followed by 'God love him/her'.

Funerals, in whatever community or culture we occupy, should not be considered synonymous with finality. For sure, they form the moment between the antagonistic and dichotomous alternatives of death and the afterlife, but they are not final. In fact, funerals are nothing, except a transitional acknowledgement of the journey between one existence and another. After all, when we mourn, it is only the living that continue to suffer. And if in that pain we turn to the Father with anger over the 'injustice' we have been subject to, we almost always forget that we all come from the source and that we must all return to the source, and as such, our anger is misplaced. Our time here is determined by the Father, and when He calls us home, we have no choice but to return. We who remain hurt because our loved ones leave before *we* think they should. But that is not our decision. That decision was made before we even got here. In some instances, it just wasn't someone's time. As children of God, saved by Christ, we must draw comfort from knowing that the next leg of journey, the final leg in many ways, has been reclaimed from the clutches of finality. We enter into paradise. There is nothing left to fear. Death has lost its sting (1 Corinthians 15:55).

219

FROM ONE CAMP TO THE NEXT: TOWARDS A TRAVELLER ESCHATOLOGY

The heat was oppressive, the crowded streets overwhelming, and the wounds of flagellation too much to bear. As the cross pressed Jesus into the dusty ground, Simon of Cyrene positioned himself underneath the instrument of death and took the weight upon his own shoulders. 'Not too far to go now. You're nearly there.' Jesus knew what was coming and that these were among His final moments. However, he kept pressing onward, knowing the joy that lay before Him. Simon, a stranger in the land, now so intimately and inadvertently involved in the crucifixion narrative, was as present as one can be. Every strike of the whip, every splinter from the wood, every drop of Jesus' spilt blood – he felt them all. In following the wounded Christ, he became figuratively and literally the first person to pick up his cross and follow Jesus. Simon's physical, mental, emotional and spiritual suffering collided, as he watched Jesus hobble towards the execution site. But soon, it would be over.

Partaking in Christ's *suffering* exists only here, in the present and temporal (human) form (2 Timothy 2:8 – 9; 1 John 5:13 – 14; John 3:16). The ending of said suffering and what follows next draws in two themes: Firstly, the decisive intervention by God in human history. Secondly, the 'final' condition and location of those subject to God's intervention. The intervention (or 'death') represents both a new destination and the execution and realisation of the covenantal promise. However, the eschatological process is rather uncertain and the subject of much debate and tension. A number of notable theologians (including C. H. Dodd, R. Bultmann, and Barth) propose an immediacy to anything apocalyptical in eschatology narratives. In short, anything that is going to come to some cataclysmic end in this life must have all futuristic elements (and thus any futuristic scope) eliminated. This could apply to anything from something relatively minor such as our bodies, all the way to something incredibly significant such as Christ's kingdom – the Kingdom of God. With that in mind, we see that Barth opts to take biblical eschatology and reinterpret it in the scope of *eternity*, whilst Bultmann reinterprets biblical eschatology in the scope of *humanity*. Meanwhile, in a move towards biblical historicity, Dodd proposes that the Kingdom of God had arrived with Christ's ministry and thus should be considered as 'realised eschatology'.[218] For Gypsies and Travellers, the nomadic transition continues in this equation of *human finality* and *realised eschatology*. It does this by drawing through a series of specific and culturally unique sacraments[219] – an actualisation or 'conclusion' of the passion and crucifixion elements of the Cross event. This 'movement' towards another settlement (in this instance: death; eternity; heaven; a resting place) is reminiscent of the collective procession from camp to camp.

Christ remains central to the entire process of death. This doesn't however make our metaphysical 'embrace' of the suffering of Christ redundant. Far from it. Our death (or the moment when the crucifixion is complete per se) is not the beginning of a transition into a place devoid of the Cross but rather a development and progression of the 'Cross event' metanarrative. In this way, remaining with the crucified but now resurrected Christ, the deceased partakes in *all* that Christ has to offer – through life and death, with the liberation 'prize' so to speak the partaking in the spiritual, the physical and the metaphysical resurrection. The significance being (both theologically and ecclesiologically), with particular emphasis on Gypsies and Travellers, that the Christological centring of faith becomes an example of a lived-out, revised liberation[220] narrative; 'looking to Jesus, the founder and perfecter of our faith, who for the joy that was set before him endured the cross, despising the shame, and is seated at the right hand of the throne of God' (Hebrews 12:2). In this context

---

[218] Livingstone, 2006, pp. 177 & 200.
[219] The particular sacraments in question are discussed in the previous section *'Death and Funerals'*.
[220] Liberation' in the sense of, a liberation theology.

the mirroring and witness-bearing of Christ's suffering should not be misunderstood as an extension of Christ's suffering. It is instead a liberative action by virtue of its fostering towards intimacy with Christ as opposed to an embracing of 'the world' (John 17:14; Romans 12:2). In this space the eschatological aspect of the Kingdom of God can be both realised *and* hope-filled, with a Traveller eschatology simultaneously occupying the history of the world, serving as a current event in Christian proclamation, and operating prophetically as a lens of social transfiguration. A new powerful metaphorical motif of the Gypsy clinging to the foot of the Cross provides a demonstration of the continual and corporate power of the Cross to alleviate human suffering through divine suffering in *this* life, whilst serving as a hope and a promise for the next life through the power of the resurrection. 'To return to the theology of the cross means…comprehending the crucified Christ in the light and context of his resurrection, and therefore of freedom and hope'.[221]

Nomadism continued: Journey through to the Resurrection

The nature of a hoped-for resurrection brings our attention back to the idea of perpetual movement; of a continual nomadic state. And as our suffering enters its winter, the grace that so lovingly enabled us to exist on this Earth with authenticity, now changes our focus, as we begin to look towards our resurrection and all that that may entail. What will the nature and composition of the resurrection look like, and what will the structure of said resurrection dwell in or emerge from? Heaven, the grave, something else perhaps? With some fortune, the specifically Christological question of when and how a resurrection will occur is catechised when interpreted through a lens of nomadism. This is partially owing to the perceived temporal and accessible composition of the first stage of the afterlife (1 Samuel 28:1-25; 1 Chronicles 10:13-14). In this sense, language that speaks

---

[221]   Moltmann, 2015, p. xx.

of a 'final resting place' becomes relatively unhelpful and possibly obsolete. Indeed, the centrality of the Cross event in a Traveller theology implies that the *resurrectional* element is the conclusion – not the Paschal Triduum (Matthew 12:40; Jonah 1:17; Luke 23:54 – 56; Luke 24:1) nor any conceptions of an immediate 'Heaven'.

This corresponds with N. T. Wright's exposition of the intertestamental Jewish (including Jesus') thought on death and that of the early Church, where the resurrectional element is the return or a new replacement of the body 'some time after death'; 'It is, in fact, life *after* life after death'.[222] Death, by virtue of the life *before* it and the resurrected existence *after* it, becomes a process and existence of its own. Whilst ascertaining the conditions and the makeup of the temporal sphere of death is open to many interpretations, the provision of hope for an existence in and after death is supported by numerous scriptures. And as always, hope can and often does appear in the most unlikely of places. For example, whereas many would read 1 Samuel 28:1 – 25 as a description of the forbidden interaction with those in a state of death, given the earlier parts of this chapter, it's easy to see how for some Gypsies and Travellers, such an interaction in the text both affirms the hope-filled continual process of life after the moment of death, and the taboo-nature of death in the community. Indeed, interpreting 1 Samuel 28 through Christ's eyes (as opposed to the background context of an ancient middle eastern battle) is not a green light for clairvoyance, but a reclaiming of a passage from the 'Fatherly fear' of 'don't do this', to the 'Fatherly reassurance' 'there is a place waiting for you after this world'. We all want to have reassurance of loved ones waiting for us and of a continuation of life, even if that life is markedly different from the one we currently experience. Yet once again many of us dampen our own hope by seeking confirmation of our doubts. It's no different to looking in the mirror and seeing anyone other than a beautiful, complete and fully loved child of God.

[222]   Wright, 2002, p. 619.

If you seek doubt you'll find it every time. Christ came to give us hope. If you seek hope and positivity, even in the places of condemnation, you'll change the world – you'll change *your* world.

SUMMARY

This leg of our journey began with the end of someone else's. Yet, in many ways, their journey was only just the beginning. We've spent much of this book looking at areas and themes and aspects of life that are being reclaimed and reimagined through the unlimited scope of Christ. Death is no exception; nor is the world beyond which we see yet we dwell in every day. For in the places that many 'righteous' folks readily condemn or fear to tread, are others like you and me, also seeking to traverse and navigate through life and, well, death. This principle is broad and applicable far beyond the examples seen in this chapter. Our call is to outreach, our reward is learning, and our response is and must be love.

Traversing these planes forces us to contend with the reality that we exist in different forms – flesh and spirit. Where and how those different forms exist, interact, appear and dwell are, it would seem, the subject of differing experiences. What is certain however, is that death is not final but a temporal 'act' or movement; a completion of sorts – a boarding gate between the purgatorial-esque proving ground of life and a paradise we cannot even begin to imagine. The Cross event remains central, as we witness the continual suffering of the marginalised, transformed into an event of liberation through the hope of the resurrection and the embracing of the Cross. 'Conventional' liberation theology narratives that liberate through a form of escape, are resisted. For whilst liberation can set us free from the punishment of the Cross, clinging to the feet of Christ and picking up our own cross is a road to experiencing intimacy with Christ in *this* life. In this way, death truly does lose its sting.

Light, not darkness, awaits us. Like waking from slumber and wiping away the tiredness from our eyes, so is life after this. Returning to the source of life itself, our 'rest' becomes our metamorphosis, as rest becomes restoration, and restoration becomes our next destination. A new eternal journey awaiting; a new adventure. For now, we are here. Our eschatological hope, however, is placed beyond this phase of temporality and is located in the paradoxical permanence of promised continuity, and found in the hope of a new (remade, restored and redeemed) Earth and a new Heaven, manifested in the resurrection of a new body; immortal, pure, and with Christ. This is our promise. This is our hope. This is our God.

CHAPTER ELEVEN
PACK UP AND MOVE ON: FINAL THOUGHTS

'But what about you?' he asked. 'Who do you say I am?'
(Matthew 16:15)
'May the God of endurance and encouragement grant you to live in
such harmony with one another, in accord with Christ Jesus.'
(Romans 15:5)

EARLY DAYS

Andy was a brilliant tutor with a wicked sense of humour. Messy grey hair, always wearing a tweed jacket that looked like it had seen its fair share of years, and smoking at least 30 cigarettes a day; a proud working class guy serving as a bridge to middle class possibilities. I'd returned to education as an adult to study for a diploma that would enable me to attend university. My local college was host to a mixture of similar hopefuls who wanted to better their chances in life, and a large number of younger students learning trades such as brick laying and hair dressing. Andy, my personal tutor, taught many of the subjects I studied each day. This meant that lessons and lectures often blended into each other, sewn together by Andy's amusing life stories, anecdotes and rants. On one occasion, Andy explained how he'd given a presentation at a conference at Oxford University. Oxford University?! We all sat up, eyes widened and ears twitching.

Those two words – 'Oxford' and 'University' weren't something often mentioned inside these four walls. Andy had been to, in his words, 'the hallowed and ornate halls of Oxford University'. 'But I wouldn't want to work there', he dismissively stated. 'When you're there, it's clear you're somewhere else – a different class; definitely not working class. Besides which, I don't have a doctorate. None of us have doctorates and never will. But you'll have good degrees in a couple of years, and that'll be all you need.' As I walked home that day, I couldn't shake off Andy's words. I thought to myself, 'how could *he* know whether anyone in our class (literally and figuratively) was capable or incapable of getting a doctorate?'. I stewed as I recalled his dismissal of a particular future based on who we were or were perceived to be. Someone else's experience or perception of themselves was shaping their expectations and opinions of others. It was all too familiar. Besides which, my understanding of how God saw me and knew me – despite all my faults, flaws and inadequacies, meant that if God wanted me to bloody walk down the 'hallowed halls of Oxford University', then I bloody well would. (I'm still waiting for an invite.)

Before we started off this Traveller Theology journey, we dug into the semantics of why '*Traveller*', rather than 'Gypsy' or 'Roma' or 'Showman' or a plethora of other titles. Stepping back a little, it should have been clear that the concern from the GRT community is that regardless of which ethnic identifier one uses, that there are social, political, historical and religious consequences. As a result, some people change the ethnic banner they identify under, depending on how they believe they will be perceived in a certain area or situation. However, a communal encounter with Christ in fourteenth-century Greece set into motion the true value by which the community is worth. Seven centuries of marginalisation, two hundred years of slavery, and one genocide later, and through it all and under every label Christ still remains faithful. So much so, that once Gypsies found their voice in the twentieth century, a global church movement was born.

Finding Faith

For many years, it was believed that Gypsies didn't have a recognisable religious identity. It couldn't have been further from the truth. Early gorger-written books and articles highlighted an exotic nature to GRT religious and spiritual practice, often resorting back to belittling accusations of superstitions and palmistry being the pinnacle of Gypsy faith. Such condemnation seemed a little unfair considering gorgers were almost exclusively the customers of palmistry services and probably held more superstitions *about* Gypsies than Gypsies had superstitions themselves. Thankfully, a hundred or so years after Gypsy women stopped being murdered as witches, the church in England (under a little pressure from the government) decided a more helpful approach would be to educate 'the heathen Gypsies' and convert them. For the record, this was not a more helpful approach. Granted, there were pockets of success, with the famous Rodney 'Gipsy' Smith travelling around the world leading thousands of people (predominantly gorgers) to Christ. But the Victorian billboard days of 'Come and see the Gypsy; hear him talk!' were coming to an end, and with that, the briefly trusted voices of a few key Romanies were all but lost to history.

A stirring began in 1950s France. Somewhere in the French countryside, the Gospel came to life in the Gypsy community and rapidly began spreading through the camps and lanes. Evangelical Pentecostalism was taking hold, and the result was a revival among Gypsies. The tsunami of faith was unstoppable, and over the next 40 years, its waves hit the shores of many other countries around the world. Ecumenical Gypsy networks began forming, and it wasn't long before Gypsy-led Churches and Church bodies began springing up. The Christ that had been present in GRT communities from day one was coming to the fore, boldly and powerfully. Revivals are interesting things: they're infrequent, they're often met with scepticism, they're wished for yet rarely welcomed, they're undoubtedly transformational, they serve both the people they emerge from and many people around them, and they usually only make sense after they've finished. The Gypsy revival was no different.

Realistically, the revival lasted for nearly 50 years, ending somewhere around the turn of the twenty-first century. However, its ending didn't come with a falling away or a reduction of zeal. Instead it evolved into a Mark 16:15 moment. Many Gypsies and Travellers who had rediscovered or recently encountered Christ were faced with a dilemma. The rapid growth of remote GRT Churches in the late 80s and early 90s wasn't sustainable in the face of ever-increasing political challenges to traditional Gypsy nomadism that had steadily rolled in since the 1970s. With many now living in fixed housing, Gypsy and Traveller Christians spread into the wider gorger Church network, taking pews in every denomination in the land. There was, however, a trade off. In exchange for the GRT fervour of faith, generosity of person, and evangelical persuasion, was the acceptance of the receiving church's doctrines and dogma. Whereas this was still mostly a 'safe' trade off and an opportunity for personal and religious growth, it came with the risk of diluting the unique ethnic qualities of the new Church member. The risk was real but the benefits to both Gypsy and non-Gypsy cultures was immense. Integration was the hope; assimilation was the fear. There's a lesson in there: If you have a person or family from a distinct minority or marginalised collective join your congregation, remember that other than loving on them, God has most likely sent them to you to add to the tapestry of your Church. So, listen to them, get to know them, proudly and excitedly introduce them to the Church, and learn from their experience with God's creation.

ON THE ROAD

In 2017, a tragedy happened in London when 72 people died as a result of a fire in a residential block of flats named Grenfell Tower. Many in the tower were impoverished, unable to convey the position of their social and financial destitution among the incredible wealth that surrounded them. Survival meant ensuring the next meal arrived. Surviving was never meant to be defined by the ability to escape a towering inferno. Beyond this, even the language highlights the disparity of difference under our very noses. Who could even begin to fathom that in twenty-first century England there are people having to 'survive'? Yet there are many under this banner, dwelling in the Edgelands of so-called civilised society. In the instance of the Grenfell tragedy, it was physically among many other communities. In the instance of Gypsies and Travellers, often it is often geographically at the physical margins of our communities. There are some historical and indeed theological reasons for this phenomenon and they are discussed in this book. However, there can be no doubts that the social, political and religious responses have collectively bought us to this position of the included and the excluded. And behind each of those 'responses' are fellow humans, like you and me; we are all responsible.

Transgressions – Real and Imagined

Still, we will offer opinion. Sometimes the privilege of knowing how to wield a pen or construct a verse in public leads us to believe that we are both kind and virtuous in what we say and think. But until our intentions are in alignment with the manifest realities of our neighbour's suffering, we are but proud peacocks with good intentions. If fear is holding you back from getting dirt under your nails, pray for courage. Have you ever been to a Traveller site or inside the home of a Gypsy or Roma person? For a very small number of you, that answer will be yes. For many however, the closest you will have knowingly come would be either incidentally or accidentally passing by a site, or seeing images on a television programme or newspaper. Yet, despite this lack of tangible engagement, it seems that so many are able to describe with visceral detail the fallibility and faults of an entire ethnic group. Lack of knowledge creates fear, and fear fuels fantasy – it's the very embodiment of anxiety. As a result, mislabelling, misconceptions, multifaceted oppression, covert and overt racism, unwarranted hatred, demonization, murder and even capital punishment have been some of the responses towards GRT people the world over.

Early on, this book attempted to bring some light to areas that are often avoided or glanced over, namely under the banner of 'sin'. When communities, particular races and minority groups are ostracised, a common yet sinister parasite is almost always present, in the form of stereotyping. Often, the best method in dealing with stereotypes is to simply ignore the narrative and place any and all value judgements through a lens of objectivity and compassion. If action is needed, it will soon make itself known. Sometimes, however, addressing accusations head-on allows for a healthy negotiation to take place, where theological deconstructionism offers an interpretation of praxis. In this instance, the dichotomous alternatives were either the creation of an apologetics, which is essentially like saying, 'You know all those horrid accusations that you made? Well, they're all true but this is why they happened.' Or, the other option, was the total avoidance of talking about sin in the community – alleged or otherwise. But this creates further issues; firstly, by effectively denying that within minority communities that there are any problems; and secondly, by missing the opportunity to dissect and examine what constitutes sin in the community and how it is understood and treated. God calls us to go into all the world – that includes the parts that don't look or feel good. However, it's in those parts that we often find glimmers of hope and something worth fighting for. In this instance, that glimmering object was the purity code.

Clean and Unclean

Mokhhadi is a seldom-used term and any talk about its application or absence is often equally as scarce. However, the idea of *mokhhadi* – of 'pure' and 'impure', of 'proper' and 'taboo', of 'acceptable' and unacceptable', is an intrinsic vascular system that has been present in most of GRT culture since its inception. As part of the reclamation and salvaging process that we have taken in this theological journey, it made sense to sharpen the direction of these terms that clearly lean towards right and wrong, and reimagine them in their present context, rather than their somewhat pan-Hindu origins and Middle-Age application. As such, terms such as 'blessing', 'curse', 'virtue' and 'sin' become helpful ways to understand and expand the conversation around *mokhhadi*. The result of course, is that Christ's implicit invitation into GRT ideological praxis becomes explicit, providing a synchronicity between the Gypsy adoption of Christianity during the early days of the diaspora and the twentieth-century 'baptism' in France and Europe.

With the idea of clean and unclean, we are immediately confronted with the concept of separation, distinctiveness and different worlds. This concept is of course universal, stretching far beyond just the world of Gypsies and Travellers. Indeed, as children of God, we are called to be in the world but not of it; we are set apart. Our duty however, as Christians, is to remember that everyone around us are also children of God, and that the Father waits for them with open arms in anticipation of their return. He loves them as much as He favours us. In the instance of GRT people, I introduced the comparison to the 'mulatto' – the 'less than', the 'white other'. When we see or speak of others who are not like us, who dwell in the Edgelands, we must be careful that we do not place ourselves on pedestals, riding waves of superiority bolstered by the belief that we occupy a higher class, possess a greater intelligence, and practise a superior ideal. There is no discrimination towards us from the grace that breathed life into our lungs or the decay that consumes the dead. Why then should we feel it is right to place ourselves above anyone else? Love is powerful because it unifies through the struggle of difference. Love is powerful because it respects borders but overcomes barriers. Love is powerful because it purposively moves between our islands of difference, never remaining static but always transitioning one God-inspired symphony and the next. Love and life are movement.

Restless Feet

'There's some Travellers just turned up on the green near the pub. Do you reckon they'd be offended if I went to ask if they need anything? The other locals are being a bit crappy to them.' The phone call from a dear friend was not the first of its kind that I'd received in the past. Requests asking for advice had arrived in many shapes and sizes from numerous acquaintances over the past few years, most often from teachers who'd had Traveller children join their class, but calls of this nature were reasonably rare. Contrary to populist belief, Travellers parking up and setting up home on private or public land doesn't happen much these days, and as discussed in this book, those that do only represent a very small number of GRT people; GRT people who are officially homeless and often extremely vulnerable. Moreover, it is an explicit demonstration of an historical cultural norm of nomadism that in itself is indicative of a collective *movement* reaching far beyond what the eye can see, seeping into the depths of values, beliefs, ideology, and faith. Nomadism in GRT culture signals so much more than simply physically moving from one place to another.

Our journey through this life is just that – a journey. That journey can never be merely metaphorical, nor can it be halted, paused or reversed. Regardless of our relationship with life, we are all either moving towards, travelling away, or waiting for something to arrive. At times this movement is recognisable through our work, as we see in the motif of the sojourner. At other times it is observable through our relationships, through the process of ageing, through our understanding and through our walk of faith. We are all sojourners in one way or another, taking the purposeful movement of our mind, our flesh and our spirit and rehoming them in new and evolving stages in the arena of our life. Of course, there is rest in and amongst the permanent impermanence; tired feet and weary minds require recuperation, and even God took at least one day off a week. If we yearn for stillness, we must remember that we must rest in God, within whom that stillness is made manifest. For in the eternal nature of God, the idea of 'never-ending' has to eventually be brought to nought; it is there and only there that whilst we occupy this mortal coil can we truly experience stillness. For now however, when God instructs us to be still (Psalm 46:10), it is not a direction to cease movement but an instruction for our hearts to be calm amidst the enemies and stresses of this world. For many of us, that rest tangibly takes place in our houses, our homes, our camps.

God among Us

Paradoxically, it's in and around the home that we become aware of the nomadic nature of our existence, which is most often seen through our presentation or 'performance'. Performance, in the Christian Traveller or Gypsy sense, could be the cleaning of the home, the preparation of the property, the dressing of the entrance and garden, the exuberant dress, or a myriad of other things. When understood through the liturgical nature of a lived-out Christianity, these performative elements become symbolic, and, at least in its contemporary guise, the place where the motif of nomadism is best found. For *all* of us, it is the home that becomes the dwelling place for the Divine; for whilst the Church hosts worship, it is the home that hosts life.

Movement and purity continue to be the undercurrents to the home. For many of us, the closest we get to speaking to the transitional nature of lives in our homes is through doors and coats by the doorway, passports in the drawer, suitcases in the loft, and a car on the driveway. For *some* Gypsies and Travellers however, this is escalated somewhat, with horse traps and carts outside, and one's accommodation being a mobile home or caravan. Still, in many ways the physical nature of the home environment is way down the list, so to speak, compared to the 'home' in which God is welcomed. For God doesn't discriminate; God is as much at home in the homeless as He is among the wealthy. Through our possessions and our environment, we have the opportunity to welcome, acknowledge and worship the Creator. But in our bodies, our minds, and indeed our lives, we are able to take that one step further and hand them over to God. This point was made a little more explicit through the 'Mosaic Camp' analogy that I introduced. Through the Gypsy and Traveller camp, the intentionality of worship in the mediums described above move from implicit to explicit. Where we make that transition and to what degree is up to us; that is, until we realise that we were never able to give back to God what was His in the first place. We may go through many transitions in our lives – from childhood to old age, from unskilled to skilled, and from marriage to divorce. But the most important transition we will ever be on, is the journey from God and back again.

How we navigate that journey is in-part dependent upon the world we create and occupy and the realities of existence – existence that is acknowledged, understood or otherwise. At times, negotiation between ourselves and God will take place through prayer, whilst at other times our spirits will stir because of a movie we've just watched or a book we have read. Our 'things' therefore become, or at least have the potential to become, channels through which we experience God. Chalices, patens, and altar cloths are replaced by photos, ornaments and decoration, whilst hymns and sermons present themselves through our language and our communication with the wider world. These symbols and conduits help in understanding ourselves and others, and more widely our position among *all* of creation – both our present 'material' condition and time beyond time. It is beyond the material that we truly occupy; much of the rest – our worries, our possessions, and our infirmities are, as Thomas Aquinas would say, just straw. Beyond that beginning and past that end is the Father, with creation occupying the centre, held tightly in His hands. Our time in His hands is His time, and the time of the eternal is no time at all.

THIS IS WHO WE ARE

'I'm so rubbish at History though, I'm definitely going to mess this up and be in trouble with the teacher.' My daughter who was about halfway through her first year at secondary (High) school, was panicking a little about a homework project due the next day. Knowing that she'd had the whole of the half term holiday in which to complete the work, I attempted to relieve the tension with some first-class dad-joke humour. 'It's okay beautiful, you don't need to worry about history – it's all in the past.' Naturally, I immediately laughed out loud in a self-congratulatory manner at my comedic contribution. 'You get it? History, it's in the past. Cos, you know, it's gone, and …' She just glared at me, seemingly, I assume, because my lighting quick response was so amazing it had warped her mind. Either way, her predicament highlighted a fundamental point in our human condition: how we remember and understand the past can and does affect our present. But unlike my daughter's history homework, our past isn't merely and abstractly located in some ancient or mediaeval period; our past is often within touching distance, just beyond our immediate memory like the dream we scratch and claw to remember upon waking but never fully grasp. Going a little beyond that, we sometimes find ourselves living in the past of our parents and grandparents, mimicking their behaviours and values, nursing and rehearsing their pasts, and living their truths. And all this with very little in the way of questioning why we hold these truths to be our own.

Discovering, realising, or unearthing truths can often be uncomfortable but is always beneficial. The refining fire of honesty allows for a deconstruction of the unhelpful narrative of exclusivism that permeates many cultures, groups of people, and religious and social ideas, and with that comes new life and new opportunities. In the instance of this book, that journey of refining went down the route of challenging the concepts of pure lineage and 'pure Gypsy blood'; concepts that were created by people beyond the camp walls, much to the detriment of many inside those walls. I proposed that the fallibility of pure bloodlines and lineage could be recovered, reclaimed and repurposed by embracing the ultimate reality of those bloodlines: foundations and heritage exist by, through and because of the *grace* of God. In this way, those at the margins of society, or even those at the margins of the margins – the mulatto and the didikais, are rightfully understood as complete, as valid, as equal and as loved as anyone and anything else in God's creation.

Heartbeats and Silence

Our entire God-experience (or life), revolves in and around Christ. Not just our heritage, but our identity – Christian and cultural. Everything is in relation to Him. Everything. But we do not get to pick and choose the terms of that relationship: We are called to pick up our cross every day, and in doing so, we accept both the affectionate characters of grace and salvation alongside participation in the brutality of the crucifixion and the process of atonement. In clinging to the cross of the crucified Jesus, we are able to endure the suffering of attachment in this life and look with hope towards the resurrection in the next. It's Christ who is our centre and by whom the pains of death and the despair in suffering are dissolved. Christ not only redeems our past but He secures our future, reclaiming our eternal lives from what the thief has stolen and what rust and moths have destroyed (Matthew 6:19-21). For Heaven is a kingdom that is at hand and salvation is for the present. And so in the chaos of our temporal storm, Christ serves as our anchor, for both individuals and entire communities. Christ does what Christ does; reaching into the material with His outstretched arms, saving the lost, the vulnerable, the widow, the refugee, the poor, the destitute, the lost and the hurting. A little over 700 years ago, Christ did the same thing for a wandering people fleeing war and searching for hope. Salvation came then; redemption comes now.

However, the journey, for *all* of us, continues. For so long in the developed world we have feared death and hidden the eyes of our mind's attention from both death and its inevitable arrival. Make no mistake – many rightfully have some concern and apprehension about the closing of the door to this life. Fear of the unknown grips all of us at different points; from our first flight in a plane, to saying 'I do' to a proposal. Not knowing what is beyond that which we currently experience is scary; so much so that it has become a taboo in the Western world. Within the Gypsy and Traveller world, whilst natural human fears remain, death is not a taboo but rather is the subject to multiple taboos. Its grip has been weakened, and rather than being a 'thing', it has become a transitional 'moment', forcing the question – death, where is your sting? (1 Corinthians 15:55). Death is only a problem for the living. The silence of absent loved ones leaves us with the pain of grief – a pain which only we the mortal living suffer. Those who no longer suffer with us, journey onward, returning to the source and being made whole. It is *us* the living that should rest in peace, whilst our dearly departed rise in glory. We were made through Him and by Him, and it is to Him we return.

Time for Bed; We've got an Early Start

There'll be no more tea tonight; the fire has reduced to a dimming bed of coals and its heat has left us for another day. We've had a long day and we've told many a story. Stories that need to be heard; some old, some new. But the good thing with stories you see, is that you can give them away as many times as you like and yet they'll always stay with you. Our story started out about a Father who heard His children cry and who cried for His children. When He spoke to us all those years ago, He gave us a love letter. How extravagant and marvellous and detailed must this letter be! We could barely contain our excitement. But when we opened the letter, all it said inside was 'Jesus'. 'Look a little closer', He said. Between each letter was a small mirror; so small that we could only see ourselves in the reflection. We all tried to look in them at the same time, but to no avail. We had to take turns to share with the others what we could see. With that, the Father smiled, gently placed His hand on our shoulder and said, 'I'll be waiting for you'. It dawned on us; 'Jesus' wasn't the story – Jesus was the author. *We* were and are the story. He wrote it *all* for us. And just like the little mirrors, every chapter and every paragraph and every line, we could see Him looking back at us. Through our torment, He held us in His fatherly arms. In our crying out, His Spirit ministered to us and wiped away every tear. And in our joy and our communion with one another, He sat there, eating with us. Our past was His past; our history was His story; and our life was and is His life. We go from Him and return to Him. Always travelling, always moving camp, always ready to hit the road again. With the wind behind us and the Son in front of us, we journey onwards. For who knows what adventures lay just beyond that hill and what stories await us. Stories of hope, stories of a future. A good story. A Traveller story.

BIBLIOGRAPHY

WORKS CITED

Acton, T. (1974) *Gypsy Politics and Social Change: The Development of Ethnic Ideology and Pressure Politics among British Gypsies from Victorian Reformism to Romany Nationalism*. London: Routledge.

Acton, T. (Ed. S. Cranford) (1979) 'The Gypsy Evangelical Church', in *The Ecumenical Review (Journal of The World Council of Churches)*, Vol. 31 (No. 3), pp. 11 – 17.

Acton, T. (2017) 'The European Forgettory: The Deconstruction of Forgetfulness. The Historian's Contribution to Breaking the Cycles of History', in Buchsbaum. T and Kapralski. S, (Eds.) *'Beyond the Roma Holocaust: From Resistance to Mobilisation'*. Krakow, Poland: The Universitas Society of Scientific Papers Authors and Publishers.

Antonio, E. (2012) 'Black Theology and Liberation Theologies', in Antonio, E. and Hopkins, D. (Eds.) *The Cambridge Companion to Black theology*. Cambridge: Cambridge University Press.

Atkin, A. (2014) *The Philosophy of Race*. Abingdon, Oxon: Routledge.

Bantum, B. (2010) *Redeeming Mulatto: A Theology of Race and Hybridity*. Waco, Texas: Baylor University Press.

Barber, D. (2007) 'The Particularity of Jesus and the Time of the Kingdom: Philosophy and Theology in Yoder', in *Modern Theology*, Vol. 23 (No. 1), pp. 63 – 89 (Accessed 04/02/17). Available at: http://onlinelibrary.wiley.com/doi/10.1111/j.1468-0025.2007.00353.x/pdf.

Barth, F. (1969) 'Introduction', in Barth, F. (Ed.) *Ethnic Groups and Boundaries: The Social Organisation of Cultural Difference*. Boston: Waveland Press.

Beckford, R. (1998) *Jesus is Dread: Black Theology and Black Culture in Britain*. London: Darton, Longman and Todd.

Bhopal, K. and Myers, M. (2008) *Insiders, Outsiders and Others: Gypsies and Identity*. Hatfield: University of Hertfordshire.

Bourdieu, P. (1989) 'Social Space and Symbolic Power', in *Sociological Theory*, Vol. 7 (No. 1), pp. 14 – 25 (Accessed 24/01/17). Available at: http://www.soc.ucsb.edu/ct/pages/JWM/Syllabi/Bourdieu/SocSpace SPowr.pdf.

Bultmann, R. and Ogden, S. (Ed) (1989) *New Testament Mythology and Other Basic Writings*. Philadelphia, US: Fortress Press.

Burns, J. and Newman, C. (2012) *Romans: Interpreted by Early Christian Commentators*. Cambridge: Wm. B. Eerdmans Publishing Co.

Calvin, J. (1848) *Commentaries on the First Book of Moses called Genesis: By John Calvin*. Edinburgh: The Edinburgh Printing Company.

Cameron, J. (2014) *Racism and Hate: An American Reality*. Bloomington, IN: AuthorHouse LLC.

Carrizo-Reimann, A. (2011) 'The Forgotten Children of Abraham: Iglesia Evangelica Misionera Biblica Rom of Buenos Aires', in *Romani Studies*, Vol. 21 (No. 2), pp. 161 – 176. Liverpool: Liverpool University Press.

Cheng, P. (2011) *An Introduction to Queer Theology: Radical Love*. New York: Seabury Books.

Clark, C. and Greenfields, M. (2006) *Here to Stay: The Gypsies and Travellers of Britain*. Hatfield: University of Hertfordshire Press.

Cone, J. (1986) *A Black Theology of Liberation*. New York: Orbis Books.

Crawley, H. (2004) *Moving Forward: The provision of accommodation for Travellers and Gypsies.* London: IPPR.

Dawson, R. (2000) *Gypsy Codes and Taboo.* Derbyshire: Blackwell Publishing.

DfES. (2003) *Aiming High: Raising the Achievement of Gypsy Traveller Pupils.* Nottingham: DfES Publications.

Dingwall, B. (2015) '*Travellers Fight Back at Council*' [Image] (Accessed 02/01/17). Available at: https://www.pressandjournal.co.uk/fp/news/aberdeen/714510/travellers-fight-back-at-council-bid-to-kick-them-off-aberdeenshire-camp/.

Donaldson, L. (2015) 'When the Media Misrepresents Black Men, the Effects are Felt in the Real World', in *The Guardian* (Accessed 10/02/16). Available at: http://www.theguardian.com/commentisfree/2015/aug/12/media-misrepresents-black-men-effects-felt-real-world.

Douglas, M. (1966) *Purity and Danger: An Analysis of the Concepts of Pollution and Taboo.* London: Routledge.

Enz, M. (2006) 'The Mulatto as Island and the Island as Mulatto in Alexandre Dumas's Georges', in *The French Review*, Vol. 80 (No. 2), pp. 383 – 394 (Accessed 08/07/16). Available at: http://www.jstor.org/stable/25480659.

Fagge, N. (2011) '*Travellers' Real Homes are Back in Ireland*' [Image] (Accessed 02/01/17). Available at: http://www.dailymail.co.uk/news/article-2038299/Dale-Farm-eviction-Travellers-homes-Ireland-NOT-homeless.html.

Farmer, P. (2013) *In the Company of the Poor: Conversations between Dr Paul Farmer and Father Gustavo Gutiérrez.* New York: Orbis Books.

Fraser, A. (1995) *The Gypsies (2nd Edition).* Oxford: Blackwell Publishing.

243

G4S / HMPS. (2016) 'On Road: A Celebration of GRT writing From HMP/YOI Parc' (Accessed 25/01/17). No publisher. Available at: http://www.g4s.uk.com/~/media/Files/United%20Kingdom/CSR %20content/On%20Road%20-%20A%20Celebration%20of%20 GRT%20writing.pdf.

Gheorghe, N. (1999) 'The Social Construction of Romani Identity', in Acton, T. (Ed.) Gypsy Politics and Traveller Identity. Hertfordshire: University of Hertfordshire Press.

Haigh, C. (2006). 'The King's Reformation: Henry VIII and the Remaking of the English Church'. The English Historical Review, **Vol.** CXXI (No. 494), pp. 1455 – 1457. Oxford Journals On-Line (Accessed 20/10/14). Available at: http://ehr.oxfordjournals.org/content/CXXI/ 494/1455.full.pdf+html.

Hancock, I. (2000) 'Standardisation and Ethnic Defence in Emergent Non-Literate Societies: The Gypsy and Caribbean Cases', in Acton, T. and Dalphinis, M. (Eds.) Language, Blacks and Gypsies. London: Whiting and Birch.

Hancock, I. (2001) 'The Romani Element in Non-Standard Speech by Yaron Matras. Review by: Ian Hancock'. Anthropological Linguistics, Vol. 43 (No. 4), pp. 515 – 519. JSTOR On-Line (Accessed 08/10/14). Available at: http://www.jstor.org/stable/30028817.

Hancock, I. (2013) We are the Romani People. Hatfield: University of Hertfordshire Press.

Horne, S. (2014) 'What Travellers Believe and Why it Matters to the Church and Educational Providers', BA (Hons), Unpublished· Canterbury Christ Church University.

Horne, S. (2019) Gypsies and Travellers: A Teacher's Guide. Bedford, England: Amazon Publishing.

Horne, S. (2019) 'Cerefino Giminéz Malla: Gypsy Saint – Christian

Martyr', in Prentis, S. (Ed.) *Every Tribe: Stories of Diverse Saints Serving a Diverse World*. London: SPCK Publishing.

Howitt, D. (1986) *The Mass Media and Social Problems*. Oxford: Pergamon Press.

Kee, A. (2008) *The Rise and Demise of Black Theology*. London: SCM Press.

Keet-Black, J. (2013) *Gypsies of Britain*. Oxford: Shire Publications.

Knapton, S. (2015) 'My Big Fat Gypsy Wedding was Accurate Portrayal of Gypsy Life, High Court Rules', in *The Telegraph Online* (Accessed 04/03/17). Available at: http://www.telegraph.co.uk/news/uknews/law-and-order/11425292/My-Big-Fat-Gypsy-Wedding-was-accurate-portrayal-of-gypsy-life-High-Court-rules.html.

Lazell, D. (1970) *From the Forest I Came: The Story of Gipsy Rodney Smith M.B.E.* London: Concordia Press.

Lee, R. (2001) 'The Rom-Vlach Gypsies and the Kris-Romani', in Weyrauch, W. (Ed.) *Gypsy Law: Romani Legal Traditions and Culture*. London: University of California Press.

Lewis, C.S. (2012) *Mere Christianity*. London: Collins.

Liégeois, J-P. and Gheorghe, N (1995) *Roma / Gypsies: A European Minority*. London: Minority Rights Group.

Livingstone, E. (2006) *Oxford Concise Dictionary of the Christian Church*. Oxford: Oxford University Press.

Locke, S. (1997) *Travelling Light: The Remarkable Story of Gypsy Revival*. London: Hodder and Stoughton Religious.

Martin, C. (2008) 'Television Media as a Potential Negative Factor in the Racial Identity Development of African American Youth', in *Academic Psychiatry*, Vol. 32 (No. 4), pp. 338 – 342. Psychiatry On-Line

(Accessed 09/02/16). Available at: http://search.proquest.com/openvi ew/2074515cbbc80b67ff79891271096f07/1?pq-origsite=gscholar.

Maslow, A. (1943) 'A Theory of Human Motivation', in *Psychological Review*, Vol. 50 (No. 4), pp. 370 – 396 (Accessed 01/04/16). Available at: http://www.researchhistory.org/2012/06/16/maslows-hierarchy-of-needs/.

Mayall, D. (1988) *Gypsy-travellers in Nineteenth-century Society.* Cambridge: Cambridge University Press.

Maximoff, M. (1965) 'The Evangelical Gypsies in France', in *Journal of the Gypsy Lore Society*, 3rd Series (XLIV).

McFarlan, D. (2003) *Dictionary of the Bible.* New Lanark: Geddes and Grosset.

McGrath, A. (2011) *Christian Theology: An Introduction 5th edition.* Oxford: Wiley-Blackwell.

McVeigh, R. (1997) 'Theorising Sedentarism: The Roots of Anti-Nomadism', in Acton, T. (Ed.) *Gypsy Politics and Traveller Identity.* Hatfield: University of Hertfordshire Press.

Merz, A. and Theissen, G. (1999) *The Historical Jesus: A Comprehensive Guide.* London: SCM Press.

Moltmann, J. (2004) *The Coming of God: Christian Eschatology.* Minneapolis, MN: Augsburg Fortress.

Moltmann, J. (2015). *The Crucified God (2nd Edition).* London: SCM Press.

Moschella, M. (2016) *Caring for Joy: Narrative, Theology, and Practice.* Boston, US: Brill Publishers.

Muncey, T. (2010) *Creating Autoethnographies.* London: SAGE Publications.

National Council of Churches (1998) *The Holy Bible: New Revised Standard Version (Cross-Referenced Edition)*. Collins, London.

Okely, J. (1998) *The Traveller-Gypsies*. Cambridge: Cambridge University Press.

Pawson, D. (2007) *Unlocking the Bible*. London: HarperCollins Publishers.

Pickering, W. (2009) *Durkheim's Sociology of Religion: Themes and Theories*. Cambridge: James Clarke and Co Ltd.

Pym, R. (2004) 'The Pariah Within: Early Modern Spain's Gypsies', in *The Journal of Romance Studies*, Vol. 4 (No. 2), pp. 21 – 35. Oxford: Berghahn Journals.

Rapport, F., Wainwright, P., and Elwyn, G. (2005) 'Of the Edgelands: Broadening the Scope of Qualitative Methodology', in *Medical Humanities*, Vol. 31 (No. 1), pp. 37 – 43 (Accessed 01/10/17). Available at: http://mh.bmj.com/content/31/1/37.long.

Richardson, J. and Ryder, A. (2012) *Gypsies and Travellers: Empowerment and Inclusion in British Society*. Bristol: The Policy Press.

Ridley, L. (2014) 'Meet the Born-Again Christian Gypsy Leading a Cultural Revolution', in *The Huffington Post UK Edition* (Accessed on 01/11/15). Available at: http://www.huffingtonpost.co.uk/2014/10/30/gypsy-church-light-and-life-jackie-boyd_n_6075434.html.

Schechner, R. (2006) *Performance Studies: An Introduction (2ⁿᵈ Edition)*. London: Routledge.

Shirley, J. (1968) *A Parisian Journal, 1405 – 1449*. Oxford: Oxford University Press.

Shoard, M. (2002) 'Edgelands', in Jenkins, J. (Ed.) *Remaking the Landscape: The Changing Face of Britain*. London: Profile Books.

Silverman, C. (1988) 'Negotiating "Gypsiness": Strategy in Context', in *The Journal of American Folklore*, Vol. 101 (No. 401), pp. 261 – 275. JSTOR (Accessed 04/03/20). Available at: https://www.jstor.org/stable/540467?seq=14#metadata_info_tab_contents.

Siu, P. (1952) 'The Sojourner', in *American Journal of Sociology*, Vol. 58 (No. 1), pp. 34 – 44. JSTOR (Accessed 16/02/15). Available at: http://www.jstor.org/stable/2771791?seq=1#page_scan_tab_contents.

Spurgeon, C. (1890) 'Camp Law and Camp Life', in *The Metropolitan Tabernacle Pulpit*, Vol. 36 (No. 2177). Spurgeon Gems (Accessed 25/08/15). Available at: http://www.spurgeongems.org/vols34-36/chs2177.pdf.

Taylor, B. (2008) *A Minority and the State: Travellers in Britain in the Twentieth Century*. Manchester: Manchester University Press.

Taylor, B. (2014) *Another Darkness, Another Dawn: A History of Gypsies, Roma and Travellers*. London: Reaktion Books.

Tomlinson, S. (2012) '*The Gipsy Family who Made £2million*' [Image] (Accessed 02/01/17). Available at: http://www.dailymail.co.uk/news/article-2153331/Ringleader-traveller-gang-600-000-tax-benefits-scam-jailed-years.html.

Trigg, E. B. (1968) 'Religion and Social Reform among the Gypsies of Britain', in *Journal of the Gypsy Lore Society*, Volume XLVII (Third Series, No. 3 – 4), pp. 82 – 109.

Trigg, E. B. (1973) *Gypsy Demons and Divinities: The Magical and Supernatural Practices of the Gypsies*. London: Sheldon Press.

Twiss, R. (2015) *Rescuing the Gospel from the Cowboys*. Downers Grove, IL: InterVarsity Press.

University of Nottingham. (2014) *Philosophical and Theological Anthropology in the 21st Century – with Professor Charles Taylor (Part*

One) (Accessed 03/02/17). Available at: https://www.youtube.com/watch?v=fd9434IaYno.

University of Nottingham. (2014) *Philosophical and Theological Anthropology in the 21st Century – with Professor Charles Taylor (Part Two)* (Accessed 03/02/17). Available at: https://www.youtube.com/watch?v=xXyqMb0ocXI.

Volf, M. (1996) *Exclusion and Embrace*. Nashville, TN: Abingdon Press.

Walcott, D. (1974) 'The Muse is History', in Coombs, O. (Ed.) *Is Massa Dead? Black Moods in the Caribbean*. New York: Doubleday and Company.

Walls, A. (1998) 'Christianity', in Hinnells, J. (Ed.) *The New Penguin Handbook of Living Religions*. London: Penguin Books.

Watson, N. (2003) *Feminist Theology*. Cambridge: Eerdmans.

Weaver, D. (2001) 'How Sin Works', in *Journal of Religious Ethics*, Vol. 29 (No. 3), pp. 473 – 501. JSTOR (Accessed 30/09/15). Available at: http://goo.gl/m587Zy.

Webster, J. (1995) *Barth's Ethics of Reconciliation*. Cambridge: Cambridge University Press.

West, C. (2001) *Race Matters*. New York: Vintage Books.

White, J. (2003) *Campbell Bunk: The Worst Street in North London between the Wars*. London: Pimlico.

Wright, N.T. (2002) 'Jesus' Resurrection and Christian Origins', in *Gregorianum*, Vol. 83 (No. 4), pp. 615 – 635. JSTOR (Accessed 20/05/17). Available at: http://www.jstor.org/stable/23581348?seq=5#page_scan_tab_contents.

WORKS CONSULTED

Acton, T. (1971) 'The Functions of the Avoidance of Moxadi Kovels (amongst Gypsies in South Essex)', in *Journal of the Gypsy Lore Society*, Series III, Vol. 50 (No. 3), pp. 108 – 136.

Acton, T. and Mundy, G. (1999) *Romani Culture and Gypsy Identity*. Hertfordshire: University of Hertfordshire Press.

Acton, T.; Caffrey, S.; Dunn, S.; Vinson, P. (1999) 'Gender Issues in Accounts of Gypsy Health and Hygiene as Discourse of Social Control', in Acton, T. and Mundy, G. (Eds.) *Romani Culture and Gypsy Identity*. Hertfordshire: University of Hertfordshire Press.

Bantum, B. (2016) *The Death of Race: Building a New Christianity in a Racial World*. Minneapolis, MN: Fortress Press.

Barth, K. (1933) *The Epistle to the Romans*. Oxford: Oxford University Press.

Bauckham, R. (2006) *The Theology of Jürgen Moltmann*. London: T&T Clark.

Cone, J. (1969) *Black Theology and Black Power*. New York: Harper & Row.

Dillmann, A. (1905) *Gypsy book: Issued for Official Gebrauche on behalf of KB Ministry of the Interior by the Security Bureau of the Police Directorate K. München*. Munich: Munich Wild.

Easton, B. (1893) 'Stranger and Sojourner (In the Apocrypha and the New Testament)', in *Bible Hub* (Accessed 02/04/15). Available at: http://biblehub.com/topical/s/stranger.htm.

Ekblad, B. (2005) *Reading the Bible with the Damned*. London: Westminster John Knox Press.

Ekblad, B. (2011) 'Reading Scripture for Good News that Crosses

Barriers of Race/Ethnicity, Class, and Culture', in *Interpretation: A Journal of Bible and Theology*, Vol. 65 (No. 3), pp. 229 – 248. SAGE (Accessed 10/12/15). Available at: http://journals.sagepub.com/doi/abs/10.1177/002096431106500302.

Gockel, M. (2017) 'Constructive Theology, the Cross of Christ, and the Praxis of Liberation', in *Dialog: A Journal of Theology*, Vol. 56 (No. 3), pp. 238 – 232 (Accessed 01/08/17). Available at: http://onlinelibrary.wiley.com/doi/10.1111/dial.12333/pdf.

Gutierrez, G. (1973) *A Theology of Liberation*. New York: Orbis Books.

Izuzquiza, D. (2009) *Rooted in Jesus Christ: Toward a Radical Ecclesiology*. Cambridge: Wm. B. Eerdmans Publishing.

Kenrick, D. and Puxon, G. (2009) *Gypsies under the Swastika*. Hatfield: University of Hertfordshire Press.

Klappert, B. (1971) *The Resurrection of the Crucified*. Neukirchen-Vluyn, Germany: Neukirchen Publishing House.

Liégeois, J-P. (1994) *Roma, Gypsies, Travellers*. Strasbourg: Council of Europe Press.

Moltmann, J. (2000) *The Trinity and the Kingdom of God: The Doctrine of God*. London: SCM Press.

Moltmann, J. (2002) *Theology of Hope*. London: SCM Press.

Nouwen, H. (2010) *The Wounded Healer*. London: Darton, Longman and Todd.

Oppenheimer, H. (1983) *The Hope of Happiness*. London: SCM.

Pannenberg, W. (1998) *Systematic Theology: Volume Three*. Edinburgh: T&T Clark.

Pannenberg, W. (2004) *Anthropology in Theological Perspective*. London: T&T Clark International.

Pinn, A. (1995) *Why, Lord?: Suffering and Evil in Black Theology*. New York: Continuum International Publishing Group.

Pinn, A. (2003) *Terror and Triumph: The Nature of Black Religion*. Minneapolis, US: Fortress Press.

Rahner, K. (1966) *Theological Investigations: Volume Four*. London: Darton, Longman and Todd.

Rawls, J. (1971) *A Theory of Justice*. Cambridge: Harvard University Press.

Reid, W. (1997) 'Scottish Gypsies / Travellers and the Folklorists', in Acton, T. & Mundy, G. (Eds.) *Romani Culture and Gypsy Identity*. Hatfield, Herts: University of Hertfordshire Press.

Ridholls, J. (1986) *Travelling Home: God's Work of Revival among Gypsy Folk*. Basingstoke: Marshall Pickering.

Smith, R. (1905) *Gipsy Smith: His Life and Work*. London: National Council of the Evangelical Free Churches.

Thompson, T. (1922) 'The Uncleanness of Women among English Gypsies', in *Journal of the Gypsy Lore Society*, Series III, Vol. 1 (No. 1), pp. 15 – 43.

Viljoen, F. (2014) 'External Cultic Tradition and Internal Ethical Purity in Matthew 15', in *In die Skriflig*, Vol. 48 (No. 1), pp. 1 – 12. AOSIS Publishing (Accessed 10/09/19). Available at: https://indieskriflig.org.za/index.php/skriflig/article/view/1818/2668.

Volf, M. (1990) 'On Loving with Hope: Eschatology and Social Responsibility', in *Transformation*, Vol. 7 (No. 3), pp. 28 – 31. JSTOR Online (Accessed 11/06/20). Available at: https://www.jstor.org/stable/43052319?seq=1#metadata_info_tab_contents.

West, C. (2000) 'A Grand Tradition of Struggle', in *The English Journal*, Vol. 89 (No. 6), pp. 39 – 44. JSTOR Online

(Accessed 20/10/19). Available at: https://www.jstor.org/stable/821261?origin=crossref&seq=2#metadata_info_tab_contents.

Weyrauch, W. (2001) *Gypsy Law: Romani Legal Traditions and Culture*. London: University of California Press.

Woolford, P. (1976) 'The Gypsies for Christ Movement', in *Romani Kongeri* (No. 1), pp. 1 – 4.

Woolford, P. (1977) 'Gypsies for Christ', in *Romani Kongeri* (No. 3), pp. 1 – 4.

United Bible Societies (1981) 'Bibliosko Nevipe', in Romani Newsletter (No.1).

Wright, N. T. (2016) *The Day the Revolution Began: Rethinking the Meaning of Jesus' Resurrection*. London: SPCK.

Zimmerman, E. (2007) *Practicing the Politics of Jesus: The Origin and Significance of John Howard Yoder's Social Ethics*. Telford, PA: Cascadia Publishing House.